# MotoGP
## Season Review 2009
### Julian Ryder

Published in November 2009

A catalogue record for this book is available from the British Library

ISBN 978 1 84425 722 5

Library of Congress catalog card no 2009928034

Haynes Publishing, Sparkford, Yeovil, Somerset BA22 7JJ, UK
Tel: +44 (0) 1963 442030
Fax: +44 (0) 1963 440001
E-mail: sales@haynes.co.uk
Website: www.haynes.co.uk

Haynes North America, Inc., 861 Lawrence Drive, Newbury Park, California 91320, USA

Printed and bound in the UK

This product is officially licensed by Dorna SL, owners of the MotoGP trademark (© Dorna 2009)


**Managing Editor** Mark Hughes
**Design** Lee Parsons
**Sub-editor** Kay Edge
**Special Sales & Advertising Manager**
David Dew (david@motocom.co.uk)
**Photography** Front cover, race action, bike side views and portraits by Andrew Northcott/AJRN Sports Photography, except: Neil Spalding 20-21, 23-24, 28-37 (details); Martin Heath 22


**Author's acknowledgements**

Thanks to:

Toby Moody, Martin Raines, Neil Spalding, Andy Ibbott, Peter Clifford, Andrew Northcott, Martin Heath, Frank Weeink, Dave Dew and his crew, Tom Jojic, Bradley Smith and family, Danny Webb, Scott Redding and James Toseland; special thanks to Wayne Rainey for the Foreword

# CONTENTS
MotoGP 2009

MotoGP
Valentino Rossi
**WORLD CHAMPION**
YAMAHA
2009

World Superbike
Ben Spies
**WORLD CHAMPION**
YAMAHA
2009

World Supersport
Cal Crutchlow
**WORLD CHAMPION**
YAMAHA
2009

British Superbike
Leon Camier
**BRITISH CHAMPION**
YAMAHA
2009

# Yamaha Rules

# And you can too

What a year it's been for Yamaha Racing - Championships for MotoGP, World Superbike and Supersport, plus the crown in British Superbike too.
In the words of Motorcycle News, 'Yamaha's Greatest Day' (Sunday 25th October 2009). As we know, racing improves the breed. Look at the technology transfer to our supersport bikes - crossplane crank, YCC-I, YCC-T, engine management just to name a few of Yamaha's innovations. Well all of that and more is available right now on our YZF-R1 and R6, and with the full-sized YZF-R125 for those starting off on their R-Series experience, the choice is clear.
Visit your local authorised Yamaha dealer now - you will find yourself a deal that just can't be beaten, and be part of Yamaha's winning team.

**YAMALUBE**

*R-Series*
www.yamaha-motor.co.uk

YAMAHA

# FOREWORD
## WAYNE RAINEY

I'm really pleased to see Yamaha sweeping the board again with all three titles – it's an amazing achievement. What can you say about Valentino that hasn't already been said? It's amazing that he's never missed a GP in his career. He's a racer at heart, he still has the desire to be the fastest every time

He goes out there and he still has fun, that's what you've got to admire. Maybe I lost sight of that side of things, and didn't have enough fun at the end of my career.

When you set out to win the World Championship, you must maximize all the performance out of the machine, your engineers, and ultimately yourself. Every race is a battle that you must go through to win the war, which is the World Championship. When Valentino looks back on this championship, I'm sure it will be very gratifying for him. Not only did he beat his team-mate, it turned out to be his biggest rival this year. As a racer to beat your team-mate is very personal.

As for Jorge, there's no doubting his speed. Maybe he has to work a little on his technical set-up and his consistency, and if he accomplishes that next year, I'm sure Rossi might not have as much fun.

I would like to congratulate everyone on the team and especially Lin Jarvis, the general manager – he not only managed two teams within one, but he was able to make Yamaha a bigger threat for 2010.

Looking forward to next year.

*Wayne Rai*

# WAYNE RAINEY
## WORLD CHAMPION 1990, 1991, 1992

Wayne at the corner that bears
his name on the run down from
Laguna Seca's Corkscrew

# THE SEASON

MAT OXLEY

# THE SHARKS ARE CIRCLING

**The 2009 MotoGP season was dominated by one team and two riders. The reigning king held on to his crown but sometimes he had to ride outside his comfort zone to stay on top**

Imagine for a moment that you're Valentino Rossi. Your world title is under threat as you launch into qualifying for the Portuguese GP at Estoril. You're riding outside your comfort zone like never before, teetering on the very brink of disaster in an effort to outpace your fastest rival. Barrelling into the 130mph kink on to the back straight the Bridgestone front slick runs out of grip and you get that stomach-churning falling feeling, like the earth is opening up beneath you. Somehow the tyre regains traction and you save the day, but you feel sick in the stomach and giddy in your head. You ride back to the pits to discuss another set-up tweak with your crew. Then it hits you – the only reason you're riding like this and taking horrible risks is because your bosses have fallen in love with some young upstart from Mallorca.

Then you start thinking about your multi-million-pound motor yacht moored in Ibiza and how keen you are to continue enjoying your hard-won luxury lifestyle for many years to come. You don't want to get hurt. But with your team-mate Jorge Lorenzo doing great things aboard the YZR-M1 (the bike you developed!) you have no option but to keep taking risks. Unless, of course, you roll over and admit defeat: 'Wave the white flag' as Rossi likes to say.

The internecine conflict at Fiat Yamaha was the story of the 2009 MotoGP season. The team-mates dominated because the factory M1 was comfortably the best bike on the grid, and its superiority gave Yamaha reasons to be cheerful and cause to be deeply concerned in equal measure. Rossi's and Lorenzo's most memorable duels – Catalunya, Sachsenring, Brno and Indy – were real edge-of-the-seat affairs. Anything could have happened, even a blue-on-blue disaster.

The duel for the title seesawed this way and that, both

**Above** Valentino waves the flag at Assen to celebrate his 100th win

**Top right** There were plenty of tense conferences with Jerry Burgess through the season

**Right** Celebrating the ninth championship in Sepang with another chicken-related joke

men taking turns at the top of the points table and both crumbling under the pressure more than once. Rossi crashed in three races, the first time he'd done that since his rookie premier-class season in 2000, a statistic that tells the story in itself. Lorenzo crashed out on no fewer than four occasions. It was like watching two heavyweight boxers fighting punch drunk, each taking it in turn to land a devastating blow, only for his rival to reel back two paces and then stagger forward once more to counter-attack with another stonking right hook.

It was a vicious duel, fierce enough to have Rossi wondering why he should stay with Yamaha when they were making life so hard for him. Late in the year he started dropping heavy hints that he might quit the marque. Quite simply, it seemed to be a case of 'this team isn't big enough for the both of us'.

Lorenzo, however, wasn't convinced by Rossi's tantrum. He was sure his team-mate was doing nothing more than rattling Yamaha's cage, strengthening his case for a better deal when he starts negotiating his 2011 contract. 'To me, this is very similar to a family, when you have a mum and two children,' says Lorenzo. 'One of the children says "I want more food" or "I want more toys", so mum brings more food or more toys. In Spain we have a saying: "He who doesn't cry, doesn't eat." This is what Valentino is doing.'

Lorenzo is a fascinating character, a highly intelligent racer with the attitude of a handsome, slightly cocky and very keen apprentice. He makes no secret of his keenness to be the boss, and he's happy to draw on all kinds of sources to achieve his goal, from everyday family life to fellow racers, from books on ancient Greek history to

works on eastern yogic teaching. This mélange of influences makes him a very unusual 22-year-old motorcycle racer indeed.

Perhaps Lorenzo has yet to read any William Blake, but he would appreciate the early nineteenth-century British artist and poet's most famous line: 'The road of excess leads to the palace of wisdom.' Such words would seem to justify Lorenzo's over-exuberance and too frequent crashes, but he does need to start learning from them very soon if he's to win the MotoGP crown. Self-assured and knowing, Lorenzo can seem a bit serious at times, but he's a funny man too. When someone asked him at Assen if he might one day match Rossi's achievement of 100 GP wins, he replied: 'Yes, but maybe only on my PlayStation.'

Lorenzo changed everything for Rossi. This was a whole new scenario for the rider who seems able to cope with anything. Rossi has taken on all-comers – Max Biaggi, Sete Gibernau, Casey Stoner and Nicky Hayden – but this was the first time he had battled a team-mate. Well, almost. In 1998 he rode factory Aprilia 250s alongside Loris Capirossi and Tetsuya Harada, but back then he was the rookie, so it was radically different from 2009. Even then, Rossi didn't like racing his team-mates. 'The atmosphere in Aprilia was terrible and I had two foxes for team-mates,' he said. The following year Aprilia made sure its favoured son got the factory team all to himself. Yamaha would never do such a thing: they are busily preparing for their post-Rossi era with Lorenzo, and now Ben Spies, 2009 World Superbike Champion, is at the front of the queue too.

Rossi found himself in trouble early in 2009, the new short-wheelbase M1 apparently better suited to his shorter

team-mate. And there were moments, like Estoril, where he got his set-up wrong and had his worst ride in years, which suggested his team were riding a knife edge on machine set-up. 'The 800s are very critical on settings,' explained crew chief Jeremy Burgess. 'They don't have the torque to put the weight on to the rear tyre like the 990s. You've got to have grip on the front and the rear all the time. They're a lot more delicate to set up than the 990s.'

In the end Rossi did come out on top, but it was a near-run thing with three races to go when just 18 points separated the pair. And if Rossi had lost the battle it would have been the first time he'd been beaten on 100 per cent equal terms. When in 2006 he lost the title he had held for five years, he did so because of engine and tyre failures; when he was defeated in 2007 his rival had a significant machinery advantage.

Yet how long will it be before the youngsters do get the better of the old man? There's no doubt they're closing in on the 30-something like young lions circling the ageing leader of the pride. Rossi preferred a marine-life analogy, likening his rivals to sharks: 'If I am not strong, I know that Casey and Jorge will eat me in one bite,' he said when things weren't going so well after the first few races. 'They look at me with a little bit of blood flowing and maybe they think, "okay, now is the time".'

Of course, Stoner has already made the kill on Rossi, but he was a long way off winning another title in 2009. His season started well enough with two wins from the first five races, but then he mysteriously fell ill. Stoner copped a lot of flak for taking time off (most notably from legends Kevin Schwantz and Wayne Gardner, both famous for riding injured), but his decision to miss three races was

entirely vindicated by his stunning speed on his return.

Typically, Stoner remained enigmatic about the whole episode, refusing to pinpoint the root cause of his health problems. Journalists (and some gnarled old veterans) love a vacuum of information, so there was a torrent of speculation, some of it laughably lurid. The most likely cause of his sickliness was post-viral fatigue triggered by the virus he suffered during June. PVF can develop into the much more serious chronic-fatigue syndrome (sometimes known as ME) if not quickly treated with complete rest. This alone seemed to fully justify his mid-season 'holiday'.

Some critics suggested Stoner was stressed, that he was sick of racing, or rather that he was sick of the hassle of a MotoGP lifestyle; and there's no doubt that Stoner truly hates the media and PR chores that are the lot of today's racer. 'I am here to race and this is what I want to do and the rest of it is just murder to me,' he says. 'Some people enjoy the media but I hate attention, I hate people talking about me. It's really something I dislike, it's difficult for me to handle. I'd really just prefer to be a little mouse in a corner, forgotten about.'

In fact, the spiky little Aussie was more relaxed than ever in 2009; indeed, he speculated that might have been the cause of his problems. 'Maybe I've been too relaxed this year and my body's decided to shut down and say "okay, you're relaxing too much".'

When Stoner was on track and fully fit, he was as fast and furious as ever. His talent, just like his illness, was plain for all to see. Many onlookers like to throw doubt on Stoner's ability, insisting he'd be nowhere if he couldn't grab a fistful of throttle and leave the rest to Ducati's

**Top left** Dani Pedrosa, injured for half the season but still dangerous

**Left** Ducati remain the factory most likely to put a dent in Yamaha's domination

**Above** Young sharks Lorenzo and Stoner eye-up a potential victim

**Above** World 250 Champion Hiroshi Aoyama, coming to MotoGP in 2010, along with the rest of the top four – Marco Simoncelli, Alvaro Bautista and Hector Barbera

**Below** Every race is a home race for Valentino, here celebrating with the Sachsenring marshals

hi-tech rider aids. During 2009 it was nice to hear that particular myth exploded. 'If you look at our data traces, you'll see that Casey uses less throttle than me,' explained new team-mate Hayden. 'He controls the [rear-end suspension] pumping by working the throttle, he doesn't just twist the grip and go.'

Stoner's 2009 season was further complicated by a new and radical machine. The carbon-fibre-framed GP9 was immediately competitive, the stiffer chassis allowing the suspension to work more effectively, with less of the 'pumping' that used to tie the machine in knots. And yet Ducati spent the whole year racking their brains to realise the bike's full potential. Maybe the GP9 was too stiff, because Stoner's big issue was corner-exit traction. All season his crew swapped back and forth between carbon and aluminium swingarms, the more malleable aluminium unit apparently offering better drive.

At the same time Ducati were working hard to transform the Desmosedici from Stoner special to everyman racer. In 2008 they were able to blame Marco Melandri for his woeful results on the GP8, but when Bologna new boy Hayden started struggling, they had to hold their hands up and admit that the Ducati/Bridgestone package did, after all, have a technical problem.

The Ducati's problem is that age-old racing Catch 22: the bike has to be ridden hard to make the tyres work, but how can the bike be worked hard before the tyres work? Ducati Corse boffin Fillipo Preziosi went some way to addressing the problem by tweaking the chassis and

softening the electronics. Hayden did score one podium on the bike, but most mortals still struggled to make friends with the Duke.

Honda could only dream of having Ducati's problems. The world's biggest motorcycle manufacturer won just three MotoGP races in 2009, bringing its total from the 800cc era to seven victories. During the same three-year period, Ducati have won 21 races, Yamaha 24.

No wonder the atmosphere was gloomy in the Repsol Honda garage. Pedrosa rarely got close to the Ducati and the Yamaha, while new recruit Dovizioso rarely got close to Pedrosa. Both men made no secret of the fact that the RCV wasn't up to it. They complained of serious corner-entry instability, Dovizioso insisting that only a full redesign, right down to basic engine architecture, would get Honda back on the pace.

During 2009, MotoGP's Fab Four – Rossi, Lorenzo, Stoner and Pedrosa – gave us the best racing we'd ever seen from the 800s, which to some extent took our minds off the problems that trouble the category of kings. The

grid still had too many vacancies, and those in charge of MotoGP burned much midnight oil in their quest for a solution. The proposal to limit each rider to one bike seemed like an easy way of doubling the size of the grid, until teams pointed out that they'd still need a spare bike for each rider, even if it was stacked in parts bins in the back of the truck.

Dorna's subsequent suggestion that privateer teams should be allowed to use tuned 1000cc streetbike engines was treated as a joke up and down pit lane. The MSMA insisted they wanted the grid to remain 100 per cent prototype, for engine development purposes, so the factories were asked to go away and name an affordable price for prototype 800cc engines which could be leased to private teams to house in their own chassis. When the factory bosses returned from their ivory towers, their idea of 'affordable' was €700,000 for a season's supply of engines. No wonder it didn't take much longer for Dorna's 1000cc street proposal to gain serious traction.

Final regulations have yet to be decided, but it seems likely that MotoGP may return to litre engines once the current 800cc formula expires at the end of 2011. Of course, it won't strictly be a return to 1000cc, since the original four-stroke limit was 990cc. Switching to a full litre limit would allow private teams to run commercially available street-based engines while factories use 1000cc prototypes, some of them no doubt based on their old 990s. Lower costs and bigger grids aren't the only hopes resting on the 1000s; the theory goes that the peaky 800s cause processional races, whereas torquey 1000s should encourage closer racing and more overtaking.

Engines weren't the only subject on the agenda during 2009. Tyres and electronics were also major talking points. The first year of MotoGP's single-tyre rule went off well, with only a few grumbles of complaint, most of which Bridgestone addressed. In fact by mid-season tyres were no longer much of a talking point – they were black, round and doing their job – a good thing in one way but probably bad for headline-hungry tyre supplier Bridgestone.

Electronics were a more controversial talking point. Rossi and others made no secret of the fact that they would rather compete alone, without a little black box riding shotgun, correcting their mistakes. Rossi, in particular, bemoans the fact that rider aids have taken the fun and the fight out of racing.

'With the 500s and 990s, the exit of corners was very hard work because slide, wheelie, change gear, slide, wheelie, change gear, always controlling the bike, fighting with the wheelie and the slide,' says the World Champion. 'Now is full gas, brrraaaaaa! You have the anti-wheelie and the traction control and you go. It is for this reason that the

bikes are not so close during the races because the rider cannot make the difference anymore. With the electronics every rider can use 100 per cent of the drive.'

MotoGP did get back on track in 2009 with some unforgettable battles, most memorably at Catalunya where Rossi achieved the first last-lap winning pass of the 800 era. But the world's premier bike racing series still needs work to be as good as it can be. In the meantime, there's much to look forward to in 2010: the novelty of the new Moto2 series and the arrival in MotoGP of Ben Spies, Marco Simoncelli, Alvaro Bautista, Aleix Espargaro, Hector Barbera and Hiroshi Aoyama.

**Top** Stoner's 'welcome back' press conference at Estoril. He seemed much more at ease with the media than usual

**Above** World Superbike Champion Ben Spies – coming to MotoGP in 2010

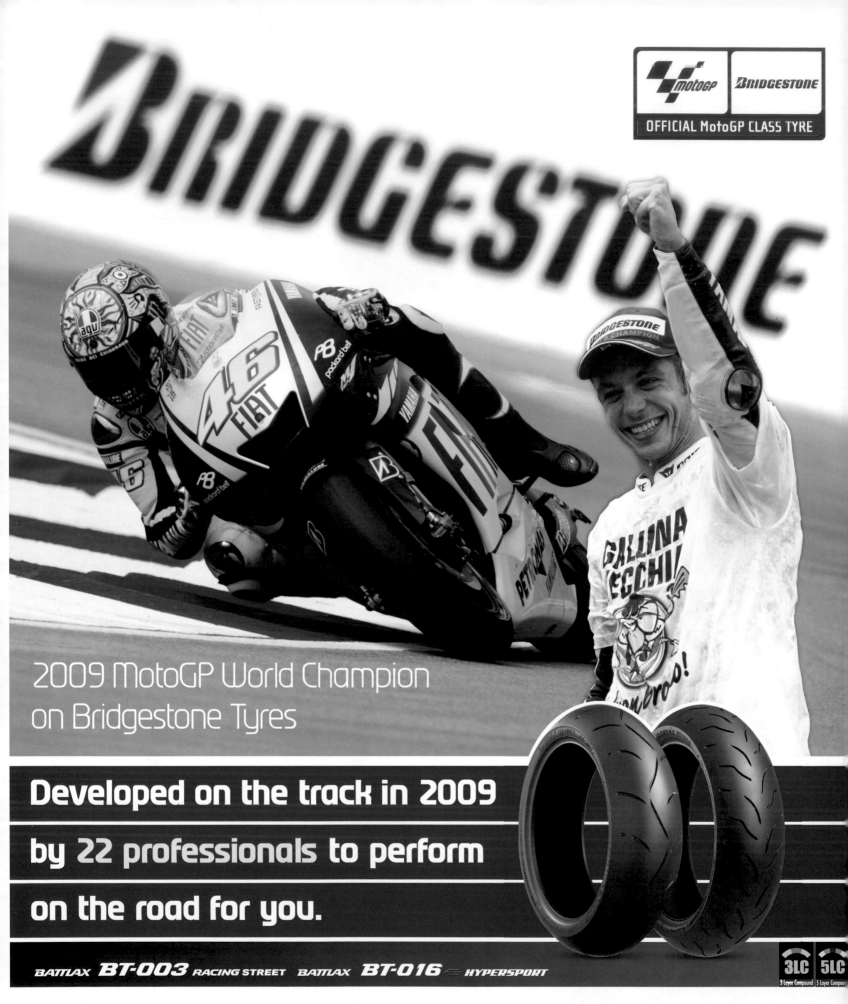

# RIDERS' RIDER OF THE YEAR 2009

**VOTED FOR BY** Alex de Angelis, Niccolo Canepa, Loris Capirossi, Andrea Dovizioso, Colin Edwards, Toni Elias, Aleix Espargaro, Sete Gibernau, Nicky Hayden, Mika Kallio, Jorge Lorenzo, Marco Melandri, Dani Pedrosa, Randy de Puniet, Valentino Rossi, Casey Stoner, Yuki Takahashi, Gabor Talmacsi, James Toseland and Chris Vermeulen

VALENTINO
ROSSI

107 POINTS

The man who wins the championship isn't always the one his opponents think is the best. To find out who the MotoGP riders judge to be the fastest of them all, for the sixth year running we polled every rider who has taken part in more than one race. They named their top six men, we counted the votes. Here are the results

This was the year of the four 'Aliens' – Valentino Rossi, Jorge Lorenzo, Casey Stoner and Dani Pedrosa. Not surprisingly, the voting reflects the domination of that quartet. Neither is it surprising that Rossi received the majority of first-place votes. Of the 19 men who could have voted for him, only two chose not to put him first.

Lorenzo was the overwhelming choice for second place, but third was a closer call. Ten voters put Stoner third, but Pedrosa and Colin Edwards also got significant support. Where would Casey have been but for his sabbatical? You have to believe he would have been a lot closer to the Fiat Yamaha riders. As for Dani, his peers seemed decidedly underwhelmed. His votes were grouped in third and fourth, although he did get one first place, which just kept him ahead of Colin Edwards, who was on more people's voting papers than anyone save Rossi. The measure of just how well Colin rode this year is that his score was

**2**nd
JORGE
LORENZO
84 POINTS

**3**rd
CASEY
STONER
64 POINTS

**4**th
DANI
PEDROSA
59 POINTS

**5**th
COLIN
EDWARDS
56 POINTS

**6**th
ANDREA
DOVIZIOSO
15 POINTS

**7**th
MARCO
MELANDRI
10 POINTS

**8th** LORIS CAPIROSSI 10 POINTS

**9th** NICKY HAYDEN 9 POINTS

**10th** ALEIX ESPARGARO 6 POINTS

right up there with the 'Aliens' and well clear of the rest.

This is the most polarised voting seen in the six-year history of Riders' Rider of the Year. The names of the top four plus Edwards appear on nearly everyone's ballot paper, although one young rookie decided to get random and ignore the top men. He put Aleix Espargaro first, Edwards second and Marco Melandri third. Marco was a popular choice, as was Loris Capirossi; they tied on points but Marco gets precedence thanks to a higher individual placing – second against fourth.

Compared with last year, John Hopkins and Chris Vermeulen drop out of our top ten while Marco Melandri returns for the first time since 2007 and Aleix Espargaro makes his debut – not bad for a youngster who just took four replacement rides.

It's always instructive to see who the MotoGP riders place higher than their final position in the World Championship table. They put Stoner above Pedrosa, the reverse of their championship finishing order, as well as Melandri in seventh (tenth in the championship), Capirossi eighth (ninth in the championship) and Nicky Hayden ninth (13th in the championship). And then there was Espargaro, 18th in the championship, who got tenth on a tiebreak with his team-mate, Mika Kallio.

Toni Elias, who finished seventh in the world, doesn't make it into our top ten, and neither does his Gresini Honda team-mate Alex de Angelis – who nobody voted for! In fact the votes were spread across fewer riders than ever before, reflecting the dominance of the big four and the universal respect for Colin Edwards' riding this year. The points gap between Colin in fifth and Andrea Dovizioso in sixth is a good deal greater than the single point that separated them in the final table.

## RIDERS' RIDER
### PREVIOUS RESULTS

|  | 2004 | 2005 | 2006 | 2007 | 2008 |
|---|---|---|---|---|---|
| **1** | Rossi | Rossi | Capirossi | Stoner | Rossi |
| **2** | Gibernau | Capirossi | Rossi | Rossi | Stoner |
| **3** | Biaggi | Melandri | Pedrosa | Pedrosa | Lorenzo |
| **4** | Edwards | Hayden | Hayden | Hopkins | Pedrosa |
| **5** | Nakano | Edwards | Melandri | Vermeulen | Dovizioso |
| **6** | Capirossi | Gibernau | Stoner | Hayden | Hayden |
| **7** | Tamada | Nakano | Roberts | Melandri | Capirossi |
| **8** | Hopkins | Hopkins | Hopkins | Guintoli | Hopkins |
| **9** | Barros | Biaggi | Checa | Capirossi | Edwards |
| **10** | Hayden | Barros | Vermeulen | De Puniet | Vermeulen |

# TECHNICAL REVIEW

NEIL SPALDING

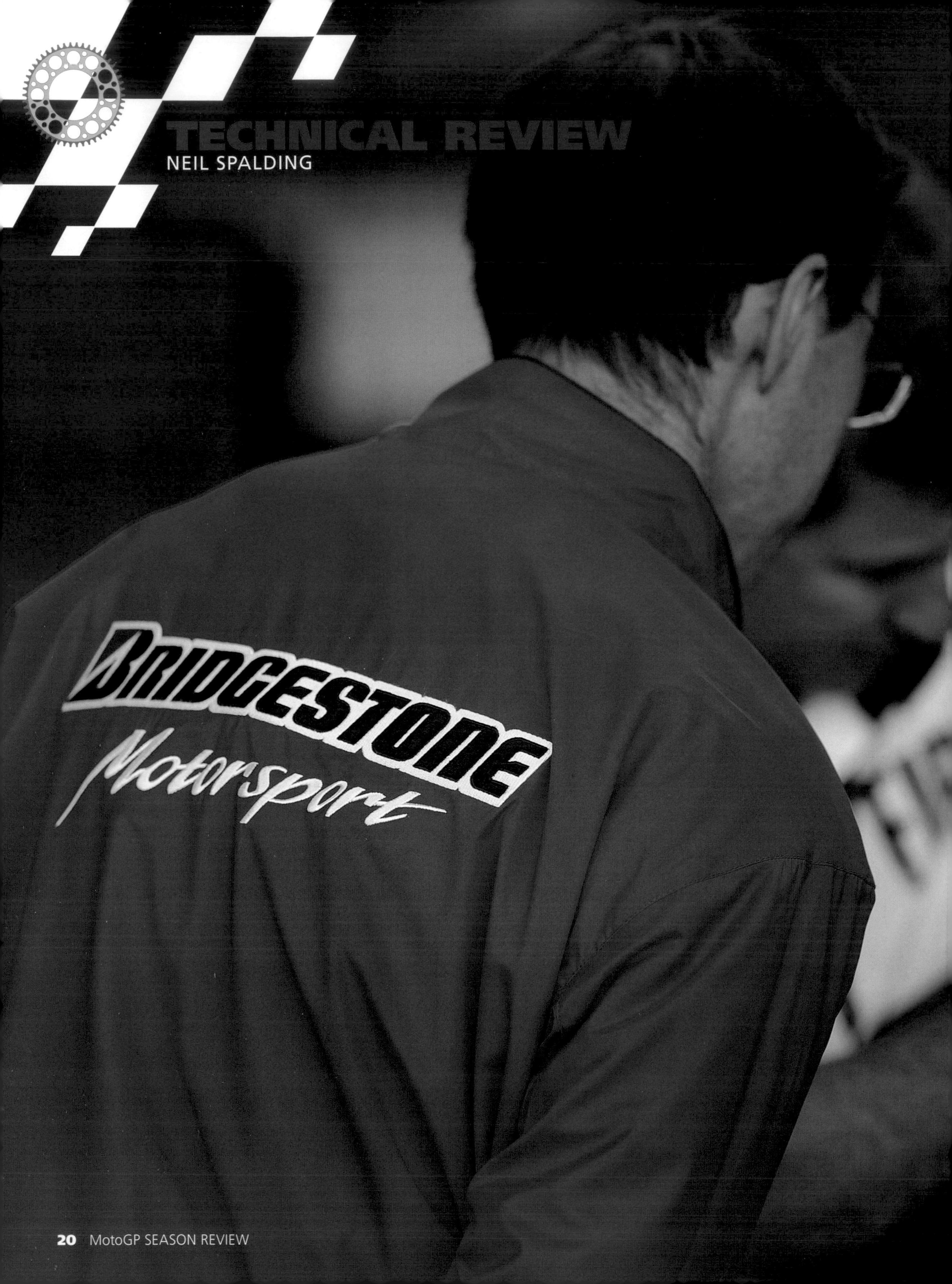

# THE TYRE DESIGNS THE BIKE

**In five short years Bridgestone have gone from also-rans to double World Champions, and now – in their first year as the MotoGP series control tyre – the whole of pit lane is re-equipping to make the best use of their tyres**

The 2009 season was the first time Grand Prix motorcycle racing has had a control tyre. In fact, it's the first time the use of any specific equipment has been mandatory. From the promoter's point of view the logic of the decision was compelling. There were only two tyre suppliers, and one of them kept getting things wrong, sufficiently so for the promoter to believe his show was in danger.

The decision, however, has had side-effects: as all the tyres respond similarly to the same circumstances, variety in the races is reduced; and, critically, bikes have to be redesigned to make best use of the tyres – not a cheap thing to do in a recession – and inevitably they will be designed to have similar 'tyre-pleasing' characteristics. Bridgestone won the contract to supply the tyres just as the world's stock markets went off a cliff; if the deal had been up for negotiation just four weeks later the chances are it would have happened very differently.

Control-tyre racing is very different from open-tyre competition. Bikes have to be made to work with the tyres, not the other way round, and that means the characteristics of the tyres matter. In addition, Bridgestone couldn't suddenly make more tyres. They have a very specialised factory making MotoGP tyres and it was at full capacity in 2008. For 2009, therefore, the number of tyres available to each team had to drop so that the total number supplied to the paddock remained similar to the number brought to each race in 2008.

The tyres Bridgestone supplied were closely related to their best ones; not exactly the same, mind you, more of a 'safe and easy-to-produce' version. Gone at most circuits were the multiple-compound specials, and all the tyres seemed to be based on a construction that was designed

Rossi is again World Champion on Bridgestones: using Yamaha's redesigned M-1, he was one of the first to understand and deal with the differences between the 2009 tyres and the 2008 versions

**Above** The original 2003 Ducati's weight distribution allied to Michelins necessitated some spectacular cornering techniques

**Below** As soon as Michelin were away from Europe their competitive advantage disappeared – Bridgestone and Ducati moved quickly to fill the gap

not to retain heat particularly well so it would be less likely to overheat and chunk. They were definitely from the same family of tyres that had won two World Championships, though, first with Casey Stoner on a Ducati, then with Valentino Rossi on his Yamaha, and they had some very specific design characteristics.

This story starts a long, long time ago in a little town in northern Italy – Bologna, to be precise. A small company, well versed in production-based Superbike racing but unused to Grand Prix prototype racing, decided that it was time to make a full-on commitment to the top class. Ducati was the factory and the class was MotoGP, and this new take on GP racing comprised big 990cc four-stroke bikes instead of the ubiquitous 500cc four-cylinder two-stroke machines.

The main reason for the change to four-stroke

motorcycles was to combine factory research and development budgets with promotional ones. At a stroke, more money would be available for racing, while things learned on the track would be of use on the road – and the bikes would at least make similar noises to the roadsters. Factories such as Ducati would never have considered the two-stroke formula, but a four-stroke one was most certainly feasible.

In 2002 the first bikes were very similar, in chassis terms at least, to the old two-stroke machines, and they used developments of the Michelin tyres that, at the time, ruled the roost. Development was frenetic over the first three years of the new class, with only Honda's design seeming to have been right first time – and all the time Michelin stayed on top.

Ducati made their debut in the second year of the new class, in 2003. They had decided to build something similar, in architectural terms at least, to their road bikes – a 90-degree V – but for MotoGP it was a four-cylinder design instead of their Superbike twins. The Desmosedici was a revelation, leading in its first race and winning in its first year. However, subtle it was not. Designed to make as much power as was usable, the bike's wheels spun and slid their way through that first season.

It looked tremendous, but it wasn't necessarily the best or the fastest way round a racetrack. Ducati's interpretation of the 90-degree V can best be called an L-four, with the front cylinders pointing directly at the front tyre while the rear pair are almost vertical. Compared to the tightly designed opposition, this layout pushed the heavy crankshaft backwards and put a lot of weight towards the back of the bike. As a result, there was considerable weight on the rear tyre and not enough on the front. To make the bike turn, it was easier to lengthen the swingarm, thus taking some weight off the rear and allowing the tyre to spin, lowering the pressure on the front tyre by getting half the corner completed with the rear end way out of line.

For 2004 it was decided that a 50/50 front/rear weight distribution would allow the tyres to grip and would make sure that the power was used more effectively. All the electronics were moved backwards, the fuel tank was situated further back than before, and a new shorter swingarm was introduced. At the final pre-season test, a new and more powerful screamer engine turned up too. Loris Capirossi was fourth fastest and set the highest top speed with a stunning performance that few who saw it will forget. Edgy, erratic and barely under control, the bike clearly gripped and fired out of the corners but it really didn't look as though it could keep that up for a full race distance.

The next few months were painful, as Ducati sought to understand their predicament. Longer swingarms arrived very quickly, returning weight distribution to the slightly front-heavy arrangement the Michelins liked. Initially weights were added to the bike to experiment with different distributions, closely followed by the electronics and fuel moving forwards once more. New motors were built, with 'soft pulse' irregular firing order crankshafts that seemed to make the power more usable. Wheelspin returned and suddenly this MotoGP game didn't seem so easy after all.

No-one gets far in any form of racing unless some victories can be delivered; it doesn't have to be many, but a few are vital. For 2006 Ducati played the joker: they signed with Bridgestone. This confused everyone. Why walk away from Michelin? Ducati had won many Superbike championships with Michelin rubber, and at the time they were clearly the best. The answer came in two parts. Bridgestone had been working away, accumulating knowledge and technology for the previous four years, first with a test team with a Honda 500 and then with the Team Roberts triple in 2001. They were already supplying Kawasaki and Suzuki, but with Ducati came the promise of seriously competitive power.

Bridgestone had also understood Michelin's strategy: practise hard, analyse the data and make special race tyres on Saturday night. And they'd seen the flaw, because Michelin couldn't use this strategy outside Europe. Ducati understood, too, that if they had reasonable tyres for non-European GPs, where all the Michelin runners would be likely to have ineffective rubber, then they just might win a couple of races.

Tohru Ubukata is Bridgestone's Manager of Motorcycle Race Tyre Development: 'We learned a lot from Ducati. They formed a special test team just for us. Ducati brought a development team, proper full race machinery, and Shinichi Itoh, a really good test rider who gives excellent feedback. We understood that to beat Michelin we had to build a tyre with a wider range and better performance; we had to do both. We had a lot of data, a lot of knowledge, but to ensure the direction of our development was right we needed a bike out there on the track. We had to test on all the circuits.'

The first half of the 2005 season was painful as Bridgestone struggled to find tyre designs, profiles and rubber compounds that suited the Ducati. Overall rolling diameters kept going up. As soon as Ducati built a new, bigger rear hugger they would have to cut it back to suit the newest batch of tyres that were even bigger than

before. In the wet and cold of Shanghai and Donington the Bridgestones were particularly bad, but slowly Bridgestone found their direction and on the 'flyaway' races at the end of the year Ducati went on a winning spree.

Now there was a full-on, high-tech, money-no-object tyre war. For 2006 Michelin fought back with new, more grippy tyres that suited the Honda more than the Yamaha, giving Honda the grip they craved and Yamaha a fit of chatter. Bridgestone formed more test teams so they could run experimental tyres on each circuit just before each race. They had a pair of designs that allowed the Ducati to be a bit heavy on the back and light on the front. They continued to have an advantage away from Europe, and towards the end of the year the Bridgestone/Ducati combination was getting seriously competitive on Michelin's home turf as well.

For 2007 came the start of the 800cc class, and a new rule to try to limit costs. Tyre numbers would be restricted, and all the tyres would have to be chosen before the start of practice. Michelin was giving up its 'Saturday night special' advantage in exchange for Bridgestone cutting back on their ruinously expensive MotoGP bike-equipped test teams. This was also the year Ducati went back to the drawing board, the first time that their bike had been seriously redesigned. Their 800, though, was different. It still had a 90-degree V, but the cylinders were rolled back and the gearbox and cylinder heads were redesigned for a more compact engine. The chassis was also different, with an abbreviated front birdcage and a carbon seat support. Bridgestone collated all their data, too, and built tyres that both suited the Ducati's weight distribution and worked in the longer cornering arcs that the 800s preferred.

**Above** New HRC race boss Shuhei Nakamoto was quite open about the difficulties Honda faced in redeveloping their chassis

**Below** Ducati set up Bridgestone with their own test team – veteran Shinichi Itoh was the test rider who gave the tyre company the required feedback

**Bottom** The Bridgestones were designed to work well in conjunction with the slightly rearwards weight distribution of the Desmosedici

Ducati and Bridgestone were on the attack. They'd built a bike that now had the power, the fuel efficiency and the right tyres. The rear carcass construction was firm and its multi-compound rubber was grippy, allowing Casey Stoner, Ducati's aggressive new number two, to load on the power at the corner apex and blast out of corners. The super-grippy front also kept him on the bike going into corners – something he hadn't excelled at on his Michelin-shod Honda the year before. Over in the Michelin camp there was disarray. With a history of building specialised tyres for specific conditions on the eve of a race, they simply couldn't produce tyres of sufficiently broad spectrum to suit the variables of weather and temperature that could be encountered a couple of weeks after manufacture. It was halfway through the season before Michelin lucked in on a tyre construction that worked, and they were as surprised as their teams when it performed well!

The die was cast. Michelin needed more tyres to be allowed in the initial selection to guarantee having something that would work on the day, so the tyre rule was rewritten. But it was too late. Rossi had watched Stoner's Ducati from the best seat in the house all the way through the previous year, and he understood what he was seeing: a stable rear carcass that allowed hard acceleration earlier in the corner than he could dream about. He wanted Bridgestones, the same ones he had seen in action on Stoner's Ducati, whatever the political cost – and he got them.

Initial tests went well for Valentino. Yamaha reacted strongly to his call for a better bike – advanced 'flying on the ground' electronics went on to a more powerful and fuel-efficient PVRS engine – and the Bridgestone tyres seemed 'nice'. The first race was a disaster, though, because Stoner disappeared into the distance as Rossi's tyres lost grip and spun up halfway through the race. He was even beaten by his new team-mate on a Michelin-shod bike. That certainly wasn't in the script.

Over the next few races MotoGP was treated to a Burgess-led piece of rolling development as the Yamaha's chassis was reconfigured to work with the Bridgestones. By the fourth race Rossi was on race-winning pace, and he was never headed again. The rest of the paddock now started to take a real interest. Kawasaki and Suzuki, as well as the Gresini Honda team, had all been on Bridgestones for years, but none of them had made the gains Yamaha had accomplished in just four races. However, they were on different 'families' of Bridgestones and they were trying to develop them to work with their chassis. Kawasaki and Suzuki could do whatever they wanted, but Gresini were operating with customer Hondas, and this meant they were trying to develop Bridgestone tyres to work on a chassis designed for Michelins.

By mid-season Suzuki understood enough to make a new chassis that let them use the RJ fronts and LX rears of the Ducati family of Bridgestones. Kawasaki, too, were hard at work, but it was to be 2009, as the Hayate team, before they could make use of the single family of Bridgestones that really worked. Gresini were gifted a prototype 2009 Honda chassis to see if it could deal with the combination of Bridgestone's firm rear carcasses and their soft and grippy front tyres.

Then Michelin dropped the ball. Over a three-race period in the middle of 2008 their tyres simply failed to

work, to the extent that the show was damaged and a furious promoter decided he had had enough of the vagaries of tyre competition. MotoGP was to be run with a single tyre supplier. And at Motegi Bridgestone was confirmed as the single supplier for 2009. After quickly working out the logistics, it was obvious that Bridgestone couldn't make any more tyres than they had in 2008, so, with a whole paddock to supply, each team would have even less choice than they'd had in 2007.

The control tyre was confirmed as being based on the Ducati/Rossi family of tyres, with the rear based on the LS carcass developed for circuits that had long corners where the full race tyres could overheat. These LS tyres had thinner tread on the edges to make sure the rubber couldn't overheat. The thinner rubber retained less heat but also lost its heat more easily, so although the tyres worked well over a broad range, the rider and his crew needed to make sure they had a chassis setting that worked heat into the tyres and then kept it there.

With the knowledge gained in 2008, each factory at least had an idea of what would have to be done to make their bikes work on the new tyres. Weight would have to go back, shorter swingarms would be required, and different chassis flexibility would be needed.

## CONTROL IS EVERYTHING!

Yamaha and Ducati had the easiest time. Yamaha had the opportunity to redesign their bike so it had the full benefit of Rossi's work in 2008. It took until Catalunya, however, for both teams to realise that there were sufficiently different aspects to the 2009 tyres to require some careful management of the height of their bikes' centre of gravity. Both Yamaha and Ducati were moving their seat heights up and down to slightly change the angle of lean required to hold their speed through the corners, and to encourage enough pitching forwards and backwards to generate the necessary tyre carcass heat.

Bridgestone's Ubukata-san explained the different specification: 'To cope with the need to supply so many bikes we cannot make so many different specifications, which means the tyres have to have a broader performance and that is why performance is a little bit less. The tyres feel stiffer, especially to riders coming from Michelin, but our tyre grips very hard and it is this that the rider can feel. When he first tried our tyre Valentino said the tyre is very stiff, and he wants more soft, but I explain our view and he tries it longer and he now understands. Our front tyre is the same. It is very stable under braking, all the way into the corner.'

Other teams took longer to sort out settings that would work. Kawasaki couldn't change much, although their design team had left some very carefully thought-out optional chassis in the parts bin for the Hayate team to use. Suzuki were still experimenting with getting the tyres to heat up quickly at the end of the season, having debuted a new 'high engine' chassis in Brno.

It was Honda who had the biggest job to do. They debuted a new chassis at the test after Catalunya, and it became standard equipment immediately. The works team chewed their way through four different swingarm designs. For years Honda had had a tyre partner who built tyres to work with their chassis design, but now they were having to redevelop their chassis to work with the control Bridgestones. Weight was effectively moved back, the front was pushed out and the rear shortened – not as much as the Yamaha, but it was still a significant change.

But let us consider what we have: a Honda designed with a 77-degree (or thereabouts) V4 engine, and a balancer shaft to make the smaller angle work; an airbox balanced on top of the engine because there was no room to get it down inside the V; and a fuel load pushed down and below the rider's seat as there was no room for large amounts of fuel around the airbox. All this was in order to get the engine weight forward enough to deliver the Michelins' front weight bias preference. So now a front weight bias wasn't required, wouldn't it be better to have a wider 90-degree V, get the inlets down inside the V and move the fuel up and forward? The result would be a better airbox, more centrally located fuel and more power, with no need for a balancer shaft.

And isn't that just about where we started, back in Bologna?

**Above** Bridgestone technicians mark the softer of the tyre options so spectators at the track and in front of their TVs can tell who's using what

## REGULATIONS

*Under the new-for-2009 single-supplier tyre regulations, Bridgestone bring a choice of two compounds of slick for both the front and rear. The selection is made from soft, medium, hard and extra-hard compounds. There's no choice of wet-weather rubber: Bridgestone bring one treaded tyre, front and rear, for rain conditions.*

*On the data pages for each Grand Prix you will find Bridgestone's selection in a panel next to the track map, and each rider's choice for the race is featured in a column in the results table below the 𝓑 logo.*

**BRIDGESTONE**

TYRE OPTIONS
FRONT SOFT (S) / MEDIUM (M)
REAR SOFT (S) / MEDIUM (M)

# THE BIKES
## 2009 MotoGP MACHINERY

# YAMAHA
## M-1 2009

**1** All the riders continued on the 48mm through-rod TTX-TR Ohlins forks. The large leg diameter gave stability under very hard braking but required a 'flexible' top triple clamp to ensure the fork legs could move slightly at high angles of lean to maintain some suspension

**2** The M-1's side beams were cut away to increase flex at the rear, again at full lean, to counteract the effect of the very stiff carcass of Bridgestone's rear control tyre

**3** Yamaha's class-leading electronics system received revised twin gyroscopes this year, mounted as before on the top of the air intake

**4** The Bridgestones needed more static weight on the rear and that meant a new, shorter swingarm. The control tyres also needed different levels of chassis flex compared with the old Michelins. Rossi used a very weak swingarm in '08, but to go with the revised main frame the '09 swingarm was a little stronger. The combined effect of frame and swingarm is more flex spread over a longer distance

**D**uring 2008 Yamaha had really pulled out the stops: new engines with reliable pneumatic valve springs; advanced ride-by-wire systems with predictive and learning capabilities; and, in Rossi's case, a new chassis/swingarm mix to optimise their bike's performance on the all-conquering Bridgestones. For 2009, therefore, it was a case of filling any remaining gaps and fine-tuning the chassis to the tyres.

Rossi had used a shorter swingarm in 2008 in combination with a steering head adjusted to its 'maximum forward' position, effectively to move the weight of the engine backwards. To make up for the fact that its sides were shorter, this swingarm was also more flexible, to enhance grip when the bike was right over at full lean. For 2009 the entire chassis was modified to optimise weight distribution for the Bridgestone tyres, and Yamaha saw fit to strengthen the swingarm a little and deliberately weaken the side beams of the main frame. The reasoning was simple: by spreading the flex over a greater area they achieved more predictable flex when the bike was at full lean. Yamaha also changed the seating position, allowing the rider to slide forward 20mm and lowering the seat by 6mm, but it quickly became apparent that this wasn't an improvement and from Catalunya onwards the seating position reverted to the 2008 set-up.

The second area where Yamaha felt the need for improvement was mid-range power. Ducati clearly stole a march on their opposition in 2008 with a variable-length inlet system. This changed the harmonic frequency of the inlet port at different revs, or, to put it another way, allowed the engine to develop better power in several different rev zones by optimising the length of the inlet port as the throttle position and revs changed.

In Yamaha's case (as with Ducati last season) it allowed the factory to spread the range of really good power over a wider rev range, effectively creating a better mid-range. In addition to an easier power band, the wider range allowed the teams to gear the bike to use less revs in certain corner sequences, and this saved fuel which could then be used to advantage on the rest of the lap. In the latter half of the season, when the five-engines-for-seven-races rule was in force, it appeared Yamaha chose to rein back on the ignition timing a little to make the engine output slightly less aggressive and to lower the chances of any failures.

# HONDA
## RC212V 2009

**1** All the Hondas this year used their Pneumatic Valve Recovery System (PVRS), which allowed higher revs to be used reliably. The customer bikes had their peak revs reduced at the start of the year to limit service costs

**2** The works bikes had new air intake systems that breathed through the side of the frame. Look carefully and you can see this bike also has the early full-section side beams

**3** By mid-season Honda had found out enough about the needs of their new tyres to weaken the main beams by cutting away an area at the bottom of the back of the beam and strengthening the front engine mounts by welding in additional plates

**4** From Assen onwards there were new swingarms. Here we see the third type used on Dovizioso's bike during the year, and he was to use one more before the season was over

This year's Honda was another evolution of the 'second half of 2008' pneumatic valve-spring bike. Honda have now tried three times to bring pneumatic valve-spring engines to MotoGP, but all have been too aggressive and difficult to handle. The problem was compounded this season by having to build a bike to suit the Bridgestone control tyres – tyres that wouldn't be developed to suit Honda's preferences. The control tyre for 2009 was a variant of those used in 2008 by the Ducatis and Rossi. It seemed to prefer a pronounced rearwards weight bias to work the very stiff rear tyre carcass, which in turn allowed the bike to accelerate very hard off corners. Honda tried several different swingarms, both shorter and more flexible versions, as well as new rear linkages, but it wasn't until Catalunya that a modified chassis was seen. Over the next few races a motor with more mid-range and two different swingarms started to make a difference.

At Brno Honda surprised everyone by testing Ohlins suspension. The experiment was sufficiently successful to have Honda team Dovizioso with Ohlins for the rest of the year, although it wasn't known whether there was a big performance improvement with the Swedish suspension or if Showa were perhaps withdrawing from racing because of the global financial slowdown.

The fairings and air intake systems on the works bikes were new as well. Last year's chassis had its air intake under the nose, a simple scoop on top of the radiator; this season saw a duct down the side of the bike and through the side of the chassis, requiring a new airbox and fairing upper.

This year the customer bikes were replicas of last year's works pneumatic-valve bikes, albeit with the usual Honda slight detuning for reliability and to cut down servicing costs. The customer bikes, of course, didn't benefit from the chassis development undertaken by the factory team to make the bikes work with the Bridgestone control tyres.

# DUCATI
## DESMOSEDICI D16-09

**1** Ducati's brilliantly elegant carbon 'stressed airbox' chassis bolted directly into the middle of the vee and replaced the old airbox and steel tube birdcage chassis

**2** This year Dorna's electronics were attached more securely, and needed to be when you saw how fast the fork position gets changed during practice

**3** From Catalunya, Ducati raised the seat pads; here the red portion of the seat is 20mm thicker than at the start of the year and there's also a further angled spacer under the seat pad

**4** Carbon-fibre swingarms were debuted in Qatar but gave a different feel to the rider; all year the riders would try both swingarm types on the Friday of each GP and decide which would be better for the circuit

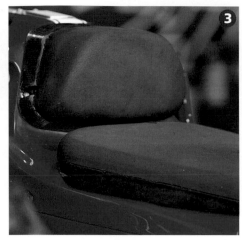

**D**ucati's new carbon chassis looked like a big airbox that had been reinforced with the 'through-the-headstock' air intake added on. This design had the combined airbox/chassis bolting into the middle of the V, which required new engine castings, and meant the chassis/airbox/engine assembly was perhaps 50mm narrower than before, potentially allowing the whole bike to be made smaller in the future. For the first round at Qatar, carbon swingarms were also introduced on the works bikes.

Ducati have been struggling with the 'only Casey Stoner can ride the bike' problem, for in three years of MotoGP Ducati 800s there has been only one 'non-Stoner' win and just a sprinkling of rostrum finishes. Ducati's initial position of 'ride it and get used to it', which led to Marco Melandri's disastrous experience in 2008, only changed at Catalunya when Nicky Hayden began to post top-ten results.

After 'discussions' with Hayden's management (who include ex-Team Roberts manager Chuck Aksland) changes were made. Raising the rider 20mm with a new higher seat pad and footpegs made the bike pitch forwards and backwards more under braking and acceleration, working heat into the tyres more quickly and giving the rider a greater feeling of security. By Indianapolis, when he finished third, Hayden was sitting 30mm higher and starting to look like he could work with the bike.

Ducati also worked hard to change their traction control and throttle strategies. Stoner had ridden the bike for over a year with serious suspension pump – it seems likely that it was connected in some way with the throttle system – and certainly something was introducing a low-frequency pulse into the rear suspension. It may have been something Casey Stoner could ride round, but Hayden simply pronounced the bike unrideable – and it started to sound even more malevolent as the year went on, with greater use being made of Ducati's impressive-sounding 'cylinder interrupt' strategy to cut power. As this machine-gun noise is the sound of unburnt fuel igniting in the exhaust system, it cannot be very fuel-efficient and also means that fuel previously kept back for power on the straights is no longer available.

# SUZUKI
## GSV-R XRG-2

**1** Suzuki used the same swingarm this year as in '08, but after tests of a new chassis, which raised the front of the engine 20mm, the axle position was moved fully forward

**2** For 2009 Suzuki were on to their fourth version of the Mitsubishi ECU, but it was still nowhere near as sophisticated as Yamaha's

**3** Suzuki used mufflers for the first time, citing some improvements in performance. They didn't seem to make the bikes any quieter though

**4** Suzuki's pneumatic-valve 75-degree V4 received a power upgrade halfway through the year

The Suzuki looked promising at the start of the season, but then failed to transfer those positive early test results to the actual races.

Suzuki decided to move their riders' positions around. A seat that allows more movement side to side and a more relaxed riding position lets the rider weight the bike more easily and more accurately. That can make a massive difference to the feel of the bike once the rider, inevitably, starts to tire halfway through a race.

Last year Suzuki switched to the 'rear weight biased' Bridgestones preferred by the Ducatis and Rossi. The move required a new frame that raised the front of the engine and moved the fuel back and down, making the bike more rear weight biased, at least when the fuel tank was full. The 2009 season started with an upgrade and a second design was debuted at Brno, raising the motor even higher in the chassis and allowing the swingarm to be run at its shortest. This modification seemed to be a reaction to the need to 'work' the control versions of Bridgestone's tyres quite hard in order for them to retain the heat needed to make them perform well.

Suzuki have always gone their own way with electronics. Uniquely, their ECU is made by Mitsubishi, but it seems to remain a generation behind the Marelli equipment used by several of the other manufacturers. The Suzuki team were left quite despondent when they realised that Yamaha's ECU was capable of self-correcting during a race; clearly the Suzuki system was nowhere near as advanced.

There were few obvious changes to the engine, although the bike now sported small mufflers on the pipes – not that any reduction in the noise level was noticed!

# HAYATE
## KAWASAKI ZX-RR 2009

**1** Kawasaki's first proper ride-by-wire system used a potentiometer strapped to the right fork leg to detect the rider's throttle movements

**2** Kawasaki's long-serving MotoGP project leader Yoshimoto Matsuda (left) paid his own way to the Jerez pre-season test; his project was shut down just three days later

**3** Kawasaki built at least two versions of their new chassis to give the Hayate team something different to try in testing

**4** The Kawasaki gained a backwards-rotating crank, and a different engine position; four races into the season a second-place finish proved that lessons had been learned

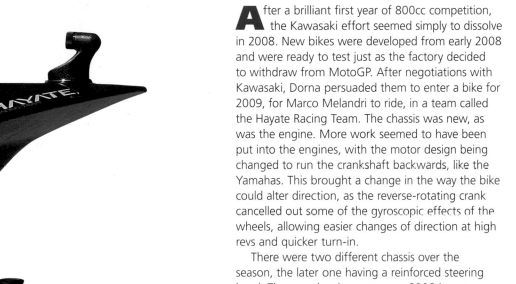

**A**fter a brilliant first year of 800cc competition, the Kawasaki effort seemed simply to dissolve in 2008. New bikes were developed from early 2008 and were ready to test just as the factory decided to withdraw from MotoGP. After negotiations with Kawasaki, Dorna persuaded them to enter a bike for 2009, for Marco Melandri to ride, in a team called the Hayate Racing Team. The chassis was new, as was the engine. More work seemed to have been put into the engines, with the motor design being changed to run the crankshaft backwards, like the Yamahas. This brought a change in the way the bike could alter direction, as the reverse-rotating crank cancelled out some of the gyroscopic effects of the wheels, allowing easier changes of direction at high revs and quicker turn-in.

There were two different chassis over the season, the later one having a reinforced steering head. The actual swingarms were 2008 items, with the main modification being the removal of the black paint! The other main change was the throttle system, extensively tested in 2008 by the Kawasaki test team with rider Olivier Jacque. This was Kawasaki's first full ride-by-wire system and allowed the traction control, wheelie control, lean-angle sensors and throttle butterfly controls to be fully integrated.

# THE SEASON IN FOCUS

Every MotoGP rider's season analysed, from the World Champion to the wild-card entry whose race lasted less than a lap

| | | |
|---|---|---|
| 1 | Valentino Rossi | 306 |
| 2 | Jorge Lorenzo | 261 |
| 3 | Dani Pedrosa | 234 |
| 4 | Casey Stoner | 220 |
| 5 | Colin Edwards | 161 |
| 6 | Andrea Dovizioso | 160 |
| 7 | Toni Elias | 115 |
| 8 | Alex de Angelis | 111 |
| 9 | Loris Capirossi | 110 |
| 10 | Marco Melandri | 108 |
| 11 | Randy de Puniet | 106 |
| 12 | Chris Vermeulen | 106 |
| 13 | Nicky Hayden | 104 |
| 14 | James Toseland | 92 |
| 15 | Mika Kallio | 71 |
| 16 | Niccolo Canepa | 38 |
| 17 | Gabor Talmacsi | 19 |
| 18 | Aleix Espargaro | 16 |
| 19 | Sete Gibernau | 12 |
| 20 | Ben Spies | 9 |
| 21 | Yuki Takahashi | 9 |
| 22 | Michel Fabrizio | – |

# 1 VALENTINO ROSSI
## FIAT YAMAHA TEAM

His ninth world title, the seventh in the premier class, in what he said was his toughest season. Want to know how hard he was riding? Can you recall him falling in three MotoGP races in a season?

For the first time ever, Valentino had to deal with a fast team-mate who refused to be intimidated. The last-corner move at Catalunya wasn't just about winning the race. It was about asserting his ultimate authority, especially over Jorge Lorenzo, just as it was in 2008 with Casey Stoner through the Corkscrew at Laguna Seca – the race that put Rossi back on top of the championship, a position he never gave up.

There were tough races as well as the usual quota of wins. Apart from the crashes, his streak of wins at

Mugello came to an end and at Estoril his crew for once failed to give him a bike with which he could win. But against those errors must be balanced epic wins in Spain, Germany and Catalunya, and the demolition job at Assen to bring up his 100th career victory, a total surpassed only by Giacomo Agostini with 122. Rossi has 103 in all classes.

The fact that Valentino didn't win any of the last four races shows how tough the competition was this season. Seeing Rossi pushed to the limit by Lorenzo, Stoner and Pedrosa was the fascinating core of the 2009 season.

Anyone who doubted Rossi's motivation at the age of 30 had their doubts firmly quashed. Old chickens really can still lay eggs.

**NATIONALITY** Italian
**DATE OF BIRTH** 16 February 1979
**2009 SEASON** 6 wins, 13 rostrums, 7 pole positions, 6 fastest laps
**TOTAL POINTS** 306

# 2 JORGE LORENZO
## FIAT YAMAHA TEAM

In his second year as a MotoGP rider Jorge proved he had the outright speed of his team-mate but, as he often said himself, he didn't have the experience.

Lorenzo beat Rossi fair and square in Japan and Portugal as well as taking advantage of his rival's errors in France and Indianapolis. Four wins and second overall, leading the championship along the way, isn't bad for your second season in MotoGP. However, when it came to wheel-to-wheel combat, Valentino was able to beat Lorenzo handily – although Jorge's win in Japan was an exception to that rule. Lorenzo's qualifying was also stellar – he failed to start from the front row just once in 17 races.

Jorge also made mistakes, but, as he said, when you're racing at lap-

record pace every lap of every race that will happen. What was amazing was his ability to instantly block out mistakes that would terminally damage the confidence of most riders. He crashed on the warm-up lap at Mugello and didn't know if he'd have a spare bike when he came into the pits, yet he finished second and in front of his team-mate. He followed up his crashes at Jerez and Brno, chasing Stoner and Rossi respectively, with resounding victories, apparently unfazed by any pressure. He also continued with his showmanship and the planting of 'Lorenzo's Land' flags, and the spaceman colour scheme at Estoril was a stroke of genius.

Jorge will only get faster and with an extra year's experience he will be even more dangerous in 2010.

**NATIONALITY** Spanish
**DATE OF BIRTH** 4 May 1987
**2009 SEASON** 4 wins, 12 rostrums, 5 pole positions, 4 fastest laps
**TOTAL POINTS** 261

**ITALIAN LEGENDARY PROTECTION**

Carmi e Ubertis Milano

Dainese and AGV together
A History rich in World Champions:

Giacomo Agostini, Barry Sheene, Angel Nieto, Kenny Roberts, Marco Lucchinelli, Fausto Gresini,
Luca Cadalora, Troy Corser, Manuel Poggiali, Max Biaggi, Valentino Rossi.

# 3 DANI PEDROSA
## REPSOL HONDA TEAM

**NATIONALITY** Spanish
**DATE OF BIRTH** 29 September 1985
**2009 SEASON** 2 wins, 11 rostrums,
2 pole positions, 5 fastest laps
**TOTAL POINTS** 234

For the second year in a row Dani missed most of pre-season testing with a nasty injury. He was far from fit when the season started and, frankly, three rostrums in the first four races constituted a minor miracle. He looked like he should have been in hospital right up to the Italian GP. A freak accident there in practice then a fast crash in the race nearly put him out of his home GP in Barcelona, where he struggled to sixth place with the help of painkillers – although he'd taken so many of these for so long that they were starting to lose effectiveness.

After another crash at Assen, thankfully without further injury, his season started to improve. He didn't need the pills any more and a surprise win at Laguna Seca saw him claw back enough points to be within range of third place overall at the final round. Dani's second win of the year coupled with Stoner's misfortune saw him achieve that objective.

It was brave season. Eight rostrum finishes as well as the two wins on a bike that clearly wasn't on a par with the Yamaha or the Ducati was a triumph of bloody-mindedness. However, Dani has now won two races a year in his four years as a factory Honda rider and only has a one-year contract going forward. Things are clearly changing at HRC and Dani will have to mount a serious championship challenge in 2010 to retain the faith of HRC management. Those quibbles aside, there is no doubt that Dani deserves his status as one of the four untouchable aces of MotoGP.

# 4 CASEY STONER
## DUCATI MARLBORO TEAM

**NATIONALITY** Australian
**DATE OF BIRTH** 16 October 1985
**2009 SEASON** 4 wins, 8 rostrums,
3 pole positions, 2 fastest laps
**TOTAL POINTS** 220

Casey's year reads like the plot of a soap opera. Two wins in the first five races put him top of the table, but then a mystery illness kicked in. Suddenly, Casey couldn't do more than half a race without his strength ebbing away. Suddenly, he was fading off the pace and collapsing after races. Despite the problem, he finished on the rostrum at Catalunya after setting the fastest lap, but he looked truly awful after the race. When the symptoms reappeared at subsequent GPs, he became so concerned that he decided to take three races off to sort the problem out.

Ducati were suddenly without their 'alien', and many paddock people – including ex-champions – doubted that Casey could come back the racer he used to be. They were wrong. At Estoril Casey returned as he'd promised, qualified on the front row and finished second only to a rampant Lorenzo. Then he went home to Phillip Island and won from pole; then he went to Malaysia and won by a distance. He only lost third in the championship because of his crash at Valencia on the warm-up lap.

Vitally, there was no sign of the old sickness coming back in those final four races of the season. He still doesn't have a proper diagnosis, but he will be able to train properly again over winter for the first time in months. Expect Stoner and Ducati to be a major threat in 2010. Even after the mid-season break he was doing things on the Desmosedici no-one else could dream of. The championship missed him.

# 5 COLIN EDWARDS
## MONSTER YAMAHA TECH 3

It is impossible to overstate Colin's achievements in 2009. Not only was he by far the best of the satellite team riders, he finished ahead of one of the factory Hondas and both the Suzukis. Fifth isn't his highest-ever finish (he was fourth in 2005), but this was his most impressive MotoGP season ever.

Colin had just a single rostrum to show for his efforts, at Donington Park in the wet. He finished fourth three times and he seemed to make fifth place his own, both on the grid and in the results. In the last seven races of the year he qualified fifth six times and finished in that position three times! As Colin said, if you're the next best to those guys it's not an insignificant achievement. As usual, his consistency was exemplary. The only time he didn't finish a race was when he was knocked off at Misano by Alex de Angelis, and he qualified in the top six 13 times.

One of the benefits of still having Colin around is that journalists are guaranteed a quote. His description of the Donington Park race as '48 minutes of pure bullshit he wouldn't have wished on his worst enemy' was a real treat. It's a shame the rest of the quote is unprintable.

It wasn't a bad year for the oldest guy in the class, who was going to retire to Texas a couple of years ago to spend more time with his golf clubs. The good news is that he's staying for another season, as he has re-signed with the Tech 3 team for 2010. He will be joined there by Ben Spies, so maybe it should be called Team Texas.

**NATIONALITY** American
**DATE OF BIRTH** 27 February 1974
**2009 SEASON** 1 rostrum
**TOTAL POINTS** 161

# 6 ANDREA DOVIZIOSO
## REPSOL HONDA TEAM

Andrea's first season in the factory Honda team wasn't an easy one. He and team-mate Pedrosa complained frequently about the lack of updates for the uncompetitive RCV, and Andrea struggled to come to terms with the abrupt power delivery. There were modifications to engine and chassis later in the year, the most significant being Andrea's adoption of Ohlins suspension after the Brno test.

However, despite his win at the British GP on a treacherous track, Dovi had to suffer some surprisingly public criticism from HRC management. That victory was his only rostrum of the year and he didn't once qualify on the front row or set a fastest race lap. At the last race he also lost fifth place in the championship to Colin Edwards. Two crashes off the front of the new chassis at Assen and Laguna Seca didn't help him, and neither did a DNF at the Sachsenring with excessive front tyre wear.

Then there was the issue of his working relationship with crew chief Pete Benson, who guided Nicky Hayden to the 2006 title. By Estoril, rider power had triumphed and Benson knew he was surplus to requirements for the 2010 season. Andrea himself renewed his contract with Repsol Honda for the following season, but it's only a one-year deal. HRC said they wanted him to sign for two years but, like Pedrosa, Andrea wanted to see significant improvements in the RCV. Like his team-mate, Dovi will be hoping Honda's aggressive approach extends to the development of the bike.

**NATIONALITY** Italian
**DATE OF BIRTH** 23 March 1986
**2009 SEASON** 1 win
**TOTAL POINTS** 160

# 7 TONI ELIAS
## SAN CARLO HONDA GRESINI

**NATIONALITY**
Spanish

**DATE OF BIRTH**
26 March 1983

**2009 SEASON**
1 rostrum

**TOTAL POINTS**
115

**T**oni was supposed to have the third factory Honda, although it was really more of a collection of parts no longer needed by the Repsol team. He had real problems at the start of the year finding traction, but after Assen things improved. He got a rostrum at Brno but his next best finish was sixth. It was enough to come out on top of the close fight for seventh overall, his best finish in five years of MotoGP, but not enough to get him a ride for 2010. Toni is high on the wish list of several teams that will contest the new Moto2 class in 2010.

# 8 ALEX DE ANGELIS
## SAN CARLO HONDA GRESINI

**NATIONALITY**
San Marinese

**DATE OF BIRTH**
26 February 1984

**2009 SEASON**
1 rostrum

**TOTAL POINTS**
111

**L**ike his team-mate Elias, Alex scored one rostrum in the season, at Indianapolis, and improved vastly on his finishing position in his rookie year. And like Toni, he didn't get to keep his job despite a couple of very solid fourth places. Unfortunately there were only five other top-ten finishes. Then there was his skittling of Hayden and Edwards at Misano and a sixth-gear tailgating of Nicky (again) at Estoril. The first incident so displeased Ducati's top management that Alex was removed from the shortlist for a satellite team ride with Pramac Ducati in 2010.

# 9 LORIS CAPIROSSI
## RIZLA SUZUKI MotoGP

**NATIONALITY**
Italian

**DATE OF BIRTH**
4 April 1973

**TOTAL POINTS**
110

**L**oris only finished outside the top ten on three occasions, all of them when the conditions didn't suit the Suzuki. He was as combative as ever whatever the circumstances and as usual dragged an underperforming bike higher up the order than it should have been, like putting it on the front row at Mugello and nearly getting on the rostrum in the race. Four fifth places may not sound like much, but under the circumstances it was an admirable fight against the odds. He'll stay with Suzuki for another season and will start his 300th GP at Qatar in 2010.

# 10 MARCO MELANDRI
## HAYATE RACING TEAM

**NATIONALITY**
Italian

**DATE OF BIRTH**
7 August 1982

**2009 SEASON**
1 rostrum

**TOTAL POINTS**
108

**A**mazingly, Marco was in the fight for seventh place overall right up to the last round on the Hayate team's Kawasaki. As the bike was only on the grid to fulfil contractual obligations and received no significant upgrades all season, this was some achievement. There were also minor technical problems with things like the throttle that held him back. At least all the hard graft was rewarded with the most unexpected rostrum of the year at Le Mans, and the paddock still knows that Marco is one of the best riders out there. He will ride for Team Gresini, for the third time, in 2010.

# 11 RANDY DE PUNIET
### LCR HONDA MotoGP

**NATIONALITY**
French

**DATE OF BIRTH**
14 February 1981

**2009 SEASON**
1 rostrum

**TOTAL POINTS**
106

**A** much better season than it looks on paper. Randy's Honda was used as the testbed for the long-life engines up until Brno, so he suffered the built-in handicap of a lower rev limit than the other satellite Hondas. A nasty broken ankle from a training accident in the summer break didn't help either, especially as it came straight after a rostrum in the UK. The most impressive thing, though, was his new-found ability to get to the finish, for which the credit goes to double ex-motocross champion Yves Demaria who helped Randy this season as his personal trainer.

# 12 CHRIS VERMEULEN
### RIZLA SUZUKI MotoGP

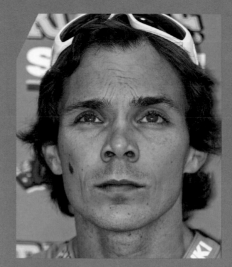

**NATIONALITY**
Australian

**DATE OF BIRTH**
19 June 1982

**TOTAL POINTS**
106

**A** horrible season in which to say goodbye to the Suzuki MotoGP team after four years that saw Chris achieve the squad's only victory. At least he had the satisfaction of being the only man to score points in every round this year, although the recalcitrant Suzuki nearly put paid to that at the last round. Even in the wet races, where he normally shines, Chris could only manage a best of sixth place, and his highest finish of the year was fifth at a dry Dutch TT. For 2010, Chris will be back in the World Superbike Championship as a factory Kawasaki rider for an attempt on the title he just missed in 2005.

# 13 NICKY HAYDEN
### DUCATI MARLBORO TEAM

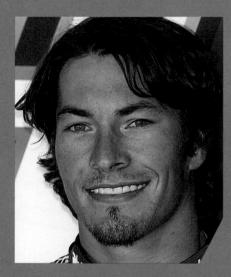

**NATIONALITY**
American

**DATE OF BIRTH**
30 July 1981

**2009 SEASON**
1 rostrum

**TOTAL POINTS**
104

**H** is time as factory Ducati rider started with a massive highside at Qatar and got worse until new electronics appeared at Catalunya on a much-modified motorcycle. From there on things got steadily better. Nicky was the victim of three first-lap incidents, the worst of which was at Misano, where he was taken out on the first corner after looking extremely competitive in practice. In Japan Takahashi rammed him and in Australia Lorenzo punted him off track. At least he got a rostrum at Indianapolis, the closest track to his home he's ever raced on – it was the least he deserved.

# 14 JAMES TOSELAND
### MONSTER YAMAHA TECH 3

**NATIONALITY**
British

**DATE OF BIRTH**
5 October 1980

**TOTAL POINTS**
92

**A** fter a promising 2008 season, James's second year in MotoGP saw him marking time rather than moving forward. He equalled his previous best finish of sixth three times, but never beat it. When things started looking good, as at Phillip Island, he got a dubious ride-through penalty. When your luck is out, it's out. Unfortunately, James had to bear comparison to the other Yamaha riders – not a comfortable position to be in. So for 2010 he does a job swap with World Superbike Champion Ben Spies and goes back to try for a third title on a third make of bike. Don't bet against him.

# 15 MIKA KALLIO
**PRAMAC RACING**

**NATIONALITY**
Finnish

**DATE OF BIRTH**
8 November 1982

**TOTAL POINTS**
71

The Rookie of the Year impressed everyone, starting the season with a brace of eighth places before things got difficult. He was back on form after the wet races in France and Italy, but then he crashed in Holland and badly damaged a finger. Mike then took over Stoner's factory Ducati when the Aussie was away for three races; he crashed it first time out while moving through the field, but then got two top-ten finishes. He returned to the Pramac team for the four final races of the year and finished with three more top-tens to make it nine in all.

# 16 NICCOLO CANEPA
**PRAMAC RACING**

**NATIONALITY**
Italian

**DATE OF BIRTH**
14 May 1988

**TOTAL POINTS**
38

The young Italian's season in MotoGP was a reward for his stint as Ducati's test rider. Not surprisingly, he found the going tough with just two finishes inside the top ten, at the Mugello track he knows so well and at Donington Park in tricky conditions. His season was brought to a premature end by a nasty injury sustained in practice for the Australian GP which necessitated a skin graft to the inside of his right elbow. He was replaced at the final three rounds by Aleix Espargaro, and the young Spaniard will take over the Pramac team's satellite Ducati ride full-time in 2010.

# 17 GABOR TALMACSI
**SCOT RACING TEAM MotoGP**

**NATIONALITY**
Hungarian

**DATE OF BIRTH**
28 May 1981

**TOTAL POINTS**
19

Talk about being thrown in the deep end. The 2007 125cc World Champion first sat on a MotoGP bike at the Catalan GP on the Saturday, his Hungarian state oil company sponsorship cash getting him the ride at Scot Honda at the expense of Yuki Takahashi. Handicapped by the testing ban, Gabor only managed four points-scoring rides in 12 races. Set-up was difficult but he could usually run with the pack in the early laps, only to lose ground in the second half of the race. His backing kept the Scot team on the grid, but Gabor won't be back in MotoGP next season.

# 18 ALEIX ESPARGARO
**PRAMAC RACING**

**REPLACEMENT RIDER**

**NATIONALITY**
Spanish

**DATE OF BIRTH**
30 July 1989

**TOTAL POINTS**
16

For a man who didn't have a GP ride at the start of the season, Aleix had a great year. He was testing Moto2 bikes in the Spanish Championship when he picked up a couple of replacement rides in the 250s, and his fourth and seventh places impressed the whole paddock. When Mika Kallio moved up from the Pramac satellite team to cover for the absent Stoner on the factory Ducati, first Michel Fabrizio and then Aleix got the ride. Espargaro rode at Indianapolis and Misano, finishing in the points both times. He replaced the injured Canepa at the last two rounds, again scoring both times and earning a full-time ride.

# 19 SETE GIBERNAU
## GRUPO FRANCISCO HERNANDO

**NATIONALITY**
Spanish

**DATE OF BIRTH**
15 December 1972

**TOTAL POINTS**
12

**S**ete returned to MotoGP after a two-year break with a new satellite Ducati team. The start of his season was affected by injury and then he rebroke his oft-damaged collarbone in practice at Le Mans. Unfortunately, the team's financial backing evaporated before mid-season and the team was disbanded. It was a sad way to say goodbye to the second most successful rider of the 990cc era and the only man before this season to push Valentino Rossi all the way in the championship. Sete did that not once but twice, but it's now unlikely we will see him race again.

# 20 BEN SPIES
## MONSTER YAMAHA TECH 3

**NATIONALITY**
American

**DATE OF BIRTH**
11 July 1984

**TOTAL POINTS**
9

**WILD CARD**

**T**he newly crowned World Superbike Champion had already signed to the Tech 3 Yamaha team for 2010 before he came to the final round of the year as a wild card. He raced three times in 2008 for Suzuki, but this was his first race on the Yamaha M-1. Although he talked down his chances, he scored an impressive seventh place at Valencia, overtaking Dovizioso six laps from the flag to hand his future team-mate Colin Edwards fifth in the final standings. Ben then backed his race up with some very impressive times in testing. Will he be the first Superbike Champ to make an impression in MotoGP? Probably.

# 21 YUKI TAKAHASHI
## SCOT RACING TEAM MotoGP

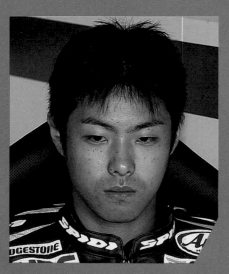

**NATIONALITY**
Japanese

**DATE OF BIRTH**
12 July 1984

**TOTAL POINTS**
9

**T**he unlucky Japanese rookie found himself the victim of circumstances in the Scot team. To put not too fine a point on it, the squad was broke and Yuki didn't have any financial backing. So when Gabor Talmacsi split from Aspar's 250 team and started advertising his considerable sponsorship budget courtesy of the Hungarian state oil company Mol – for MotoGP only, mind, not 250s – Yuki's days were numbered. He and Talmacsi both raced at Catalunya and Assen, but when he turned up at Laguna Seca Takahashi found he was unemployed. He has secured a Moto2 ride for 2010 with Tech 3.

# 22 MICHEL FABRIZIO
## PRAMAC RACING

**NATIONALITY**
Italian

**DATE OF BIRTH**
17 September 1984

**REPLACEMENT RIDER**

**D**ucati's factory Superbike rider had space in his schedule to replace Mika Kallio at Brno while the Finn deputised for Casey Stoner on the works bike. He didn't have an easy time. The considerably more violent MotoGP bike first pulled a muscle in his arm in practice and then in the race had another go and turned the pull into a torn muscle. He had to retire from the race. Michel does have a history in MotoGP: in 2004 he rode for the WCM team and was loaned to Aprilia as a replacement rider. He also replaced the injured Elias at Gresini Honda for the 2007 German GP.

# MotoGP SILVERSTONE 2010

**17-20 JUNE 2010***

> NEW CIRCUIT LAYOUT

> NEW GRANDSTANDS AND VIEWING BANKS

> TICKETS ON SALE NOW

> PRICES FROM £15

FOR MORE INFORMATION, VISIT
WWW.SILVERSTONE.CO.UK/MOTOGP
OR CALL 0844 3750 500

* DATE SUBJECT TO CHANGE

SILVERSTONE

# THE RACES
## MotoGP 2009

# QATARI GP
## LOSAIL INTERNATIONAL CIRCUIT
### ROUND 1
**April 13**

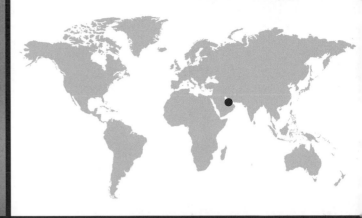

# NIGHT FEVER

**Casey Stoner and Ducati made it three in a row in Qatar, but only after a 24-hour postponement due to a desert storm**

MotoGP 2009 opened with Casey Stoner winning on a track where he has dominated since the introduction of the 800cc formula. No surprises there, but a torrential downpour moments before the race was due to start on Sunday night caused the schedule to be put back 24 hours. It was fortunate that there was no race the following weekend, or Dorna would have been unable to take up the Qatari promoter's offer of a postponement. Not everyone was happy. Stoner didn't want to race on the Monday because he thought the track conditions would be so different from qualifying that it would be dangerous. Thankfully, though, there was minimal wind overnight so very little sand was blown on to the tarmac. The new mono-tyre regulation didn't affect things either; the only duplication of track time was the extra 20-minute warm-up session.

Losail has always been an odd race to work at – the crowd is sparse and there are no motorbikes in the public parking areas – but as the 125 and 250 teams had already gone home, Monday felt even weirder than usual. Once racing got under way, however, everything felt reassuringly normal. Stoner started from pole position and was never headed. He only eased up in the final laps, maybe for reasons of fuel consumption, certainly to give his front Bridgestone as easy a time as possible. Ducati's new carbon-fibre chassis didn't appear to make the Ducati team's life any more difficult than the old steel-lattice version. Casey reported that the bike did move about a bit, but his dirt-track experience meant he was well in control. He certainly didn't look worried; in fact, he looked more relaxed than he'd ever done.

Stoner's new team-mate, Nicky Hayden, on the other

two-strokes effortlessly to the big class.

Finishing the race seven seconds behind Casey, the Fiat Yamaha team-mates started their season as they meant to go on, by beating each other up in the early laps, before Valentino Rossi got into second place on lap three, ahead of Jorge Lorenzo, only to find himself nearly three seconds behind Stoner. When Rossi pushed and closed slightly, Stoner was able to respond immediately and decisively. Rossi went through the motions of declaring himself happy with his weekend but sounded far from convincing. The gap was too big for that. Still, three Yamahas packing the places behind Stoner must have made the factory happy, with only James Toseland failing to show at the front. He ran off track early on to cap a very depressing pre-season and opening race weekend.

Honda could take encouragement from a typically gritty performance by Andrea Dovizioso – and from the fact that Dani Pedrosa was much fitter than anyone expected. However, the Spanish rider's left knee was obviously still lacking movement and he could hardly put any weight on his left leg. That was part of the reason Alex de Angelis ran into Pedrosa late in the race: Dani was very slow into the corner, as he was unable to weight the inside footpeg, and unfortunately Alex was approaching at speed and there was a coming-together. Race Direction looked at the footage, talked to de Angelis and called it a 'racing incident'. Pedrosa was less forgiving, muttering darkly about de Angelis needing to respect other riders. Given Dani's total lack of pre-season testing, though, it was no surprise that he couldn't last the pace.

**Above** Sunday night – and it rained enough in the desert for the race to be postponed. Who'd have thought it?

**Below** Monday night – and all is well again on the weather front. The MotoGP grid charges towards the first corner

hand, had an awful weekend on the track where he'd enjoyed his best pre-season test. The American managed precious little track time on Friday thanks to mechanical problems, had an engine blow on him on Saturday morning, then suffered the mother of all highsides in qualifying. He raced hurt, with stitches in his chest from where he'd been fired through his own windscreen, plus a very sore back. Second Ducati rider home was the very impressive class rookie Mika Kallio, in eighth place, transferring the style with which he won a dozen GPs on

The eyes have it as Valentino Rossi concentrates on chasing Casey Stoner

**Above** Colin Edwards' charge to fourth place put three Yamahas in the top four

**Below** Most people expected Casey to win, but they didn't expect the winning margin to be so big

## 'I SUFFERED A LOT PHYSICALLY DURING THE RACE AND DE ANGELIS GAVE ME A BIG HIT'

**DANI PEDROSA**

Pedrosa's new team-mate, Dovizioso, made an impressive debut for the works team. On a bike that hadn't shown up particularly well in winter testing, was difficult to handle on corner entry and still had far too sudden power delivery, fifth place was quite an achievement. However, Dovi was nearly 30 seconds behind the winner. More good news was that the satellite Hondas didn't seem as far off the pace as had been feared. Rossi had a view, of course, suggesting that the Honda would be a winner with him or Stoner aboard. Casey's typically trenchant observation was that the other Honda riders should shut up because when Dani was on form the Honda didn't seem slow; wait until Pedrosa is fully fit was the Aussie's advice.

The Suzuki team had their calculations thrown out by the change in track conditions, while the Kawasaki of Marco Melandri and the Hayate Racing Team looked, not surprisingly, like it needed a lot more set-up time.

As for the return of Sete Gibernau after two years away from racing, there was a sense of anti-climax as he was carrying a shoulder injury – apparently from overdoing things in the gym. Nor was there a renewal of hostilities between Sete and Valentino Rossi at the track where they'd fallen out in 2004. The pair chatted happily at the pre-race press conference and announced that they'd actually talked on the phone a couple of times in the recent past. No scandal there then.

On the face of it, the first race of the year didn't give many pointers for the rest of the season. It looked very much as if normal service had been resumed. We should perhaps have paid more attention to those three Yamahas in the top four...

# THE CARBON QUESTION

Ducati's carbon-fibre chassis won on its debut, an achievement that was as impressive as it was undersold. Maybe it was because the frame wasn't visible, but there was precious little noise made about the first victory for a composite chassis in the premier class of motorcycle racing. Quite why it has taken so long for motorcycles to go where cars have been for decades is a bit of a mystery. Heron Suzuki did experiment back in 1984 with a honeycomb-composite RG500 chassis, but it was horribly efficient at transmitting vibration and way too rigid.

In the past few years, the relative stiffness of various chassis parts has been the area that has most occupied the factories' design engineers, so the desired properties of a frame are much better understood now. Ducati also had two other advantages. First, their consultant Alan Jenkins was a pioneer of carbon fibre in F1 and brought decades of understanding of the material to Bologna. Second, Ducati's V4 already had a thumping great carbon-fibre airbox sitting over the engine. It was a simple matter, comparatively speaking, to adapt the design so that it was large enough to bolt the swinging arm to the rear and the forks to the front without the need for extra chassis parts. Ducati have never used the industry-standard twin-beam aluminium deltabox design; in fact, they've never used an aluminium frame. All their bikes have two hallmarks without which customers

wouldn't consider them to be true Ducatis. First, there is desmodromic valve operation and, second, the lattice chassis is fabricated from short, straight lengths of steel tubing. The frame has become more and more vestigial over the years, and while customers wouldn't have accepted a (Japanese-style) alloy fabrication, they couldn't object to Ducati pioneering composite materials technology in motorcycle racing.

While the chassis obviously worked first time out, there seemed to be some debate over the swinging arm. The team would experiment with both aluminium and carbon designs over the following races.

**Above**
Ducati's new carbon-fibre chassis is barely visible; it is little more than a reinforced airbox between the cylinder heads and the headstock
© Ducati Corse

**Below** Jorge Lorenzo was happy with third but not with the distance between himself and the two men in front

**BRIDGESTONE**
TYRE OPTIONS
FRONT: SOFT (S) / MEDIUM (M)
REAR: SOFT (S) / MEDIUM (M)

MotoGP TISSOT SWISS WATCHES SINCE 1853
OFFICIAL TIMEKEEPER

# QATARI GP
## LOSAIL INTERNATIONAL CIRCUIT

### ROUND 1
April 13

# RACE RESULTS

**CIRCUIT LENGTH** 3.343 miles
**NO. OF LAPS** 22
**RACE DISTANCE** 73.546 miles
**WEATHER** Dry, 22°C
**TRACK TEMPERATURE** 26°C
**WINNER** Casey Stoner
**FASTEST LAP** 1m 55.844s, 103.887mph, Casey Stoner
**LAP RECORD** 1m 55.153s, 104.510mph, Casey Stoner, 2008

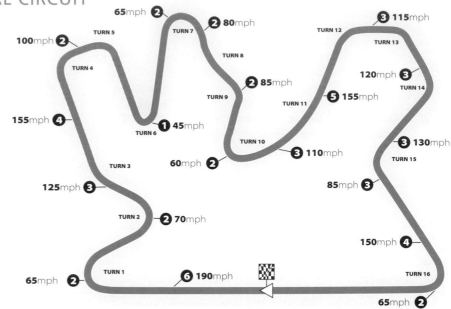

## QUALIFYING

| | Rider | Nationality | Team | Qualifying | Pole + | Gap |
|---|---|---|---|---|---|---|
| 1 | Stoner | AUS | Ducati Marlboro Team | 1m 55.286s | | |
| 2 | Rossi | ITA | Fiat Yamaha Team | 1m 55.759s | 0.473s | 0.473s |
| 3 | Lorenzo | SPA | Fiat Yamaha Team | 1m 55.783s | 0.497s | 0.024s |
| 4 | Dovizioso | ITA | Repsol Honda Team | 1m 55.977s | 0.691s | 0.194s |
| 5 | Capirossi | ITA | Rizla Suzuki MotoGP | 1m 56.149s | 0.863s | 0.172s |
| 6 | Edwards | USA | Monster Yamaha Tech 3 | 1m 56.194s | 0.908s | 0.045s |
| 7 | De Puniet | FRA | LCR Honda MotoGP | 1m 56.358s | 1.072s | 0.164s |
| 8 | Vermeulen | AUS | Rizla Suzuki MotoGP | 1m 56.493s | 1.207s | 0.135s |
| 9 | De Angelis | RSM | San Carlo Honda Gresini | 1m 56.790s | 1.504s | 0.297s |
| 10 | Kallio | FIN | Pramac Racing | 1m 56.852s | 1.566s | 0.062s |
| 11 | Melandri | ITA | Hayate Racing Team | 1m 56.962s | 1.676s | 0.110s |
| 12 | Elias | SPA | San Carlo Honda Gresini | 1m 57.225s | 1.939s | 0.263s |
| 13 | Toseland | GBR | Monster Yamaha Tech 3 | 1m 57.510s | 2.224s | 0.285s |
| 14 | Pedrosa | SPA | Repsol Honda Team | 1m 57.729s | 2.443s | 0.219s |
| 15 | Gibernau | SPA | Grupo Francisco Hernando | 1m 57.899s | 2.613s | 0.170s |
| 16 | Hayden | USA | Ducati Marlboro Team | 1m 58.215s | 2.929s | 0.316s |
| 17 | Takahashi | JPN | Scot Racing Team MotoGP | 1m 58.784s | 3.498s | 0.569s |
| 18 | Canepa | ITA | Pramac Racing | 1m 58.999s | 3.713s | 0.215s |

## FINISHERS

**1 CASEY STONER** Third dominating win in a row in Qatar, with any wrist worries dispelled by the way Casey led the whole race from pole. Slowed his pace towards the end to conserve the front Bridgestone, and because of the rate he was using fuel, yet still won by nearly eight seconds.

**2 VALENTINO ROSSI** Didn't get the good start he needed to stay with Stoner's Ducati, but happy to start the season better than a year ago. Had a strong run mid-race when he closed Casey down a little, but knew his tyres would suffer if he maintained that pace so settled for 20 points.

**3 JORGE LORENZO** Like his team-mate, had some minor problems with grip due to the effect of the rainstorm on the track's surface. Dropped to sixth before fighting back to third. Happy to be on the rostrum but only too aware of the gaps to Rossi and Stoner.

**4 COLIN EDWARDS** A bad start, only getting past Dovizioso shortly after mid-race, and by then Lorenzo was long gone. Concentrated on being smooth and not abusing his tyres, coming home in fourth and proving that his form in pre-season testing wasn't illusory.

**5 ANDREA DOVIZIOSO** The Honda had obvious problems with stability going into corners and aggressive power delivery, so fifth place after running as high as third

was a respectable result – but Andrea was well aware of the performance gap to the Yamahas and Stoner's Ducati.

**6 ALEX DE ANGELIS** Only two seconds behind the works bike after a bad start was a great result. Knew the rostrum was out of reach but had charged through the pack to sixth before half-distance. Came together with Pedrosa in alarming fashion but Race Direction decided he wasn't culpable.

**7 CHRIS VERMEULEN** Both Suzukis suffered from a lack of front-tyre grip plus chatter that only appeared on the Monday. Like Loris, Chris got a good start, then the problems with the front were followed towards the end of the race by similar trouble with the rear tyre.

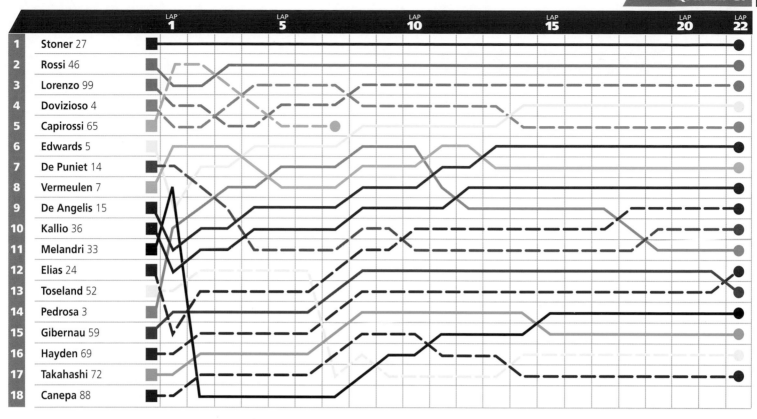

| | LAP 1 | LAP 5 | LAP 10 | LAP 15 | LAP 20 | LAP 22 |
|---|---|---|---|---|---|---|
| 1 | Stoner 27 | | | | | |
| 2 | Rossi 46 | | | | | |
| 3 | Lorenzo 99 | | | | | |
| 4 | Dovizioso 4 | | | | | |
| 5 | Capirossi 65 | | | | | |
| 6 | Edwards 5 | | | | | |
| 7 | De Puniet 14 | | | | | |
| 8 | Vermeulen 7 | | | | | |
| 9 | De Angelis 15 | | | | | |
| 10 | Kallio 36 | | | | | |
| 11 | Melandri 33 | | | | | |
| 12 | Elias 24 | | | | | |
| 13 | Toseland 52 | | | | | |
| 14 | Pedrosa 3 | | | | | |
| 15 | Gibernau 59 | | | | | |
| 16 | Hayden 69 | | | | | |
| 17 | Takahashi 72 | | | | | |
| 18 | Canepa 88 | | | | | |

## RACE

| | Rider | Motorcycle | Race Time | Time + | Fastest Lap | Av Speed | B |
|---|---|---|---|---|---|---|---|
| 1 | Stoner | Ducati | 42m 53.984s | | 1m 55.844s | 102.865mph | M/M |
| 2 | Rossi | Yamaha | 43m 01.755s | 7.771s | 1m 56.093s | 102.556mph | M/M |
| 3 | Lorenzo | Yamaha | 43m 10.228s | 16.244s | 1m 56.936s | 102.220mph | M/M |
| 4 | Edwards | Yamaha | 43m 18.394s | 24.410s | 1m 57.116s | 101.899mph | M/M |
| 5 | Dovizioso | Honda | 43m 21.247s | 27.263s | 1m 56.433s | 101.787mph | M/M |
| 6 | De Angelis | Honda | 43m 23.867s | 29.883s | 1m 57.281s | 101.685mph | M/M |
| 7 | Vermeulen | Suzuki | 43m 27.611s | 33.627s | 1m 57.416s | 101.539mph | M/M |
| 8 | Kallio | Ducati | 43m 28.739s | 34.755s | 1m 57.510s | 101.495mph | M/M |
| 9 | Elias | Honda | 43m 33.465s | 39.481s | 1m 57.849s | 101.311mph | M/M |
| 10 | De Puniet | Honda | 43m 36.268s | 42.284s | 1m 57.947s | 101.203mph | M/M |
| 11 | Pedrosa | Honda | 43m 42.510s | 48.526s | 1m 57.121s | 100.962mph | M/M |
| 12 | Hayden | Ducati | 43m 42.867s | 48.883s | 1m 58.273s | 100.948mph | M/M |
| 13 | Gibernau | Ducati | 43m 46.199s | 52.215s | 1m 58.104s | 100.820mph | M/M |
| 14 | Melandri | Kawasaki | 43m 50.363s | 56.379s | 1m 57.990s | 100.661mph | M/M |
| 15 | Takahashi | Honda | 43m 54.270s | 1m 00.286s | 1m 58.665s | 100.512mph | M/M |
| 16 | Toseland | Yamaha | 44m 08.962s | 1m 14.978s | 1m 57.807s | 99.954mph | M/M |
| 17 | Canepa | Ducati | 44m 09.012s | 1m 15.028s | 1m 59.170s | 99.952mph | M/M |
| | Capirossi | Suzuki | 13m 49.501s | 15 laps | 1m 57.290s | 101.562mph | M/M |

## CHAMPIONSHIP

| | Rider | Team | Points |
|---|---|---|---|
| 1 | Stoner | Ducati Marlboro Team | 25 |
| 2 | Rossi | Fiat Yamaha Team | 20 |
| 3 | Lorenzo | Fiat Yamaha Team | 16 |
| 4 | Edwards | Monster Yamaha Tech 3 | 13 |
| 5 | Dovizioso | Repsol Honda Team | 11 |
| 6 | De Angelis | San Carlo Honda Gresini | 10 |
| 7 | Vermeulen | Rizla Suzuki MotoGP | 9 |
| 8 | Kallio | Pramac Racing | 8 |
| 9 | Elias | San Carlo Honda Gresini | 7 |
| 10 | De Puniet | LCR Honda MotoGP | 6 |
| 11 | Pedrosa | Repsol Honda Team | 5 |
| 12 | Hayden | Ducati Marlboro Team | 4 |
| 13 | Gibernau | Grupo Francisco Hernando | 3 |
| 14 | Melandri | Hayate Racing Team | 2 |
| 15 | Takahashi | Scot Racing Team MotoGP | 1 |

**8 MIKA KALLIO** A very impressive first race in MotoGP. Didn't get a good start but stayed calm and maintained his rhythm to finish just over a second behind Vermeulen at the flag.

**9 TONI ELIAS** Happy with a top-ten finish after struggling with set-up all weekend. 'If you'd have offered me ninth on Friday, I'd probably taken it!'

**10 RANDY DE PUNIET** One of many who was confident after qualifying, in Randy's case on the third row. Then found the rain had changed conditions radically. His problem was with the front tyre: 'I never had the same feeling as in practice.'

**11 DANI PEDROSA** An amazing performance given the state of Dani's health.

Unable to ride for five weeks after surgery on his knee, so his 14th place on the grid was no surprise, but his charge up to sixth most certainly was. Faded late on as pain and lack of fitness told; also very unhappy with de Angelis after the 'incident'.

**12 NICKY HAYDEN** A painful debut for Ducati in his 100th GP, with a 130mph highside in practice leaving him with stitches in his chest and a very sore back, plus doubts about his ability to take part. Still put in his fastest laps of the weekend in the last five or six laps of the race.

**13 SETE GIBERNAU** A discreet return to competition after a two-year lay-off. Still suffering from a shoulder injury he'd picked up in training, so too early to judge the wisdom

of his comeback. At least he and Rossi resumed diplomatic relations.

**14 MARCO MELANDRI** Seriously disappointed after qualifying well, his race ruined when he overshot the end of the straight on lap two, putting himself at the back of the field by nearly nine seconds. Scoring points from that position was definitely impressive.

**15 YUKI TAKAHASHI** A quiet start to his MotoGP career. Yuki was happy to score the final point and said he learnt a lot from following Melandri for so long.

**16 JAMES TOSELAND** Suffered with stability problems all weekend but was closing on Kallio and de Puniet when an attempted

overtake by Elias put James off track at the last corner. After that, there was little chance of getting back into a points-scoring position.

**17 NICCOLO CANEPA** Not surprisingly, Niccolo was somewhat overwhelmed by his first MotoGP race.

## NON-FINISHERS

**LORIS CAPIROSSI** Lost the front on lap eight after showing well early on. The change in track conditions affected the Suzukis more than other bikes and, like his team-mate, Loris had problems with the front tyre as well as serious race-day chatter that led to his crash.

# JAPANESE GP
TWIN-RING MOTEGI

ROUND **2**
**April 26**

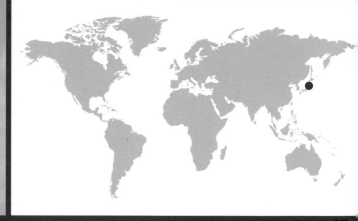

# YOUNG PRETENDER

**Jorge Lorenzo showed his team-mate what he could expect for the rest of the year**

When weather conditions, or other outside factors, make life difficult for the teams, one would certainly expect Rossi's crew, led by Jeremy Burgess, to use their massive experience to give their boy a bike that works well – and usually better than anyone else's. It looked as if that would be the story of the Japanese GP. Terrible weather followed the paddock from Qatar to Japan and ensured that race set-up would be a guessing game. The rain on Saturday was bad enough to wash out qualifying, and Sunday morning's warm-up was also wet, so when the MotoGP riders went to the grid under blue skies they had less than an hour of dry testing under their belts on tarmac that was ten degrees warmer than it had been all weekend. Just the circumstances, one might think, for Burgess & Co to work their magic.

And that's how it looked in the opening laps. Valentino Rossi bolted from the start, leaving Pedrosa and Lorenzo to fight their way through to second and third places. Jorge moved into second on lap three and immediately closed on his team-mate. His first attempt at a pass only resulted in an immediate retake, but half a lap later he went to the front on the brakes at the end of the downhill back straight, Motegi's favoured passing place. Now it was the turn of Rossi to be the stalker, although it was apparent after a few laps that Lorenzo was more comfortable than the World Champion. Both men were on Bridgestone's medium compound rear tyre, the choice of the majority of the field, so that shouldn't have been an issue. However, Rossi reported a problem in the middle part of the race that killed his corner speed. Then a mistake lost Valentino the best part of a second and all of a sudden he was under

attack from Dani Pedrosa. The Spaniard gave Honda something to smile about at their home circuit, on the 50th anniversary of their entry to GPs, while the crowd was treated to the unusual sight of Rossi being harried and passed by a Honda, although he retook second place a lap later. Valentino was then able to close slightly on Jorge, but as he said himself, 'I enjoy the last part of the race but it was too far to try and attack him.'

No-one was more surprised by Pedrosa's rostrum place than Dani himself. When he'd found himself battling with the Yamahas he thought 'maybe two laps', then 'maybe five', and so on until the flag. Given that Dani had been unable to train since October, this was, in his words, 'an unbelievable result'. Honda's second factory rider, Andrea Dovizioso, also impressed in his fights with, first, his team-mate, and then with Casey Stoner, although it was very noticeable that even in Japan both Repsol riders were surprisingly open in their criticism of the RC212V and the lack of new parts. Stoner had a difficult start to the race with a brake problem that faded as the laps rolled out, eventually enabling him to deal with Dovizioso. It was probably something as mundane as a high spot on a disc that wore down with use.

It was noticeable that Rossi was happy to chat to Pedrosa, and he congratulated him warmly in *parc fermé*; indeed, the two always exhibit animated mutual respect. Not surprisingly, Valentino didn't have such a warm exchange with Lorenzo. Jorge's win might only have been his second in MotoGP, but it was laden with significance. Of course, Rossi has been

beaten by team-mates when he has crashed, suffered mechanical maladies or been caught out in flag-to-flag races, but to finish second to the guy on the other side of the pit garage when none of those external factors had skewed the outcome was a very rare experience for him.

It was a significant win for the young Spaniard as well. His victory put him on the top of the championship table (as opposed to being joint leader) for the first time; it was also his first win on Bridgestone tyres and it was the first occasion since his maiden win in the 2008 Portuguese GP that he was the first Yamaha rider across the line. The wider significance of the race wasn't lost on anybody. Eight-times World Champion Valentino Rossi was now sharing a garage and a bike with someone who was capable not just of pressuring him but, on occasion, beating him. This was totally new territory for all concerned.

The sight of Marco Melandri winning the entertaining fight for sixth place gave hope to all the non-factory teams, and Mika Kallio's second MotoGP race resulted in

**Above** The shape of things to come for the rest of the season: the Fiat Yamaha team-mates in close combat

**Opposite** Jorge Lorenzo prepares to plant his Lorenzo's Land flag in a Japanese gravel trap

## 'I ENJOY THE LAST PART OF THE RACE BUT IT WAS TOO FAR TO TRY AND ATTACK HIM'
**VALENTINO ROSSI**

**Right** Loris Capirossi tried as hard as ever but a gamble on settings didn't pay off – he finished seventh

**Opposite** Casey Stoner was handicapped in the first part of the race by a vibration on the brakes; it wore off and he came fourth

**Below** Dani Pedrosa surprised himself with third place and upheld Honda's honour at home on the 50th anniversary of the company's first GP

another solid eighth place. Given that the Finn suffered a massive highside in practice and could only qualify 17th, this was an even better ride than at Qatar and prompted the thought that maybe a good, front-end-happy 250 rider was what the Desmosedici really needed.

What Motegi undoubtedly showed was that the top four riders – Rossi, Lorenzo, Stoner and Pedrosa (even though Dani was still physically below par) – were better than the rest by a distance. Someone, maybe Marco Melandri, although some say it was Randy de Puniet, came up with a neat phrase for the quartet. He called them 'the Aliens'. As the season unfolded, it would seem an increasingly fitting description.

# THE STRANGE CASE OF COLIN EDWARDS

At the end of the first lap Colin Edwards raised his hand to indicate he was slowing with some sort of problem. Everyone assumed it was mechanical, but it wasn't: his crew had fouled up and sent him out with the wet-weather mapping in the engine management electronics. Colin had so little power under his right hand that he was terrified of getting rammed from behind. He kept going, though, and a look at his lap times reveals astounding evidence of the sophistication of Yamaha's electronics.

On his first flying lap Colin did a time of 1m 56.383s; on lap 15 he set his best time of the race at 1m 49.397s, the sixth best personal lap of the race behind the factory Hondas, the Fiat Yamahas and Stoner's Ducati. How was this possible? How could an engine management system allow an improvement in lap time of seven seconds?

The answer is as simple as it is amazing: the system 'learnt' and altered its settings and limits as the race went on. At the start it had a limit on how much power it would allow the bike to use in each corner. As Colin started with wet settings this was well under the safe limit for the warm, dry track, so when he opened the throttle, as he said, it was 'a joke'. However, the really clever thing about Yamaha's system is that if the power allowed on any corner doesn't produce a certain amount of wheelspin, then next time around it allows the rider a little more power, and so on, until it finds the limit. It would seem that took 15 laps.

Yamaha call this system mu-Learning, as in the Greek letter 'mu', the symbol for the coefficient of friction – which the system is effectively measuring corner by corner, lap by lap. There were some shocked-looking people in pit lane when they realised just what had gone on and that Yamaha's electronics could effectively learn during a race. Colin may have been totally ticked off with finishing 12th, but there couldn't have been a better demonstration of why the Yamaha M1 was now the best all-round bike on the grid.

**Above** Colin Edwards had a dreadful race but demonstrated just how sophisticated Yamaha's electronics have become

**BRIDGESTONE**
TYRE OPTIONS
FRONT SOFT (**S**) / MEDIUM (**M**)
REAR SOFT (**S**) / MEDIUM (**M**)

**OFFICIAL TIMEKEEPER**

# JAPANESE GP
## TWIN-RING MOTEGI

### ROUND 2
**April 26**

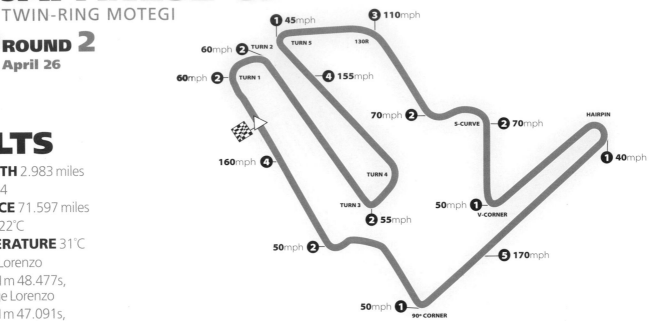

# RACE RESULTS

**CIRCUIT LENGTH** 2.983 miles
**NO. OF LAPS** 24
**RACE DISTANCE** 71.597 miles
**WEATHER** Dry, 22°C
**TRACK TEMPERATURE** 31°C
**WINNER** Jorge Lorenzo
**FASTEST LAP** 1m 48.477s, 99.002mph, Jorge Lorenzo
**LAP RECORD** 1m 47.091s, 100.288mph, Casey Stoner, 2008

## QUALIFYING

| | Rider | Nationality | Team | **FP1** | Pole + | Gap |
|---|---|---|---|---|---|---|
| 1 | Rossi | ITA | Fiat Yamaha Team | 1m 48.545s | | |
| 2 | Stoner | AUS | Ducati Marlboro Team | 1m 48.601s | 0.056s | 0.056s |
| 3 | Lorenzo | SPA | Fiat Yamaha Team | 1m 48.965s | 0.420s | 0.364s |
| 4 | Vermeulen | AUS | Rizla Suzuki MotoGP | 1m 49.382s | 0.837s | 0.417s |
| 5 | Edwards | USA | Monster Yamaha Tech 3 | 1m 49.697s | 1.152s | 0.315s |
| 6 | Capirossi | ITA | Rizla Suzuki MotoGP | 1m 49.980s | 1.435s | 0.283s |
| 7 | Dovizioso | ITA | Repsol Honda Team | 1m 50.030s | 1.485s | 0.050s |
| 8 | Melandri | ITA | Hayate Racing Team | 1m 50.123s | 1.578s | 0.093s |
| 9 | Elias | SPA | San Carlo Honda Gresini | 1m 50.209s | 1.664s | 0.086s |
| 10 | Toseland | GBR | Monster Yamaha Tech 3 | 1m 50.342s | 1.797s | 0.133s |
| 11 | Pedrosa | SPA | Repsol Honda Team | 1m 50.391s | 1.846s | 0.049s |
| 12 | Hayden | USA | Ducati Marlboro Team | 1m 50.393s | 1.848s | 0.002s |
| 13 | Takahashi | JPN | Scot Racing Team MotoGP | 1m 50.404s | 1.859s | 0.011s |
| 14 | Gibernau | SPA | Grupo Francisco Hernado | 1m 50.538s | 1.993s | 0.134s |
| 15 | De Angelis | RSM | San Carlo Honda Gresini | 1m 50.601s | 2.056s | 0.063s |
| 16 | De Puniet | FRA | LCR Honda MotoGP | 1m 50.669s | 2.124s | 0.068s |
| 17 | Kallio | FIN | Pramac Racing | 1m 51.643s | 3.098s | 0.974s |
| 18 | Canepa | ITA | Pramac Racing | 1m 51.929s | 3.384s | 0.286s |

## FINISHERS

**1 JORGE LORENZO** A second MotoGP win, 16 races after his maiden victory, gave Jorge solo leadership of the championship for the first time. It was also his first win on Bridgestone tyres. Able to run the pace he wanted throughout the race, he led from lap nine to the flag.

**2 VALENTINO ROSSI** For once Rossi and Burgess didn't get their set-up perfect, unsurprisingly as Saturday qualifying was rained off, Sunday warm-up was wet and the race was dry. Quickest from the start, Pedrosa gave him trouble mid-race, but he put some pressure on Lorenzo in the closing laps.

**3 DANI PEDROSA** A rostrum in the second race was an unexpected surprise, for Dani's knee was still giving problems and the Honda V4 was far from the equal of the Yamaha. Thought his physical condition might have prevented him using sufficient power for a podium place.

**4 CASEY STONER** Felt serious vibration from the front brakes on the warm-up lap, hindering him for the first six laps. No visible problem afterwards so it may have been a high spot that wore off as the race unfolded. Able to pass Dovizioso on the penultimate lap.

**5 ANDREA DOVIZIOSO** Much closer to the leaders than he'd been at Qatar – 9s behind as opposed to 27s – but still frustrated with his motorcycle. Getting it into corners was the most pressing of his problems.

**6 MARCO MELANDRI** Went into sixth place on the sixth lap from eighth on the grid and held off Capirossi for the rest of the race. An encouraging result for the Hayate team after the disappointment of the first round.

**7 LORIS CAPIROSSI** Like everyone else Loris gambled on set-up, and also like most he didn't get a bike that was particularly easy to ride. A second-row start was wasted when he got boxed in on the first lap, and once he got up to seventh the next group was too far away to catch.

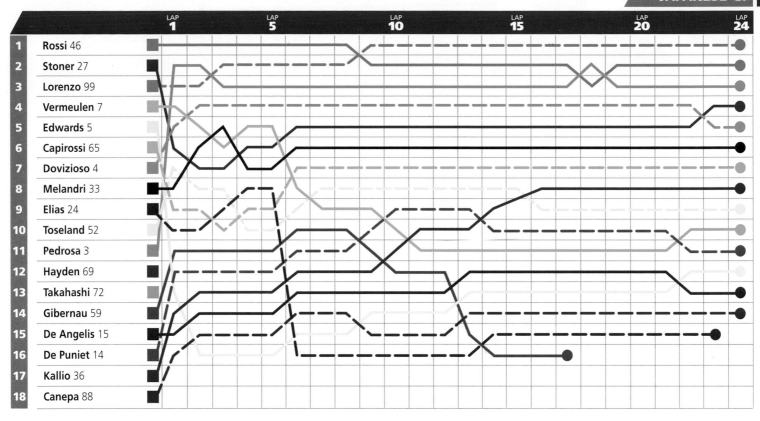

| | | LAP 1 | LAP 5 | LAP 10 | LAP 15 | LAP 20 | LAP 24 |
|---|---|---|---|---|---|---|---|
| 1 | Rossi 46 | | | | | | |
| 2 | Stoner 27 | | | | | | |
| 3 | Lorenzo 99 | | | | | | |
| 4 | Vermeulen 7 | | | | | | |
| 5 | Edwards 5 | | | | | | |
| 6 | Capirossi 65 | | | | | | |
| 7 | Dovizioso 4 | | | | | | |
| 8 | Melandri 33 | | | | | | |
| 9 | Elias 24 | | | | | | |
| 10 | Toseland 52 | | | | | | |
| 11 | Pedrosa 3 | | | | | | |
| 12 | Hayden 69 | | | | | | |
| 13 | Takahashi 72 | | | | | | |
| 14 | Gibernau 59 | | | | | | |
| 15 | De Angelis 15 | | | | | | |
| 16 | De Puniet 14 | | | | | | |
| 17 | Kallio 36 | | | | | | |
| 18 | Canepa 88 | | | | | | |

## RACE

| | Rider | Motorcycle | Race Time | Time + | Fastest Lap | Av Speed | B |
|---|---|---|---|---|---|---|---|
| 1 | Lorenzo | Yamaha | 43m 47.238s | | 1m 48.477s | 98.110mph | M/M |
| 2 | Rossi | Yamaha | 43m 48.542s | 1.304s | 1m 48.563s | 98.061mph | M/M |
| 3 | Pedrosa | Honda | 43m 51.001s | 3.763s | 1m 48.602s | 97.970mph | M/M |
| 4 | Stoner | Ducati | 43m 52.929s | 5.691s | 1m 48.635s | 97.898mph | M/M |
| 5 | Dovizioso | Honda | 43m 56.445s | 9.207s | 1m 48.732s | 97.767mph | M/M |
| 6 | Melandri | Kawasaki | 44m 17.793s | 30.555s | 1m 49.703s | 96.982mph | M/M |
| 7 | Capirossi | Suzuki | 44m 19.994s | 32.756s | 1m 49.727s | 96.902mph | M/M |
| 8 | Kallio | Ducati | 44m 26.654s | 39.416s | 1m 49.816s | 96.660mph | M/S |
| 9 | Toseland | Yamaha | 44m 30.344s | 43.106s | 1m 50.470s | 96.527mph | M/S |
| 10 | Vermeulen | Suzuki | 44m 30.483s | 43.245s | 1m 49.893s | 96.522mph | M/M |
| 11 | De Puniet | Honda | 44m 32.072s | 44.834s | 1m 50.127s | 96.464mph | M/M |
| 12 | Edwards | Yamaha | 44m 33.778s | 46.540s | 1m 49.397s | 96.402mph | M/M |
| 13 | De Angelis | Honda | 44m 40.763s | 53.525s | 1m 50.141s | 96.151mph | M/M |
| 14 | Canepa | Ducati | 45m 09.042s | 1m 21.804s | 1m 51.713s | 95.148mph | M/M |
| 15 | Elias | Honda | 44m 25.681s | 1 lap | 1m 49.949s | 92.666mph | M/M |
| | Gibernau | Ducati | 41m 40.115s | 7 laps | 1m 50.349s | 73.028mph | M/M |

## CHAMPIONSHIP

| | Rider | Team | Points |
|---|---|---|---|
| 1 | Lorenzo | Fiat Yamaha Team | 41 |
| 2 | Rossi | Fiat Yamaha Team | 40 |
| 3 | Stoner | Stoner Marlboro Team | 38 |
| 4 | Dovizioso | Repsol Honda Team | 22 |
| 5 | Pedrosa | Repsol Honda Team | 21 |
| 6 | Edwards | Monster Yamaha Tech 3 | 17 |
| 7 | Kallio | Pramac Racing | 16 |
| 8 | Vermeulen | Rizla Suzuki MotoGP | 15 |
| 9 | De Angelis | San Carlo Honda Gresini | 13 |
| 10 | Melandri | Hayate Racing Team | 12 |
| 11 | De Puniet | LCR Honda MotoGP | 11 |
| 12 | Capirossi | Rizla Suzuki MotoGP | 9 |
| 13 | Elias | San Carlo Honda Gresini | 8 |
| 14 | Toseland | Monster Yamaha Tech 3 | 7 |
| 15 | Hayden | Ducati Marlboro Team | 4 |
| 16 | Gibernau | Grupo Francisco Hernando | 3 |
| 17 | Canepa | Pramac Racing | 2 |
| 18 | Takahashi | Scot Racing Team MotoGP | 1 |

**8 MIKA KALLIO** Another very impressive performance in his second MotoGP race. Started from 17th on the grid after an enormous crash on Friday, last in the early stages, then rode past half a dozen other riders. Obviously likes Motegi, having won there three times in the smaller classes.

**9 JAMES TOSELAND** Used the soft rear tyre on Friday and stuck with it for the race, although he knew it would make life difficult in the closing stages. Boosted his confidence by holding off de Puniet and re-passing Vermeulen on the last lap.

**10 CHRIS VERMEULEN** Ran at the front early on and was shadowing Rossi when his quickshifter started malfunctioning. Thought he'd worked out

how to ride round the problem, but from lap six had to shut the throttle and use the clutch for each change. The bad-luck story of the race, but still his first top-ten finish at Motegi.

**11 RANDY DE PUNIET** Not happy when qualifying was cancelled, not least because he was 16th on the grid. Found the bike physically demanding and lacking grip from the rear tyre.

**12 COLIN EDWARDS** One of the few to use the harder rear tyre on Friday so should have had an advantage on race day, especially starting from the second row, but the wet-weather map was in his engine management system and it took ages to let him use full power. Then

lapped at top-five pace. A very strange race – and a missed opportunity.

**13 ALEX DE ANGELIS** Used his settings from Friday afternoon for the race but with the harder tyres rather than the softer option he'd practised on. It didn't work and he reported no feeling from them. Not the way Alex wanted to celebrate his 150th career GP.

**14 NICCOLO CANEPA** Another difficult weekend, but this time with the consolation of a couple of points, his first in MotoGP. His main problem was with the rear of the bike, but he was puzzled after the race because his tyre looked fine.

**15 TONI ELIAS** A cautious start. Attacked

when he had some heat in his tyres, moving past Toseland and Capirossi on consecutive laps and closing on Melandri, but a wide line going into the hairpin at the top of the circuit put him on dirty tarmac and he slid off. Remounted to take the last point despite 'that stupid mistake'.

## NON-FINISHERS

**SETE GIBERNAU** Slid off his Ducati on the 13th lap when he lost the front. He was in 12th place at the time. Got back on but retired six laps later.

**YUKI TAKAHASHI** Outbraked himself at the hairpin on the first lap, and took Hayden down as well.

**NICKY HAYDEN** An innocent victim of Takahashi's accident, taking another hard knock to the same part of his back that had suffered in his big Qatar crash. Felt happier with his team and bike than he had at the first race, but 'knew we were never looking at a great result'.

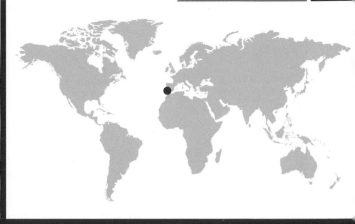

# PARADISE REGAINED

**Three races, three different winners, three different championship leaders: this time it was Valentino Rossi's turn**

After two flyaway races complicated by some extreme weather, Spain and its continual sunshine was, said Valentino Rossi, like being in Paradise. He didn't feel quite the same way after qualifying, but at the chequered flag his world was perfect again.

On Saturday Rossi wasn't happy. He qualified on the second row and had a gentle moan about the Bridgestone front tyre not being as hard as the one he and Casey Stoner used last year, and also confessed to lacking feel from the front. He was blunt in his assessment of his chances: 'I won't be able to win.' To make matters worse, Jorge Lorenzo was on pole. This wasn't what Valentino needed after events in Japan, where his team-mate had beaten him. What's more, the limited track time they'd had at Motegi, due to the weather, should have played to the strengths and massive experience of Rossi and his crew, but that simply hadn't happened. Now, under Andalusian sunshine, Rossi and his crew again failed to make the best of their bike in qualifying. There were some seriously furrowed brows on the right-hand side of the Fiat Yamaha garage, but somehow the old magic was summoned up and this time it did work.

Jerry Burgess and his team threw a major modification at Rossi's bike on Sunday morning after a lot of thinking overnight. Effectively they raised the bike's ride height so that, under both braking and acceleration, it pitched to and fro a little more, working the tyres harder in order to get some heat into them. In Sunday warm-up Valentino was fastest – just another minor miracle from JB. They even got it right for the increased track temperature on race day. Motegi had obviously been a blip.

Even the race was old-school Rossi. He didn't get the holeshot but had to work his way past Lorenzo, Stoner and Pedrosa. True to form, Dani hit the front at the first corner, pursued by Casey and Jorge. Valentino took third off his team-mate half-way round the second lap, then closed up on Stoner. The Ducati rider had never had any luck at Jerez – in fact he'd never been on the rostrum at the Spanish GP, in any class – and in recent years the Desmosedici had looked particularly unsuited to the circuit. Not any more. It took Rossi more than one attempt to get ahead. The decisive move was a near-replica of that infamous pass on Gibernau, up the inside at the final corner with that left leg waving in the breeze, a sure indication that Rossi was trying, and trying very hard. Valentino now found himself 1.33s behind Pedrosa, and that's the way it stayed for the next nine laps. Then came the charge that took him up to and past Dani on

the brakes in the stadium section. Pedrosa had no answer but he was happy, delighted even, to be able to exceed all expectations – especially his own – at his home race. He'd wanted to win, of course, but was 'very happy with the podium, and surprised too'. The Honda rider explained that when Rossi came past he just concentrated on running his own race. However, he again mentioned that the bike wasn't yet up to expectations, as did Andrea Dovizioso.

Once Rossi was ahead he pulled away, leaving the on-track interest in the group battles going on all the way down the field. It looked as if Stoner had a safe third place, but Lorenzo started to eat into the three-second gap and five laps from the flag had the margin well under a second. Stoner knew Jorge was coming and pushed again. He'd had several hairy moments in his earlier dice with Rossi and was getting a feeling of déjà vu when Lorenzo suddenly lost the

front. The Yamaha had been slower than on Friday and Saturday because of the change in track temperature, and Lorenzo did wonder if he should have 'gone more gently'. But the desire to do well in front of his home fans overrode any such caution. And, as Jorge pointed out, a rider going at the same pace as Casey is already

## 'IT'S ONLY THIRD PLACE BUT IT FEELS EVEN BETTER THAN THE WIN IN QATAR'
**CASEY STONER**

**Above** Dani Pedrosa performed above anyone's expectations in leading for over half the race

**Opposite** Thankfully everyone got through the first corner this year

**Above** A brilliant fifth place for Marco Melandri on the Kawasaki gave hope to the cash-strapped Hayate team

on the limit, so to attack him is to take a risk. Lorenzo extended this analysis to his other rivals, Rossi and Pedrosa: to race at the pace of the top men this season meant you were always taking chances.

Stoner was pleasantly surprised by his third place, countering Rossi's complaint about not having last year's tyre with an observation to the effect that everyone was

in the same situation now. However, Casey did get in his own dig about the reduced track time available, with the loss of the Friday morning session, by remarking that before the race he had thought a podium 'would be a long shot, though we had the best setting we could get in the time available'.

Randy de Puniet's fourth place after

an impressive fifth in qualifying gave hope to satellite teams, and Marco Melandri's top-five result again exceeded anyone's expectations. He beat Capirossi and Edwards fair and square in one of the group battles and said that he hoped the result would encourage Kawasaki to do some development work.

To show that normal order had been restored, Valentino treated the crowd to his first post-race stunt of the season. Actually, it was a rerun of one of his best. Ten years previously he had won the 250cc race at Jerez and on the slow-down lap he'd stopped and run into a marshals' Portaloo. He revisited 'one of the funniest jokes' to celebrate the fact he was still winning here. It was, in fact, Rossi's sixth win in the top class at Jerez and, perhaps just as significantly, it was his 64th podium on a Yamaha, putting him level with Wayne Rainey's record. And he also went to the top of the championship table. Happy days.

**Below** Randy de Puniet beat all the other Honda riders except Pedrosa on his way to a fighting and well-deserved fourth place

# HONDA ENGINES FOR MOTO2

*The shape of the 250cc replacement class, Moto2, became clearer with the announcement that the spec engine would be supplied by Honda. Originally, the idea had been floated that teams would build their own engines using off-the-shelf internal components, all of which would have to comply with very detailed regulations as to material, weight, etc. Not surprisingly, this concept was shelved because it would have been extremely difficult to police, and so manufacturers were invited to tender to supply a control engine. The crucial cost-saving measures of spec electronics and data-logging were retained, however.*

*Two factories tendered, Yamaha and Honda. It is thought that the decision went to Honda because their engine would be more of a racer than Yamaha's, which would have been a very standard R6 motor. The Honda suggestion, while obviously based on the CBR600 power unit, incorporated such racetrack necessities as a deeper sump and chamfered engine cases and would make over 150hp – although the announcement didn't specify where that power output would be measured. The engines wouldn't be available for several months, but teams were assured that if they designed their chassis with regard to standard CBR600 engine mountings they would be doing nothing wrong. Three-dimensional computer graphics of the motor were made available under a confidentiality agreement.*

*The only aspect of the deal that wasn't immediately popular in the paddock was the likelihood that the engine wouldn't have a cassette gearbox. (Only Kawasaki's 600 has one, which gave rise to an earlier rumour that Kawasaki would be the supplier.) Honda could, of course, modify their crankcases for a cassette gearbox but the add-on cost would be considerable – several thousand dollars – and that wasn't considered a viable option, although Honda did suggest that the modification might be incorporated after the 2010 season.*

*Teams were told that the deadline for some hard facts about riders, machines, sponsors, etc, would be the Portuguese GP in early October, when an entry list was due to be published.*

**Above** Aleix Espargaro on a Harris-framed Moto2 bike in the '09 Spanish Championship

© Harris Performance

# SPANISH GP
## CIRCUITO DE JEREZ

### ROUND 3
May 3

# RACE RESULTS

**CIRCUIT LENGTH** 2.748 miles
**NO. OF LAPS** 27
**RACE DISTANCE** 74.16 miles
**WEATHER** Dry, 27°C
**TRACK TEMPERATURE** 45°C
**WINNER** Valentino Rossi
**FASTEST LAP** 1m 39.818s, 99.120mph, Valentino Rossi (record)
**PREVIOUS LAP RECORD** 1m 40.116s, 98.824mph, Dani Pedrosa, 2008

Track map labels:
- 60mph — 2
- 165mph — 5
- MICHELIN
- 100mph — 3
- 45mph — 2
- PELUQUI — 2 70mph
- ENZO FERRARI — 3 110mph
- 3 95mph
- 80mph — 3
- ANGEL NIETO — 2 60mph
- 3 100mph
- 95mph — 3
- 2 45mph
- DUCADOS
- 80mph — 3 SITO PONS
- DRY SACK — 2 45mph
- 5 170mph
- EXPO '92

## QUALIFYING

| | Rider | Nationality | Team | Qualifying | Pole + | Gap |
|---|---|---|---|---|---|---|
| 1 | Lorenzo | SPA | Fiat Yamaha Team | 1m 38.933s | | |
| 2 | Pedrosa | SPA | Repsol Honda Team | 1m 38.984s | 0.051s | 0.051s |
| 3 | Stoner | AUS | Ducati Marlboro Team | 1m 39.415s | 0.482s | 0.431s |
| 4 | Rossi | ITA | Fiat Yamaha Team | 1m 39.642s | 0.709s | 0.227s |
| 5 | De Puniet | FRA | LCR Honda MotoGP | 1m 39.806s | 0.873s | 0.164s |
| 6 | Capirossi | ITA | Rizla Suzuki MotoGP | 1m 39.862s | 0.929s | 0.056s |
| 7 | Edwards | USA | Monster Yamaha Tech 3 | 1m 39.926s | 0.993s | 0.064s |
| 8 | Dovizioso | ITA | Repsol Honda Team | 1m 39.966s | 1.033s | 0.040s |
| 9 | Elias | SPA | San Carlo Honda Gresini | 1m 40.112s | 1.179s | 0.146s |
| 10 | Vermeulen | AUS | Rizla Suzuki MotoGP | 1m 40.185s | 1.252s | 0.073s |
| 11 | Melandri | ITA | Hayate Racing Team | 1m 40.381s | 1.448s | 0.196s |
| 12 | Gibernau | SPA | Grupo Francisco Hernando | 1m 40.440s | 1.507s | 0.059s |
| 13 | Takahashi | JPN | Scot Racing Team MotoGP | 1m 40.599s | 1.666s | 0.159s |
| 14 | Toseland | GBR | Monster Yamaha Tech 3 | 1m 40.670s | 1.737s | 0.071s |
| 15 | De Angelis | RSM | San Carlo Honda Gresini | 1m 40.796s | 1.863s | 0.126s |
| 16 | Hayden | USA | Ducati Marlboro Team | 1m 40.953s | 2.020s | 0.157s |
| 17 | Kallio | FIN | Pramac Racing | 1m 41.238s | 2.305s | 0.285s |
| 18 | Canepa | ITA | Pramac Racing | 1m 41.253s | 2.230s | 0.015s |

## FINISHERS

**1 VALENTINO ROSSI** Another minor miracle: the M1 wasn't performing until warm-up, when he was fastest. Fought with Lorenzo, then Stoner, then Pedrosa for his first win of the season, taking him 11 points clear in the table. Also his 64th podium for Yamaha, equalling Rainey's record.

**2 DANI PEDROSA** Another surprise result. Conceded that second exceeded all expectations, given his lack of strength and testing, but disappointed not to have won for his home fans. Led the first 17 laps, holding Rossi off for more than ten of them.

**3 CASEY STONER** First front row on a MotoGP bike at Jerez, a circuit the Ducati is always said not to suit, finishing on the podium for the first time in any class. In *parc fermé* looked as happy as if he'd won, though almost lost the front while trying to match the pace of Rossi and Pedrosa.

**4 RANDY DE PUNIET** By far his best result here (13th in 2007) and best finish since leaving Kawasaki. Fifth on the grid and fourth In the race, albeit due to a couple of crashes in front of him, came thanks to a near-faultless weekend – and proof that his new trainer, ex-motocross champ Yves Demaria, was having the desired effect.

**5 MARCO MELANDRI** A superb result for the impecunious Hayate team in Marco's

100th race in MotoGP. Won a race-long battle with Capirossi and Edwards, then expressed the hope that his impressive start to the season would encourage Kawasaki to develop some new parts.

**6 LORIS CAPIROSSI** A change of rear tyre on the line affected his performance in the opening laps and put him down to ninth. Passed Edwards and Melandri only for grip to go off and they got back in front. Fought back to fifth before running wide, but passed Colin on the last lap.

**7 COLIN EDWARDS** Never got his rear suspension setting right and temperature variations between morning and afternoon sessions further confused the issue. Adjusted his usual front-end style to get some weight

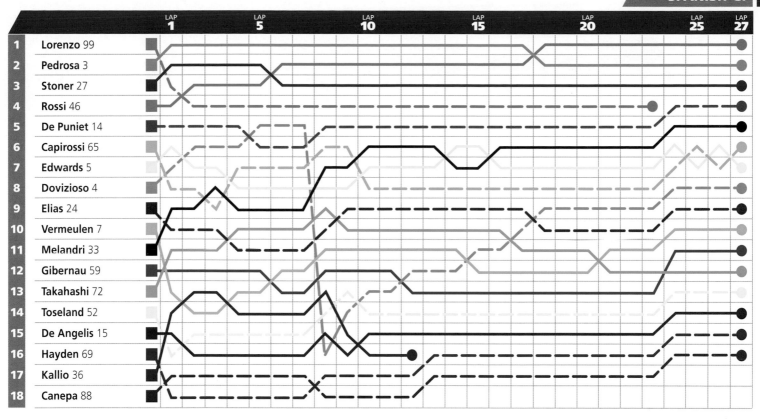

| | | LAP 1 | LAP 5 | LAP 10 | LAP 15 | LAP 20 | LAP 25 | LAP 27 |
|---|---|---|---|---|---|---|---|---|
| 1 | Lorenzo 99 | | | | | | | |
| 2 | Pedrosa 3 | | | | | | | |
| 3 | Stoner 27 | | | | | | | |
| 4 | Rossi 46 | | | | | | | |
| 5 | De Puniet 14 | | | | | | | |
| 6 | Capirossi 65 | | | | | | | |
| 7 | Edwards 5 | | | | | | | |
| 8 | Dovizioso 4 | | | | | | | |
| 9 | Elias 24 | | | | | | | |
| 10 | Vermeulen 7 | | | | | | | |
| 11 | Melandri 33 | | | | | | | |
| 12 | Gibernau 59 | | | | | | | |
| 13 | Takahashi 72 | | | | | | | |
| 14 | Toseland 52 | | | | | | | |
| 15 | De Angelis 15 | | | | | | | |
| 16 | Hayden 69 | | | | | | | |
| 17 | Kallio 36 | | | | | | | |
| 18 | Canepa 88 | | | | | | | |

## RACE

| | Rider | Motorcycle | Race Time | Time + | Fastest Lap | Av Speed | B |
|---|---|---|---|---|---|---|---|
| 1 | Rossi | Yamaha | 45m 18.557s | | 1m 39.818s | 98.268mph | H/M |
| 2 | Pedrosa | Honda | 45m 21.257s | 2.700s | 1m 39.836s | 98.171mph | H/M |
| 3 | Stoner | Ducati | 45m 29.064s | 10.507s | 1m 39.855s | 97.890mph | H/M |
| 4 | De Puniet | Honda | 45m 50.450s | 31.893s | 1m 40.432s | 97.129mph | H/M |
| 5 | Melandri | Kawasaki | 45m 51.685s | 33.128s | 1m 40.929s | 97.085mph | H/M |
| 6 | Capirossi | Suzuki | 45m 52.685s | 34.128s | 1m 40.775s | 97.050mph | H/M |
| 7 | Edwards | Yamaha | 45m 52.978s | 34.421s | 1m 41.130s | 97.039mph | H/M |
| 8 | Dovizioso | Honda | 45m 53.182s | 34.625s | 1m 40.173s | 97.032mph | H/M |
| 9 | Elias | Honda | 46m 01.246s | 42.689s | 1m 41.259s | 96.749mph | H/M |
| 10 | Vermeulen | Suzuki | 46m 03.740s | 45.183s | 1m 41.374s | 96.661mph | H/M |
| 11 | Gibernau | Ducati | 46m 06.749s | 48.192s | 1m 41.457s | 96.556mph | H/M |
| 12 | Takahashi | Honda | 46m 10.432s | 51.875s | 1m 41.064s | 96.428mph | H/M |
| 13 | Toseland | Yamaha | 46m 12.240s | 53.683s | 1m 41.243s | 96.365mph | H/M |
| 14 | De Angelis | Honda | 46m 12.498s | 53.941s | 1m 41.644s | 96.356mph | H/M |
| 15 | Hayden | Ducati | 46m 19.794s | 1m 01.237s | 1m 42.036s | 96.103mph | H/S |
| 16 | Canepa | Ducati | 46m 29.453s | 1m 10.896s | 1m 41.986s | 95.770mph | H/S |
| 17 | Lorenzo | Yamaha | 38m 40.226s | 4 laps | 1m 40.137s | 98.081mph | H/M |
| 18 | Kallio | Ducati | 20m 38.937s | 15 laps | 1m 41.582s | 95.834mph | H/S |

## CHAMPIONSHIP

| | Rider | Team | Points |
|---|---|---|---|
| 1 | Rossi | Fiat Yamaha Team | 65 |
| 2 | Stoner | Ducati Marlboro Team | 54 |
| 3 | Lorenzo | Fiat Yamaha Team | 41 |
| 4 | Pedrosa | Repsol Honda Team | 41 |
| 5 | Dovizioso | Repsol Honda Team | 30 |
| 6 | Edwards | Monster Yamaha Tech 3 | 26 |
| 7 | De Puniet | LCR Honda MotoGP | 24 |
| 8 | Melandri | Hayate Racing Team | 23 |
| 9 | Vermeulen | Rizla Suzuki MotoGP | 21 |
| 10 | Capirossi | Rizla Suzuki MotoGP | 19 |
| 11 | Kallio | Pramac Racing | 16 |
| 12 | De Angelis | San Carlo Honda Gresini | 15 |
| 13 | Elias | San Carlo Honda Gresini | 15 |
| 14 | Toseland | Monster Yamaha Tech 3 | 10 |
| 15 | Gibernau | Grupo Francisco Hernando | 8 |
| 16 | Takahashi | Scot Racing Team MotoGP | 5 |
| 17 | Hayden | Ducati Marlboro Team | 5 |
| 18 | Canepa | Pramac Racing | 2 |

over the rear and make the bike turn. Unhappy not to be in the top six.

**8 ANDREA DOVIZIOSO** Lost the rear while in fifth place chasing Lorenzo and ran off track, rejoining in 16th place. Was right behind the group fighting for fifth at the flag, but still unhappy with lack of new parts for the Honda.

**9 TONI ELIAS** Closer to the leaders than he'd been in the first two races, but scant consolation at a track where he'd finished fourth in 2006 and 2007. Rear traction, or lack of it, was the main problem.

**10 CHRIS VERMEULEN** A victim of the first-corner bunching in the middle of the pack which put him behind a couple of Ducatis. Found himself in trouble with a lack of front grip when he finally overcame their superior speed.

**11 SETE GIBERNAU** Not the result he'd hoped for back in front of a Spanish crowd, but still the second Ducati home. Sete's physical condition was only just getting to a level he was happy with.

**12 YUKI TAKAHASHI** Best result so far. Improved on his qualifying position despite first his front and then his rear tyre giving him problems in the second half of the race. Felt he was getting to understand his bike.

**13 JAMES TOSELAND** Handicapped again by qualifying low down the grid and still struggling to find a setting that

is comfortable over race distance. Said he needs to find a second a lap to be where he thinks he should be.

**14 ALEX DE ANGELIS** Suffering from a bout of 'flu all weekend. Got stuck behind Toseland, and although Alex said he was 'much faster than him' he couldn't match James's braking, so spent the race in the Yamaha's wheel tracks.

**15 NICKY HAYDEN** Still suffering the effects of his heavy crashes in the opening races. Couldn't get on with the harder front tyre and raced with the softer option, but that didn't work until he got some heat into the rubber, only setting his personal best race lap the 17th time round.

**16 NICCOLO CANEPA** Another tough weekend for the rookie. Got a good start, then hit problems with the front end. Thought he should have been two or three places higher.

IRTA test and won the 250 race the previous season when a problem with the rear brake forced him to retire.

## NON-FINISHERS

**JORGE LORENZO** Pole position and searingly fast right up to race day, when the temperature increase meant his bike didn't work as he expected: 'We don't understand why, and this is more disappointing than the crash.' Fell four laps from the flag while fourth and closing down on Stoner.

**MIKA KALLIO** Going well on the track where he was sixth fastest in the pre-season

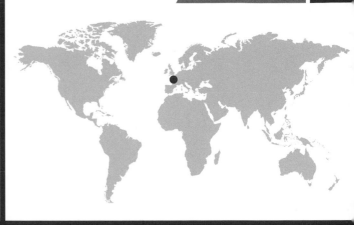

# SLIP-SLIDING AWAY

**The first flag-to-flag race of the year saw Fiat Yamaha riders finish first and last, with Marco Melandri a splendid second**

**A**nyone who thought the sunshine of Jerez meant that MotoGP had escaped the rain was brought up short on Sunday at Le Mans when a flag-to-flag race was run. For once, though, it was a race that started wet and turned dry, giving the riders and teams a whole new array of problems. The big question is always about when to change bikes. Theoretically, in a wet-to-dry race, the optimum time should be just before someone on slicks posts the fastest lap of the race so far. That happened on lap nine when Marco Melandri, who'd pitted on lap seven, started to move through the field from eleventh place towards the most unexpected rostrum finish of the season.

This wasn't just a case of Melandri striking it lucky with his timing, because he'd been up to third on wet tyres before he came in. Only three riders had pitted before him – Rossi, Pedrosa and Capirossi at the end of lap five – but these proved to be over-optimistic decisions. Valentino didn't make it round his out lap; he was caught by a damp patch invisible on the dark tarmac at Musée, and crashed. Pedrosa saw it happen and nearly fell himself. In fact, he reckoned it took at least three laps before he had any heat in his tyres.

The crash started Rossi on a bizarre progress downfield. He wrestled the bent bike back to the pits and remounted his wet machine, now with a slick on the rear, but was then penalised for speeding in pit lane. That brought him in for a ride-through penalty, and then he was in the pits again to get back on his now-roadworthy dry bike. This farrago put him two laps adrift of the field, but he persevered in the hope of picking up a point or two. It didn't happen. Valentino Rossi finished last for the first time ever – not something

## 'IS A TOTAL TURNAROUND. I HAVE TO LEARN TO BE CONSTANT, KEEP THE CALM. I DID A MISTAKE IN JEREZ, TAKE RISK AND CRASH. I WAS ANGRY BECAUSE I THOUGHT THIS YEAR I FINISH ALL THE RACES'

**JORGE LORENZO**

**Opposite** Dani Pedrosa put on a stunning late charge to pip his Repsol Honda team-mate Andrea Dovizioso to the final rostrum position

**Below** The least expected and most popular rostrum finish of the year – Marco Melandri's second place on the Kawasaki

he will be anxious to repeat. He had always intended to pit early, a decision reinforced when he saw he was losing ground to Lorenzo in the opening laps. The gap was over three seconds when Rossi went into the pits the first time.

No-one had told Jorge that it would be a good idea to pit on lap seven or eight, so he stayed out on wet tyres, feeling like he was riding a motocross bike and slightly handicapped by the fact he couldn't see his pit board. When Lorenzo finally came in at the end of lap 12 he had a lead of over 30 seconds, and he went out on his dry bike still well ahead of second-placed Melandri. The Kawasaki rider was able to close to within five seconds, but once Jorge was

confident about his tyres he pulled away again to win by 17 seconds. To lead every lap in a bike-change race is some achievement, especially after the disaster of the previous round. 'Is a total turnaround. I have to learn to be constant, keep the calm. I did a mistake in Jerez, take risk and crash. I was angry because I thought this year I finish all the races.'

The young Spanish rider nearly didn't get to start the race at all: he lined up on a 125/250 grid slot, but a sharp-eyed official noticed and he was allowed to move. Riders have been penalised for this error in recent years, so it was a lucky escape. And the late bike change? 'I trust my team.' This was, of course, his first flag-to-flag race. His race engineer, Daniele Romagnoli, waited until Jorge was losing more than a second a lap to his likely competitors before calling him in.

Lorenzo's win was as stunning as Rossi's misfortune, but the contrasting fates of the Fiat Yamaha riders somewhat overshadowed other significant rides. Dani Pedrosa might have been, in his own words, performing at less than 50 per cent fitness, but he set pole and the conditions on race day gave him a slightly easier time. In the second half of earlier races, he said, he was … words failed him and he drew a finger across his throat. He also admitted that he was on painkillers all the time and was a little worried that they were starting to lose their effectiveness. Both Rossi and Stoner were unstinting in their praise. 'I have to take Dani more seriously,' said Valentino in a conversation about potential championship challengers. Casey took a dig at other Honda riders by observing that the bike seemed quick enough when Dani was on it.

**Above** Andrea Dovizioso had to put up with another fourth-place finish; he was overtaken by his team-mate in sight of the flag

**Below** Jorge Lorenzo leads the pack into the Dunlop chicane; they didn't see him again

The Aussie also refused to join in with the general mumbling of discontent about the number and type of tyres available and the lack of dual compounds. 'Casey has a strange position on this,' said Rossi. For his part, Nicky Hayden said he would have taken a gamble on slicks from the start if a dual-compound tyre have been available, but the left side of either of the tyres on offer wouldn't have been anywhere near working temperature in the damp conditions. Stoner did have a go at his team after the race, being mightily displeased to lose out on what he thought was a genuine opportunity to do well. He found his dry bike far too stiff and had to take his hand off the throttle to back it off by a couple of clicks. There was a suggestion, though, that it was the contrast between

the softly sprung wet bike and the much stiffer dry bike that caught Casey out rather than any mistake by the Ducati crew.

Once all the pit stops had shaken out, the race settled down, save for Pedrosa's quite astonishing charge up to and past his team-mate, Andrea Dovizioso, to snatch the final rostrum position. Dani was visibly the quickest man on the track, and his corner speed and lean angle into and through the final complex was breathtaking, underlining Rossi's observation that if this was a bad Honda the competition would be 'in the shit' when they found a good one. He was doubtless thinking similarly unpleasant thoughts about his own team-mate, who was now back at the top of the championship table.

# DUCATI'S DILEMMA

There were signs that Ducati's management were becoming increasingly agitated by the belief spreading through the paddock that only Casey Stoner could ride their bike. There were several facets to their dilemma. First, new recruit Nicky Hayden was obviously having trouble adapting to both the machine and his team. This prompted the decision to give the American rider a new crew chief, Juan Martinez, and move Christian Pupulin to a fresh job overseeing data analysis. Nicky seemed happier immediately, maybe because of Martinez's better command of the English language.

Marco Melandri, who'd had a nightmare season at Ducati in 2008, had a trenchant view: 'When I had trouble they sent me to a psychologist, when Nicky has trouble they give him a new crew chief!' According to one Ducati source, Marco had constantly tried changing everything in order to find the 'genius solution'. Casey Stoner was of the opinion that the other Ducati riders should follow his lead and go for a 'simpler setting'. He also added that it was Ducati's problem, not his. However, he did explain that he was using the oldest, least intrusive electronics package Ducati had available while other riders were searching, as Melandri had, for a magic bullet that would cure all their problems. This tied in with what some very experienced technicians were now saying, that far from relying completely on his electronics Casey raced with a minimum of anti-spin control.

Getting all their riders up to speed was not Ducati's only concern. The next generation of MotoGP riders was already being recruited from the 250 class. Alvaro Bautista and Marco Simoncelli were the obvious choices, but they were being strongly linked with Suzuki and Honda, respectively. Why would they turn either of those rides down in favour of a bike that was rapidly acquiring a reputation as a career killer? Here was Ducati's real problem. While Casey Stoner was healthy everything was rosy, but what would happen if he was injured, or moved on? After all, if it were not for Stoner, how would recent history have judged the 800cc Desmosedici? Not kindly is the answer.

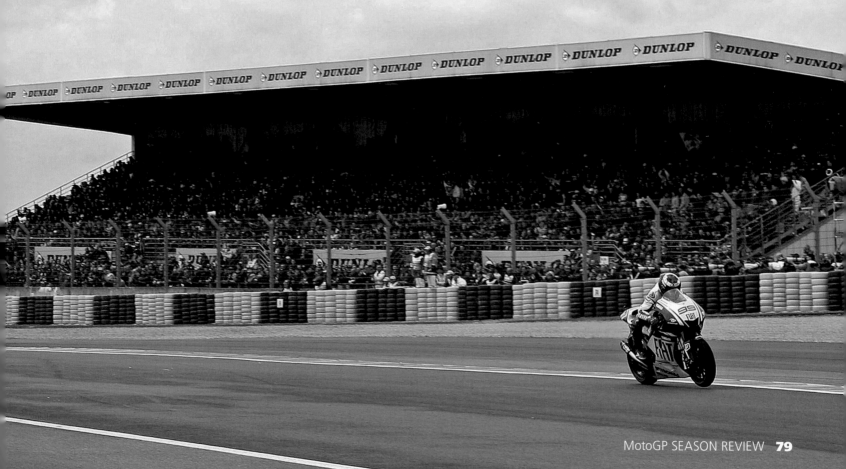

# FRENCH GP
## LE MANS

### ROUND 4
May 17

# RACE RESULTS

**CIRCUIT LENGTH** 2.600 miles
**NO. OF LAPS** 28
**RACE DISTANCE** 72.816 miles
**WEATHER** Wet, 16°C
**TRACK TEMPERATURE** 19°C
**WINNER** Jorge Lorenzo
**FASTEST LAP** 1m 35.0s, 98.496mph, Dani Pedrosa
**LAP RECORD** 1m 34.215s, 99.363mph, Valentino Rossi, 2008

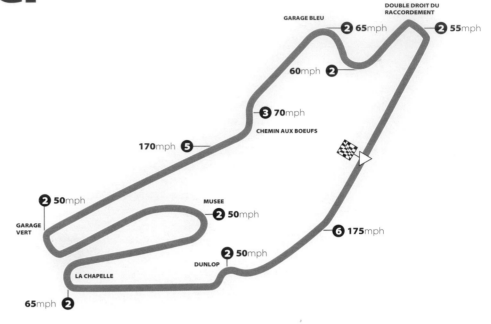

Track map labels:
- DOUBLE DROIT DU RACCORDEMENT
- GARAGE BLEU
- 65mph
- 55mph
- 60mph
- 70mph
- CHEMIN AUX BOEUFS
- 170mph
- 50mph
- GARAGE VERT
- MUSEE 50mph
- 175mph
- 50mph DUNLOP
- LA CHAPELLE
- 65mph

## QUALIFYING

| | Rider | Nationality | Team | Qualifying | Pole + | Gap |
|---|---|---|---|---|---|---|
| 1 | Pedrosa | SPA | Repsol Honda Team | 1m 33.974s | | |
| 2 | Lorenzo | SPA | Fiat Yamaha Team | 1m 33.979s | 0.005s | 0.005s |
| 3 | Stoner | AUS | Ducati Marlboro Team | 1m 34.049s | 0.075s | 0.070s |
| 4 | Rossi | ITA | Fiat Yamaha Team | 1m 34.106s | 0.132s | 0.057s |
| 5 | Dovizioso | ITA | Repsol Honda Team | 1m 34.300s | 0.326s | 0.194s |
| 6 | Edwards | USA | Monster Yamaha Tech 3 | 1m 34.330s | 0.356s | 0.030s |
| 7 | Vermeulen | AUS | Rizla Suzuki MotoGP | 1m 34.676s | 0.702s | 0.346s |
| 8 | Capirossi | ITA | Rizla Suzuki MotoGP | 1m 34.839s | 0.865s | 0.163s |
| 9 | Melandri | ITA | Hayate Racing Team | 1m 35.008s | 1.034s | 0.169s |
| 10 | De Puniet | FRA | LCR Honda MotoGP | 1m 35.399s | 1.425s | 0.391s |
| 11 | Elias | SPA | San Carlo Honda Gresini | 1m 35.431s | 1.457s | 0.032s |
| 12 | Toseland | GBR | Monster Yamaha Tech 3 | 1m 35.524s | 1.550s | 0.093s |
| 13 | Hayden | USA | Ducati Marlboro Team | 1m 35.682s | 1.708s | 0.158s |
| 14 | Kallio | FIN | Pramac Racing | 1m 35.741s | 1.767s | 0.059s |
| 15 | Takahashi | JPN | Scot Racing Team MotoGP | 1m 35.774s | 1.800s | 0.033s |
| 16 | De Angelis | RSM | San Carlo Honda Gresini | 1m 35.785s | 1.811s | 0.011s |
| 17 | Canepa | ITA | Pramac Racing | 1m 36.136s | 2.162s | 0.351s |

## FINISHERS

**1 JORGE LORENZO** Instant redemption from the Jerez disaster – and he led every lap. Out on wet tyres longer than anyone, pitted at the end of lap 12 with a 35-second lead, emerged still well ahead and won by over 17 seconds to go top of the points table. A stunning race.

**2 MARCO MELANDRI** Good qualifying, fast in the wet, pitted 'one lap too early' but kept up his momentum to give Hayate their maiden rostrum, the first for Kawasaki since de Puniet at Motegi in 2007, and Marco's first since Sepang the same year. A perfect morale boost for the cash-strapped team.

**3 DANI PEDROSA** First pole of the year. Followed Rossi into the pits early and nearly suffered the same fate, but when the track was properly dry he was awesome. Took over 10s out of his team-mate, with a last-lap pass, to make it on to the rostrum.

**4 ANDREA DOVIZIOSO** A strong second in the wet, and third when he rejoined, only to be mugged by a rampaging Pedrosa on the last lap. The first time Andrea had been in a 'flag-to-flag' race; he thought the rule 'worked well'.

**5 CASEY STONER** Not a happy race due to problems with both bikes. Lack of grip on the wet bike was followed by a steering-damper problem with the dry one. Reported the bike felt stiff and got off the gas to

slacken the damper by a click or two, after which he improved his pace.

**6 CHRIS VERMEULEN** Was contemplating changing his bike early when he saw Rossi crash and decided to stay out for a few more laps. Came in while lying fourth but lost two places in the pits. Still his best result of the season so far.

**7 COLIN EDWARDS** Lost out in the wet and for the first few laps in the dry – used the harder front tyre. Able to get past his team-mate and Capirossi once he got some heat in his slicks, but disappointed not to be in contention for a rostrum at a track that suits him and the Yamaha.

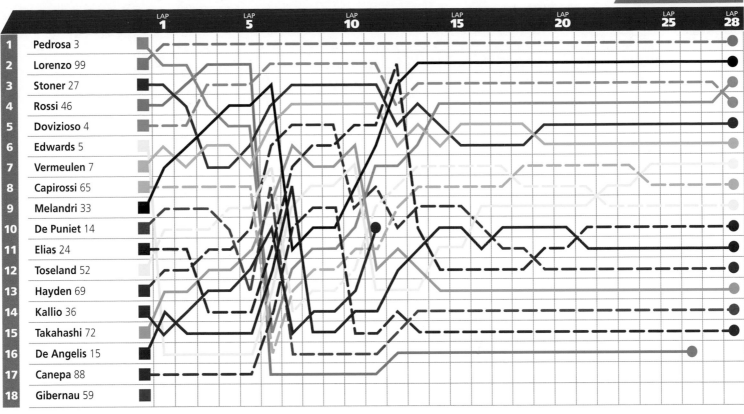

| | | LAP 1 | LAP 5 | LAP 10 | LAP 15 | LAP 20 | LAP 25 | LAP 28 |
|---|---|---|---|---|---|---|---|---|
| 1 | Pedrosa 3 | | | | | | | |
| 2 | Lorenzo 99 | | | | | | | |
| 3 | Stoner 27 | | | | | | | |
| 4 | Rossi 46 | | | | | | | |
| 5 | Dovizioso 4 | | | | | | | |
| 6 | Edwards 5 | | | | | | | |
| 7 | Vermeulen 7 | | | | | | | |
| 8 | Capirossi 65 | | | | | | | |
| 9 | Melandri 33 | | | | | | | |
| 10 | De Puniet 14 | | | | | | | |
| 11 | Elias 24 | | | | | | | |
| 12 | Toseland 52 | | | | | | | |
| 13 | Hayden 69 | | | | | | | |
| 14 | Kallio 36 | | | | | | | |
| 15 | Takahashi 72 | | | | | | | |
| 16 | De Angelis 15 | | | | | | | |
| 17 | Canepa 88 | | | | | | | |
| 18 | Gibernau 59 | | | | | | | |

## RACE

| | Rider | Motorcycle | Race Time | Time + | Fastest Lap | Av Speed | 🅱 |
|---|---|---|---|---|---|---|---|
| 1 | Lorenzo | Yamaha | 47m 52.678s | | 1m 35.855s | 91.251mph | M/S |
| 2 | Melandri | Kawasaki | 48m 10.388s | 17.710s | 1m 36.565s | 90.692mph | S/S |
| 3 | Pedrosa | Honda | 48m 12.571s | 19.893s | 1m 35.045s | 90.623mph | M/S |
| 4 | Dovizioso | Honda | 48m 13.133s | 20.455s | 1m 35.826s | 90.606mph | S/S |
| 5 | Stoner | Ducati | 48m 23.217s | 30.539s | 1m 35.289s | 90.291mph | S/S |
| 6 | Vermeulen | Suzuki | 48m 30.140s | 37.462s | 1m 36.199s | 90.076mph | M/S |
| 7 | Edwards | Yamaha | 48m 32.869s | 40.191s | 1m 35.593s | 89.992mph | M/S |
| 8 | Capirossi | Suzuki | 48m 38.099s | 45.421s | 1m 36.626s | 89.830mph | M/S |
| 9 | Toseland | Yamaha | 48m 42.985s | 50.307s | 1m 37.283s | 89.680mph | S/S |
| 10 | Elias | Honda | 48m 45.896s | 53.218s | 1m 36.563s | 89.591mph | S/S |
| 11 | De Angelis | Honda | 48m 46.228 | 53.550s | 1m 36.392s | 89.581mph | S/S |
| 12 | Hayden | Ducati | 48m 49.325s | 56.647s | 1m 36.995s | 89.486mph | S/S |
| 13 | Takahashi | Honda | 48m 49.366s | 56.688s | 1m 36.988s | 89.485mph | S/S |
| 14 | De Puniet | Honda | 49m 03.977s | 1m 11.299s | 1m 37.040s | 89.041mph | S/S |
| 15 | Canepa | Ducati | 49m 08.063s | 1m 15.385s | 1m 37.418s | 88.917mph | M/S |
| 16 | Rossi | Yamaha | 49m 28.685s | 2 laps | 1m 36.615s | 81.993mph | M/S |
| 17 | Kallio | Ducati | 20m 47.302s | 17 laps | 1m 43.297s | 82.563mph | S/S |

## CHAMPIONSHIP

| | Rider | Team | Points |
|---|---|---|---|
| 1 | Lorenzo | Fiat Yamaha Team | 66 |
| 2 | Rossi | Fiat Yamaha Team | 65 |
| 3 | Stoner | Ducati Marlboro Team | 65 |
| 4 | Pedrosa | Repsol Honda Team | 57 |
| 5 | Melandri | Hayate Racing Team | 43 |
| 6 | Dovizioso | Repsol Honda Team | 43 |
| 7 | Edwards | Monster Yamaha Tech 3 | 35 |
| 8 | Vermeulen | Rizla Suzuki MotoGP | 31 |
| 9 | Capirossi | Rizla Suzuki MotoGP | 27 |
| 10 | De Puniet | LCR Honda MotoGP | 26 |
| 11 | Elias | San Carlo Honda Gresini | 21 |
| 12 | De Angelis | San Carlo Honda Gresini | 20 |
| 13 | Toseland | Monster Yamaha Tech 3 | 17 |
| 14 | Kallio | Pramac Racing | 16 |
| 15 | Hayden | Ducati Marlboro Team | 9 |
| 16 | Gibernau | Grupo Francisco Hernando | 8 |
| 17 | Takahashi | Scot Racing Team MotoGP | 8 |
| 18 | Canepa | Pramac Racing | 3 |

**8 LORIS CAPIROSSI** A worrying race for Suzuki. Loris changed bikes early, then ran off track twice, but when the track was dry he had the same lack of grip he'd experienced in practice.

**9 JAMES TOSELAND** Up to seventh after the bike change, in his first experience of a race under these rain regulations, but he'd gone for the softer front tyre and it didn't quite go the distance.

**10 TONI ELIAS** Not fully fit after a compartment syndrome operation on his forearms. Rode with 30 stitches, was last to change bikes, and just won the duel for tenth with his team-mate.

**11 ALEX DE ANGELIS** Lost in qualifying, gambled on a big set-up change for the race, struggled in the wet and on cold slicks. Took risks everywhere and was pleasantly surprised not to have crashed.

**12 NICKY HAYDEN** Felt he'd made some progress, with new chief mechanic Juan Martinez, even though the result didn't look good. Ran fourth in the wet and eighth in the dry before Kallio's crashed bike took him off track, losing both time and places.

**13 YUKI TAKAHASHI** Happier in the wet than the dry, and had difficulty staying focused when the bike started to misbehave during the last part of the race.

A difficult introduction to MotoGP's wet-weather rules.

**14 RANDY DE PUNIET** An awful weekend at his home GP. Struggled with the conditions, like everyone else, but also destabilised by the news of the serious injuries suffered by his training partner Regis Laconi in South Africa.

**15 NICCOLO CANEPA** His second points-scoring ride of the year after a difficult weekend. Lost a lot of time after changing to the dry bike and only really got going in the final half-dozen laps.

**16 VALENTINO ROSSI** First time he'd finished out of the points and first time he had ever finished last in a GP. Crashed at the Dunlop chicane a lap after switching bikes, then yo-yo'd in and out of the pits – to get back on his undamaged bike, for a stop-and-go penalty for speeding in pit lane, to get back on his dry bike…

## NON-FINISHERS

**MIKA KALLIO** Going well on slicks when he crashed trying to overtake Hayden. Changed line to go round the outside, found a patch of water and his bike slid into the Ducati.

## NON-STARTERS

**SETE GIBERNAU** A crash on Saturday morning resulted in another break to his oft-damaged left collarbone. Went straight back to Barcelona for an operation in an attempt to be fit for his home GP.

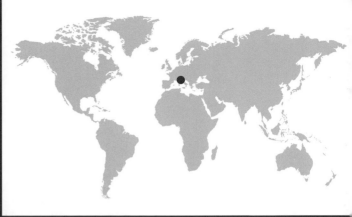

# ALL THINGS MUST PASS

**Casey Stoner gave Ducati their first win at an Italian Grand Prix and went back to the top of the table; Lorenzo beat his team-mate – again**

At last! Ducati finally won a MotoGP race at Mugello and Casey Stoner and his crew got things right in a flag-to-flag race. That meant Valentino Rossi's astonishing run of victories at the Italian track stopped at seven. Race conditions were almost identical to Le Mans two weeks previously: it was wet at the start, with the track then drying rapidly and riders pitting to change bikes as early as lap four. However, the profile of the race was a lot more complicated than it had been in France because six riders took a turn at leading: Vermeulen, Dovizioso, Melandri, Capirossi, Rossi and Stoner.

Most of the grid learned from the mistakes they had made at Le Mans which meant, in Stoner's case, not losing ground in the opening wet laps and having his dry bike set up right. Even the first men in to change bikes, with James Toseland leading the way, managed to stay on their wheels while warming up their tyres in the tricky conditions; the exception was Alex de Angelis, who crashed on his first lap on slicks. James pitted at the end of lap four and was the fastest man on track by lap seven, triggering most of the field to swap bikes over the next two laps. Melandri's and Rossi's brief stints at the front came during the laps when there was the biggest flurry of activity in pit lane. The men who led in both wet and dry conditions were Stoner and Andrea Dovizioso, who enjoyed the sensation of heading his home race for the first time. What he didn't enjoy was just failing to get on the rostrum despite coming out of the final corner alongside Valentino.

Andrea definitely enjoyed his weekend more than his team-mate did. Dani Pedrosa crashed in the race,

**Above** A quick clean-up on the grid for Lorenzo after his sighting-lap crash

**Opposite** Suzuki led a race for the first time in 2009 with Chris Vermeulen, but he couldn't maintain the pace on slicks

**Below** Chris Vermeulen leads in the early stages

but he had also managed to increase his catalogue of injuries in practice, without even falling off the bike, when a near-highside tweaked his hip hard enough for a tendon to pull away from his pelvis and take a flake of bone with it. That was the party line, anyway; there was an unofficial version which maintained he had fallen off his bicycle the previous week. As Dani looked fine at the start of the weekend, but his injured knee still prevented him riding a bike, it seems likely the 'non-crash' story may well have been correct, however strange it was.

Valentino Rossi did make an error of judgement here, but not nearly as severe as the one he'd made at Le Mans. He went with the harder slick front tyre on his dry bike and, like some others, found it took too long to get heat into the rubber, so he couldn't challenge for third place until three laps from the flag. Vale put a brave face on things, saying this was his first rostrum in this kind of race – conveniently forgetting his third place in Australia in 2006, the first flag-to-flag race.

Lorenzo's race was remarkable, however, and not just because he beat his team-mate. On the sighting lap Jorge hit a wet kerb and crashed. He got the damaged bike back to the pits just in time to go out on his second M1, avoiding having to start from pit lane by a matter of seconds. Then he had the worst start possible off pole position. It looked like launch control wasn't engaged, so the bike snaked madly off the line, and when the TV director switched to the Fiat Yamaha's rearwards-facing camera smoke was visibly coming off the Bridgestone. Moreover, Lorenzo didn't know if his mechanics would be able to get his crashed bike in a fit state to race. Not surprisingly, he didn't show at the front in the early stages as he disputed sixth place with Pedrosa and Melandri. By lap ten the crew had fitted a complete new front brake system, exhaust pipes, throttle and bodywork to the crashed Yamaha, and when Jorge got onboard he started making rapid progress. He was fourth when the field settled down and quickly despatched Dovizioso and Capirossi, although he couldn't quite get on terms with Stoner.

This was a mind-boggling display of focus and

# 'I'VE WON BEFORE IN ITALY [AT MISANO] BUT THIS WAS THE ONE I REALLY WANTED'
### CASEY STONER

concentration from a racer who only turned 22 after the start of the season. The sighting-lap crash, the bad start, the imperfectly set-up wet bike, the prospect of the dry bike not being ready … just one of those problems would have been enough to put even a world-class racer off his game. Not Jorge Lorenzo. To ignore all those traumas and still outperform his illustrious team-mate removed any doubts the critics had about his ability to challenge for the title.

As everyone had come to expect, Loris Capirossi performed a minor miracle or two at Mugello. First, he got the Suzuki on the front row for the first time this season; then he finished just over a second behind third-placed Rossi and only lost fourth place on the last lap. Team manager Paul Denning was of the opinion that the GSV could not possibly have gone any faster on that qualifying lap, and he said that in the race Loris rode 'like an animal'. The fact that Capirossi lost a rostrum finish in the final laps was so obviously due to the bike's lack of pace down the kilometre-long front straight that team manager and rider both felt able to publicly request more help from Suzuki.

Mugello is normally all about Italian riders, but this time it was about an Italian motorcycle. Ducati have won a GP in Italy, at Misano – but that was the San Marino Grand Prix. This was definitively the Italian Grand Prix, at the iconic Tuscan track, and it was the first premier-class victory ever at Mugello by an Italian machine. It was also Casey Stoner's first victory here in any class, a race both rider and team had been waiting a long time to win. 'I'm so happy,' said Casey, speaking for all the grinning folks in red shirts in the pit lane and the grandstands.

**Above** Dani Pedrosa is carried away, fortunately with no injuries other than those he already had

**Below** It took a late charge from Valentino Rossi to keep Andrea Dovizioso off the rostrum

**Opposite** Colin Edwards leads Mika Kallio and Alex de Angelis in the early stages

# THE TEAM-MATE THING

Jorge Lorenzo's second-place finish meant he had beaten his team-mate Valentino Rossi for the third time in just five races. This was not an insignificant occurrence, because finishing a race behind a team-mate used to be a rare event for Valentino. In his 123 MotoGP races, up to Mugello 2009, this had happened to him just 12 times (that is, when both he and the team-mate had finished the race), and on four of those occasions Valentino had crashed and remounted.

It is Rule One of racing that the first objective is to beat the man who shares the pit garage with you – what Wayne Rainey used to call 'the team-mate thing' – so the significance of Lorenzo's results cannot be underestimated. Before the 2009 season only two team-mates had actually won races that Rossi had also finished, the first being Tohru Ukawa in the second-ever MotoGP race (South Africa in 2002), when he and Valentino were riding for Repsol Honda. The next time it happened to Rossi was six years later, in 2008, at Estoril, when Jorge Lorenzo won a MotoGP race for the first time. And only a little way into the 2009 season Lorenzo had done it again, in Japan and France.

Valentino didn't have team-mates in his 125, 250 and 500 days, and he had few problems with his MotoGP team-mates until Jorge arrived, so

this was all a new experience for him. And things weren't about to get any easier with Lorenzo emerging as a genuine contender for the title. From Yamaha's point of view they had done the prudent thing, and invested and planned for a post-Rossi future. Later in the season Rossi would welcome rumours about Jorge decamping to Honda, which turned out to be untrue; he then started to snipe at Yamaha for having two top riders in the same team and even began giving some credence to suggestions of a one-man Ducati team for 2010. It's tricky, this team-mate thing.

**Above** Valentino was finding it harder and harder to keep calm about his very rapid team-mate

# ITALIAN GP

MUGELLO

## ROUND 5
May 31

## RACE RESULTS

**CIRCUIT LENGTH** 3.259 miles
**NO. OF LAPS** 23
**RACE DISTANCE** 74.794 miles
**WEATHER** Wet, 18°C
**TRACK TEMPERATURE** 20°C
**WINNER** Casey Stoner
**FASTEST LAP** 1m 51.186s, 105.523mph, Valentino Rossi
**LAP RECORD** 1m 50.003s, 106.658mph, Casey Stoner, 2008

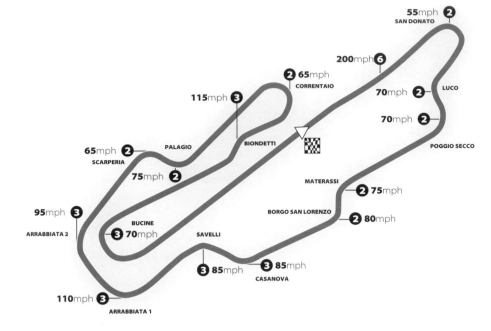

Track map: San Donato 55mph, 200mph, Correntaio 65mph, Luco 70mph, 70mph, Palagio 115mph, Biondetti, Poggio Secco, Scarperia 65mph, 75mph, Materassi 75mph, Borgo San Lorenzo 80mph, Bucine 95mph, 70mph, Savelli, Casanova 85mph, 85mph, Arrabbiata 2, Arrabbiata 1 110mph

## QUALIFYING

| | Rider | Nationality | Team | Qualifying | Pole + | Gap |
|---|---|---|---|---|---|---|
| 1 | Lorenzo | SPA | Fiat Yamaha Team | 1m 48.987s | | |
| 2 | Stoner | AUS | Ducati Marlboro Team | 1m 49.008s | 0.021s | 0.021s |
| 3 | Capirossi | ITA | Rizla Suzuki MotoGP | 1m 49.121s | 0.134s | 0.113s |
| 4 | Rossi | ITA | Fiat Yamaha Team | 1m 49.148s | 0.161s | 0.027s |
| 5 | De Puniet | FRA | LCR Honda MotoGP | 1m 49.499s | 0.512s | 0.351s |
| 6 | Edwards | USA | Monster Yamaha Tech 3 | 1m 49.547s | 0.560s | 0.048s |
| 7 | Dovizioso | ITA | Repsol Honda Team | 1m 49.648s | 0.661s | 0.101s |
| 8 | Pedrosa | SPA | Repsol Honda Team | 1m 50.073s | 1.086s | 0.425s |
| 9 | Elias | SPA | San Carlo Honda Gresini | 1m 50.078s | 1.091s | 0.005s |
| 10 | Takahashi | JPN | Scot Racing Team MotoGP | 1m 50.305s | 1.318s | 0.227s |
| 11 | Vermeulen | AUS | Rizla Suzuki MotoGP | 1m 50.405s | 1.418s | 0.100s |
| 12 | De Angelis | RSM | San Carlo Honda Gresini | 1m 50.448s | 1.461s | 0.043s |
| 13 | Canepa | ITA | Pramac Racing | 1m 50.528s | 1.541s | 0.080s |
| 14 | Toseland | GBR | Monster Yamaha Tech 3 | 1m 50.537s | 1.550s | 0.009s |
| 15 | Melandri | ITA | Hayate Racing Team | 1m 50.710s | 1.723s | 0.173s |
| 16 | Hayden | USA | Ducati Marlboro Team | 1m 50.924s | 1.937s | 0.214s |
| 17 | Kallio | FIN | Pramac Racing | 1m 51.008s | 2.021s | 0.084s |

## FINISHERS

**1 CASEY STONER** Ducati's first win at Mugello (and of an Italian GP), and Casey's first in a race where he changed bikes. Stayed out on shredded wet tyres until the perfect moment to change, handled a clutch problem, then held off a late charge from Lorenzo to go top of the table.

**2 JORGE LORENZO** Nearly missed the race by crashing on the sighting lap, got back in time to use his spare bike, then a massive wheelspin off the line put him down to tenth. Climbed up to third before changing bikes, then rode brilliantly to pass Loris and Dovi and hold off Rossi. 'I can't believe the race, it is like a movie.'

**3 VALENTINO ROSSI** So the streak of home wins ended at seven – only led for one lap when bikes were being changed. Went out on the harder slicks but it took too long to get any heat into them, though fought in the closing laps to go from fifth to third. Put a brave face on it, but finishing behind a team-mate was a rare experience for him.

**4 ANDREA DOVIZIOSO** Led his home race on both wet and dry tyres despite pitting earlier than most of the top men. Always in the hunt for a rostrum and only lost out to Rossi by a few thousandths of a second, despite being in the Yamaha's slipstream coming out of the last corner.

**5 LORIS CAPIROSSI** A magnificent effort in front of his home crowd. Started from the front row, in contention thanks to bravery on the laps either side of the bike change and even in a position to challenge Stoner for the lead. But the Suzuki simply didn't have the speed down the long straight to hold off the Fiat Yamahas and Dovi's Honda.

**6 COLIN EDWARDS** Lacked confidence in the front when the track was wet, but charged through from the back of the field once he'd got some heat in the harder dry tyres. Almost a carbon copy of his previous race in France.

**7 JAMES TOSELAND** Competitive for the first time in 2009. First to change bikes – a gamble worth taking – and once he'd got heat in the harder slicks he was fastest on the track while the rest were pitting.

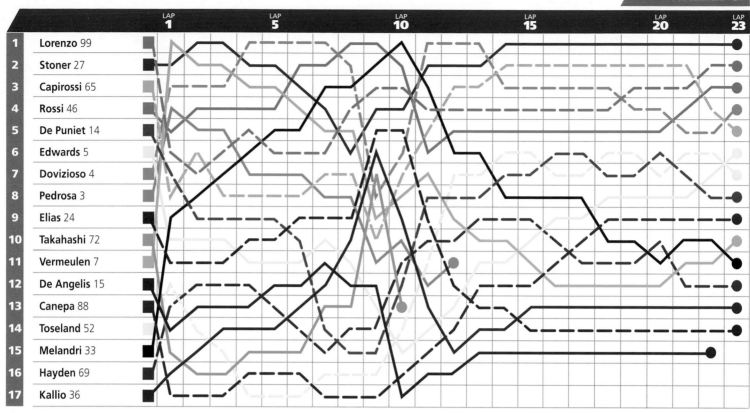

| | | | | | | | LAP 1 | | LAP 5 | | LAP 10 | | LAP 15 | | LAP 20 | | LAP 23 |
|---|---|---|---|---|---|---|---|---|---|---|---|---|---|---|---|---|---|
| 1 | Lorenzo 99 | | | | | | | | | | | | | | | | |
| 2 | Stoner 27 | | | | | | | | | | | | | | | | |
| 3 | Capirossi 65 | | | | | | | | | | | | | | | | |
| 4 | Rossi 46 | | | | | | | | | | | | | | | | |
| 5 | De Puniet 14 | | | | | | | | | | | | | | | | |
| 6 | Edwards 5 | | | | | | | | | | | | | | | | |
| 7 | Dovizioso 4 | | | | | | | | | | | | | | | | |
| 8 | Pedrosa 3 | | | | | | | | | | | | | | | | |
| 9 | Elias 24 | | | | | | | | | | | | | | | | |
| 10 | Takahashi 72 | | | | | | | | | | | | | | | | |
| 11 | Vermeulen 7 | | | | | | | | | | | | | | | | |
| 12 | De Angelis 15 | | | | | | | | | | | | | | | | |
| 13 | Canepa 88 | | | | | | | | | | | | | | | | |
| 14 | Toseland 52 | | | | | | | | | | | | | | | | |
| 15 | Melandri 33 | | | | | | | | | | | | | | | | |
| 16 | Hayden 69 | | | | | | | | | | | | | | | | |
| 17 | Kallio 36 | | | | | | | | | | | | | | | | |

## RACE

| | Rider | Motorcycle | Race Time | Time + | Fastest Lap | Av Speed | B |
|---|---|---|---|---|---|---|---|
| 1 | Stoner | Ducati | 45m 41.894s | | 1m 51.310s | 98.422mph | M/M |
| 2 | Lorenzo | Yamaha | 45m 42.895s | 1.001s | 1m 51.331s | 98.386mph | M/H |
| 3 | Rossi | Yamaha | 45m 43.970s | 2.076s | 1m 51.186s | 98.348mph | H/H |
| 4 | Dovizioso | Honda | 45m 44.023s | 2.129s | 1m 51.187s | 98.346mph | M/H |
| 5 | Capirossi | Suzuki | 45m 45.168s | 3.274s | 1m 51.980s | 98.305mph | M/M |
| 6 | Edwards | Yamaha | 46m 06.345s | 24.451s | 1m 52.179s | 97.552mph | H/H |
| 7 | Toseland | Yamaha | 46m 07.515s | 25.621s | 1m 53.233s | 97.511mph | H/H |
| 8 | De Puniet | Honda | 46m 07.940s | 26.046s | 1m 53.454s | 97.496mph | H/H |
| 9 | Canepa | Ducati | 46m 13.709s | 31.815s | 1m 53.361s | 97.293mph | M/M |
| 10 | Vermeulen | Suzuki | 46m 16.708s | 34.814s | 1m 53.473s | 97.188mph | M/M |
| 11 | Melandri | Kawasaki | 46m 16.984s | 35.090s | 1m 54.033s | 97.178mph | H/H |
| 12 | Hayden | Ducati | 46m 21.016s | 39.122s | 1m 53.710s | 97.037mph | M/M |
| 13 | Kallio | Ducati | 46m 34.356s | 52.462s | 1m 54.305s | 96.574mph | H/M |
| 14 | Elias | Honda | 46m 34.372s | 52.478s | 1m 54.296s | 96.574mph | M/M |
| 15 | De Angelis | Honda | 46m 03.967s | 1 lap | 1m 56.863s | 93.391mph | M/M |
| 16 | Pedrosa | Honda | 25m 15.529s | 11 laps | 1m 58.753s | 92.904mph | M/H |
| 17 | Takahashi | Honda | 21m 18.170s | 13 laps | 2m 03.081s | 91.796mph | H/H |

## CHAMPIONSHIP

| | Rider | Team | Points |
|---|---|---|---|
| 1 | Stoner | Ducati Marlboro Team | 90 |
| 2 | Lorenzo | Fiat Yamaha Team | 86 |
| 3 | Rossi | Fiat Yamaha Team | 81 |
| 4 | Pedrosa | Repsol Honda Team | 57 |
| 5 | Dovizioso | Repsol Honda Team | 56 |
| 6 | Melandri | Hayate Racing Team | 48 |
| 7 | Edwards | Monster Yamaha Tech 3 | 45 |
| 8 | Capirossi | Rizla Suzuki MotoGP | 38 |
| 9 | Vermeulen | Rizla Suzuki MotoGP | 37 |
| 10 | De Puniet | LCR Honda MotoGP | 34 |
| 11 | Toseland | Monster Yamaha Tech 3 | 26 |
| 12 | Elias | San Carlo Honda Gresini | 23 |
| 13 | De Angelis | San Carlo Honda Gresini | 21 |
| 14 | Kallio | Pramac Racing | 19 |
| 15 | Hayden | Ducati Marlboro Team | 13 |
| 16 | Canepa | Pramac Racing | 10 |
| 17 | Gibernau | Grupo Francisco Hernando | 8 |
| 18 | Takahashi | Scot Racing Team MotoGP | 8 |

Fought with de Puniet for sixth when the dust settled, but both caught by Edwards in the last two laps.

**8 RANDY DE PUNIET** Good qualifying and a great start followed by a very similar race to Toseland's. Cautious on the wets, changed bikes early, took two laps to get the slicks to work, then enjoyed the dice.

**9 NICCOLO CANEPA** Dead last initially in the wet, followed Toseland in for an early change, then things got better. A top-ten finish, Nico's first in MotoGP, at a first home GP was not a bad result.

**10 CHRIS VERMEULEN** Lived up to his reputation as a rainmaster by leading on the first lap, but things went wrong after he

took to his dry bike. Lack of grip at the rear going into corners was the problem, and Chris slipped from fifth to tenth.

**11 MARCO MELANDRI** Third for a few laps and even led as the pack changed bikes: he looked at ease in the wet. Unfortunately, in the dry he looked as uncomfortable as he had in practice.

**12 NICKY HAYDEN** At least there were some signs of improvement, notably his sixth in warm-up and his pace in the wet. The dry pace was respectable until he fried his rear brake trying to control wheelspin.

**13 MIKA KALLIO** In contrast to teammate Canepa, Mika was very strong in the wet but couldn't make his dry bike

work at all for two laps, even at vastly reduced speeds. 'The bike didn't follow my instructions. I nearly ran off track – at 50kph!'

**14 TONI ELIAS** Thought the wet segment would be difficult but he was wrong. Came out on his dry bike only two seconds behind Rossi and Stoner, then lost four seconds a lap for four laps and the best part of three seconds after that. A complete disaster for Fausto Gresini's team.

**15 ALEX DE ANGELIS** Fell and remounted two corners after changing to his dry bike, but knew he didn't have the set-up to repeat his heroics of 12 months previously.

## NON-FINISHERS

**DANI PEDROSA** Handicapped by a new injury to his hip, caused by a near-highside in practice (or a bicycle crash, depending on who you believe). Running midfield when he fell, fortunately without further injury.

**YUKI TAKAHASHI** Crashed soon after changing to his dry bike, thus wasting his first top-ten qualifying of the season.

## NON-STARTERS

**SETE GIBERNAU** Missed the race due to the collarbone injury from his crash at Le Mans. Hoped to recover in time for his home race at the next round, in Barcelona.

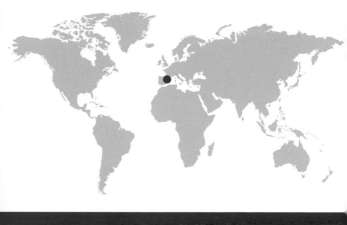

# FIGHT OF THE YEAR

**Valentino Rossi and Jorge Lorenzo gave us the best race of the 800cc era, and one of the greatest last laps ever**

Kevin Schwantz, the 1993 World Champion, was at Catalunya. He knows a thing or two about personal rivalries on track: he fought a career-long battle with Wayne Rainey, first in the USA, then in Grands Prix, with an intensity that has rarely been equalled. After one of their greatest races Schwantz could recall that his comment had been 'That was about more than five points.' He wasn't wrong. We already knew that Jorge Lorenzo was the most serious threat to Valentino Rossi's status as the dominant talent and personality in the MotoGP paddock. Now we found out just how hard Valentino was prepared to ride and how deep he was prepared to dig to put the contender in his place.

It took the best final lap to a GP anyone could remember – and that includes Jerez in 2005 – to do it. This Rossi–Lorenzo battle bears examination in detail. The Fiat Yamaha team-mates went into the 25th and last lap line-astern and nearly nine seconds in front of third-placed Casey Stoner. Lorenzo made the classic Catalunya outbraking move into Turn 1; Rossi tried his utmost to get back on the inside at the left-hander of Turn 2 but had the door shut in his face good and hard. Rossi's next attack came at the second of the two big right-handers, Turn 4. He got his nose in front for a moment but Lorenzo bit back immediately, riding a perfect defensive line up to the tight left as Rossi's left foot flapped in the slipstream – a sure indication that he was trying very, very hard. That was the last possible passing place, wasn't it? Valentino then shadowed Jorge through the stadium section and into the two fast rights that end the lap. He nearly tailgated Lorenzo in the first one, and then came the move of the season – or the move of just about any season.

**Right** No-one knew at the time just how serious the fatigue that affected Casey Stoner would turn out to be

**Opposite** Jorge Lorenzo leads in the early stages. His special crash helmet design celebrated Barcelona's Champions League victory

**Below** MotoGP got a new rider, ex-125cc World Champion Gabor Talmacsi of Hungary, on a Scot Honda

Going into the final corner, the third-gear downhill sweeper that leads on to the home straight in front of Catalunya's giant grandstands, Rossi found the speed, the space and the skill to make the cleanest of passes on the inside at a place where most people wouldn't even have dreamed a pass was possible. This was a race, a lap, a move that fans will be talking about in decades to come, and Valentino didn't hold back his emotions. On the slow-down lap he repeatedly karate-chopped the air with his right hand, reliving that pass.

The feeling, he said, was like winning at Mugello in 2006 and he admitted to 'screaming very much' in his crash helmet. Was it his best win? The battle with Casey Stoner at Laguna Seca the previous year had been more important for the championship, but this, thought Vale, was 'more exciting' and proved that 'In a battle one-to-one I am still strong.'

Lorenzo hid his disappointment well. 'Valentino was more brave than me, with more experience than me.' Ah, that line again. Rossi wasn't having it. He pointed out that it was a very difficult pass, executed with precision on worn tyres: 'I don't touch Lorenzo, I stay on line, I turn the bike.' In other words brains as well as balls, and don't you forget it.

In truth, Jorge was seething. He had predicted his own doom in an interview published in the event programme, which took the form of a corner-by-corner guide to the track. The paragraph on the final bend started with the question 'Can you pass here?' to which Jorge replied, 'No … unless you are Valentino.' He forgot his own advice: 'In the easiest corner to maintain first place he overtake me. I see the victory and I didn't close [the door].'

It was difficult, if not impossible, to take one's eyes off the two Fiat Yamahas, but there were some significant rides going on downfield. Stoner just made it to third place, despite feeling increasingly sick as the weekend went on. On the grid Casey told his mechanic that if he finished the race he would be needing a doctor, and he wasn't exaggerating. Stoner was 'dead from half-way', suffering from stomach cramps, and he could hardly stand in *parc fermé*. Nevertheless, he found the strength to fight off a late charge from Andrea

Dovizioso. Most people assumed that his malaise was a one-off event, but it would soon become apparent that it was the first indication of a serious problem that would end the Aussie's challenge for the title in 2009.

Loris Capirossi made good use of a new engine from Suzuki (or upgrade, depending on who was talking) to finish fifth, but he was much happier than he'd been with the same result at Mugello. If he had had the new motor then, said Loris, he could have been on the rostrum, and he would have been more competitive here in Barcelona if he'd been allowed to use it for the whole weekend. The Italian was fast enough to keep home-town hero Pedrosa at bay, but Dani, after his succession of injuries and the recent crash at Mugello, was just glad to finish the race. Listening to him talk about how the painkillers he'd been on for months were starting to lose their effectiveness was not a comfortable experience.

The finishing order produced a situation unique in the 60-year history of the World Championships – three riders tied on points for the lead. After six races, Rossi, Lorenzo and Stoner all had 106 points, although the table ranked them in the above order on countback. Rossi's win also moved him closer to another career landmark, because this was his 99th Grand Prix victory – and that was the reason he was pointing out Jorge Lorenzo's race number to the TV cameras in *parc fermé*. Valentino Rossi had many reasons for wanting to win, but the first person he mentioned afterwards was Jerry Burgess, whose mother had died the day before the race. Vale simply said that the victory was for him, and that without Jerry he would be nowhere near his total of 99 wins.

# 'VALENTINO WAS MORE BRAVE THAN ME, WITH MORE EXPERIENCE THAN ME'

**JORGE LORENZO**

**Above** Stoner suffered badly in the final laps but found enough strength to hold off Dovizioso

**Below** The Fiat Yamahas were never more than a second apart and usually this close for the entire race

**Opposite** Dani Pedrosa was suffering from a variety of injuries but raced to sixth in his home GP

# HAYDEN'S PROGRESS

Nicky Hayden rode a very different-looking Ducati at Barcelona, the result of some intensive work at Mugello after the Italian GP with support from factory test rider Vito Guareschi and suspension engineers from Ohlins. 'We changed everything but the grips,' said Nicky, looking happier than he'd done all season. 'I'm no poker player, but it's a lot more fun.'

As well as the radical revision of riding position, swingarm length and geometry, there was a new electronics package. Or rather it was new for Stoner, because other Ducati riders had been using it for a while. Casey's comments cast an interesting light on Ducati's electronics, which most observers have presumed the Aussie relies on more than the rest. Not so. According to team-manager Livio Suppo, Casey is really smooth on the bike whereas Nicky is more aggressive. Other teams' engineers were saying the same thing, namely that Stoner rides with very little traction or spin control.

The man himself was cautiously optimistic about the system, saying the new electronics 'calm the bike down'. Casey even put some numbers on it. He usually got '30 to 40 cuts per cycle' [a cut would be one – or maybe more – cylinder(s) dropping a spark]. With the new system it was 'thousands, like everybody else'. However, Stoner has never been a fan of too much electronic control. 'Everyone thinks I love it,' he said, with just a hint of the bitterness that used to surface far more regularly, because he felt it robbed the bike of too much power, and there was also a heavy price to be paid in fuel consumption. This might have something to do with the Ducati being unable to match the pace of the Yamahas on a track with a kilometre-long straight.

Hayden was still an uncomfortable distance behind his team-mate, but there was now cause for optimism, not least because there was an official test on the Monday after the Catalunya GP. Nicky would be able to get in some of the track time he has always needed to get to grips with new equipment.

# CATALAN GP
## CIRCUIT DE CATALUNYA
### ROUND 6
June 14

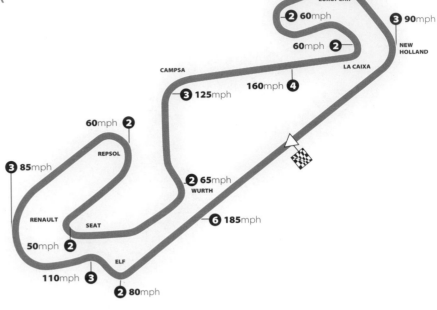

**BRIDGESTONE**
TYRE OPTIONS
MEDIUM (M) / HARD (H)
HARD (H) / EXTRA HARD (XH)

**motoGP · TISSOT** SWISS WATCHES SINCE 1853
OFFICIAL TIMEKEEPER

Track diagram labels:
- 90mph EUROPCAR
- 60mph
- 90mph NEW HOLLAND
- 60mph
- LA CAIXA
- 160mph
- CAMPSA 125mph
- 60mph REPSOL
- 85mph
- 65mph WURTH
- RENAULT SEAT
- 185mph
- 50mph
- ELF
- 110mph
- 80mph

# RACE RESULTS

**CIRCUIT LENGTH** 2.937 miles
**NO. OF LAPS** 25
**RACE DISTANCE** 73.425 miles
**WEATHER** Dry, 36°C
**TRACK TEMPERATURE** 46°C
**WINNER** Valentino Rossi
**FASTEST LAP** 1m 42.858s, 102.802mph, Casey Stoner
**LAP RECORD** 1m 42.358s, 103.304mph, Dani Pedrosa, 2008

## QUALIFYING

| | Rider | Nationality | Team | Qualifying | Pole + | Gap |
|---|---|---|---|---|---|---|
| 1 | Lorenzo | SPA | Fiat Yamaha Team | 1m 41.974s | | |
| 2 | Rossi | ITA | Fiat Yamaha Team | 1m 41.987s | 0.013s | 0.013s |
| 3 | Stoner | AUS | Ducati Marlboro Team | 1m 42.426s | 0.452s | 0.439s |
| 4 | Dovizioso | ITA | Repsol Honda Team | 1m 42.594s | 0.620s | 0.168s |
| 5 | Elias | SPA | San Carlo Honda Gresini | 1m 43.139s | 1.165s | 0.545s |
| 6 | Edwards | USA | Monster Yamaha Tech 3 | 1m 43.168s | 1.194s | 0.029s |
| 7 | De Puniet | FRA | LCR Honda MotoGP | 1m 43.175s | 1.201s | 0.007s |
| 8 | Pedrosa | SPA | Repsol Honda Team | 1m 43.207s | 1.233s | 0.032s |
| 9 | Toseland | GBR | Monster Yamaha Tech 3 | 1m 43.233s | 1.259s | 0.026s |
| 10 | Kallio | FIN | Pramac Racing | 1m 43.336s | 1.362s | 0.103s |
| 11 | Capirossi | ITA | Rizla Suzuki MotoGP | 1m 43.365s | 1.391s | 0.029s |
| 12 | Vermeulen | AUS | Rizla Suzuki MotoGP | 1m 43.411s | 1.437s | 0.046s |
| 13 | Hayden | USA | Ducati Marlboro Team | 1m 43.414s | 1.440s | 0.003s |
| 14 | De Angelis | RSM | San Carlo Honda Gresini | 1m 43.422s | 1.448s | 0.008s |
| 15 | Gibernau | SPA | Grupo Francisco Hernando | 1m 43.714s | 1.740s | 0.292s |
| 16 | Takahashi | JPN | Scot Racing Team MotoGP | 1m 43.777s | 1.803s | 0.063s |
| 17 | Melandri | ITA | Hayate Racing Team | 1m 43.792s | 1.818s | 0.015s |
| 18 | Canepa | ITA | Pramac Racing | 1m 43.991s | 2.017s | 0.199s |
| 19 | Talmacsi | HUN | Scot Racing Team MotoGP | 1m 45.833s | 3.859s | 1.842s |

## FINISHERS

**1 VALENTINO ROSSI** A superb last lap and one of the great last-corner moves made a point to his team-mate as well as giving him race victory number 99. 'One of the best and hardest wins of my career,' he said, dedicating the race to Jerry Burgess, whose mother had just passed away.

**2 JORGE LORENZO** Brilliant all weekend. Let his guard drop at what he called the 'easiest corner on the track to defend', but showed he won't be intimidated by his team-mate. At least got to enjoy carrying the colours of Barcelona's football club of which he is an ardent supporter.

**3 CASEY STONER** Given his state of health, this rostrum was as good as a win. Slightly ill on Friday but by Sunday knew he was in serious trouble: felt 'dead' half-way through the race, though found the strength to fend off Dovizioso in the closing laps. First signs of a mystery illness that would effectively put him out of contention.

**4 ANDREA DOVIZIOSO** His third consecutive fourth-place finish, 9s behind the winner and a fraction of a second off third place: 'Maybe I should have attacked Casey with six laps to go when he slowed.' Still unhappy about the delay in new parts from Honda.

**5 LORIS CAPIROSSI** Much happier with this fifth place than the previous one at Mugello. Suzuki decided, eventually, to use their new motor (or possibly upgraded parts). Still down on top-end power, but felt he'd have made the rostrum if the new motor had been available for the whole weekend.

**6 DANI PEDROSA** Still suffering from his Mugello injuries and unsure on Friday if he'd even be able to race. Did manage to get to the flag, despite yet another crash in practice, and even though he looked terrible afterwards he gritted his teeth for a more than respectable finish.

**7 COLIN EDWARDS** An uncharacteristic crash on Saturday and suffered in the heat, or rather his front tyre did. Third in warm-up, but with track temperatures up to 46 degrees when the race started it was a struggle to get

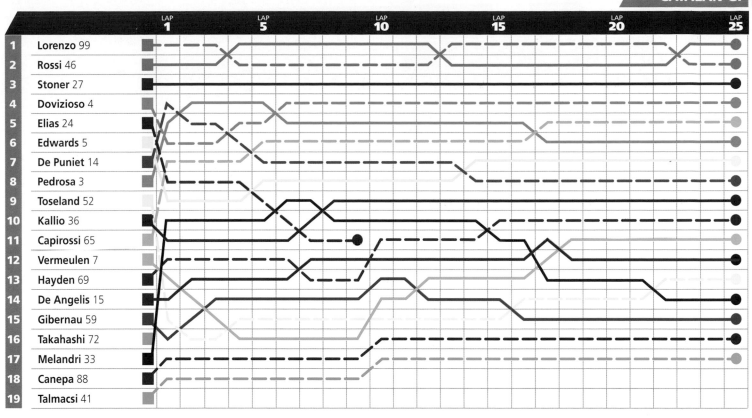

| | | LAP 1 | LAP 5 | LAP 10 | LAP 15 | LAP 20 | LAP 25 |
|---|---|---|---|---|---|---|---|
| 1 | Lorenzo 99 | | | | | | |
| 2 | Rossi 46 | | | | | | |
| 3 | Stoner 27 | | | | | | |
| 4 | Dovizioso 4 | | | | | | |
| 5 | Elias 24 | | | | | | |
| 6 | Edwards 5 | | | | | | |
| 7 | De Puniet 14 | | | | | | |
| 8 | Pedrosa 3 | | | | | | |
| 9 | Toseland 52 | | | | | | |
| 10 | Kallio 36 | | | | | | |
| 11 | Capirossi 65 | | | | | | |
| 12 | Vermeulen 7 | | | | | | |
| 13 | Hayden 69 | | | | | | |
| 14 | De Angelis 15 | | | | | | |
| 15 | Gibernau 59 | | | | | | |
| 16 | Takahashi 72 | | | | | | |
| 17 | Melandri 33 | | | | | | |
| 18 | Canepa 88 | | | | | | |
| 19 | Talmacsi 41 | | | | | | |

## RACE

| | Rider | Motorcycle | Race Time | Time + | Fastest Lap | Av Speed | |
|---|---|---|---|---|---|---|---|
| 1 | Rossi | Yamaha | 43m 11.897s | | 1m 42.874s | 101.995mph | H/XH |
| 2 | Lorenzo | Yamaha | 43m 11.992s | 00.095s | 1m 43.041s | 101.991mph | H/XH |
| 3 | Stoner | Ducati | 43m 20.781s | 8.884s | 1m 42.858s | 101.646mph | H/XH |
| 4 | Dovizioso | Honda | 43m 20.833s | 8.936s | 1m 43.276s | 101.644mph | H/XH |
| 5 | Capirossi | Suzuki | 43m 31.728s | 19.831s | 1m 43.306s | 101.221mph | H/XH |
| 6 | Pedrosa | Honda | 43m 34.079s | 22.182s | 1m 43.335s | 101.297mph | H/XH |
| 7 | Edwards | Yamaha | 43m 35.444s | 23.547s | 1m 43.771s | 101.076mph | H/XH |
| 8 | De Puniet | Honda | 43m 37.162s | 25.265s | 1m 43.433s | 101.010mph | H/XH |
| 9 | Kallio | Ducati | 43m 43.694s | 31.797s | 1m 43.883s | 100.759mph | H/XH |
| 10 | Hayden | Ducati | 43m 45.490s | 33.593s | 1m 44.047s | 100.690mph | H/XH |
| 11 | Vermeulen | Suzuki | 43m 48.580s | 36.683s | 1m 44.272s | 100.571mph | H/XH |
| 12 | De Angelis | Honda | 43m 48.771s | 36.874s | 1m 43.945s | 100.564mph | H/XH |
| 13 | Toseland | Yamaha | 43m 51.330s | 39.433s | 1m 43.898s | 100.466mph | H/XH |
| 14 | Melandri | Kawasaki | 43m 56.685s | 44.788s | 1m 43.836s | 100.262mph | H/XH |
| 15 | Gibernau | Ducati | 43m 58.651s | 46.754s | 1m 44.053s | 100.188mph | H/XH |
| 16 | Canepa | Ducati | 44m 07.770s | 55.873s | 1m 44.534s | 99.842mph | H/XH |
| 17 | Talmacsi | Honda | 44m 39.537s | 1m 27.640s | 1m 45.652s | 98.659mph | H/XH |
| 18 | Elias | Honda | 15m 45.214s | 16 laps | 1m 43.779s | 100.686mph | H/XH |

## CHAMPIONSHIP

| | Rider | Team | Points |
|---|---|---|---|
| 1 | Rossi | Fiat Yamaha Team | 106 |
| 2 | Lorenzo | Fiat Yamaha Team | 106 |
| 3 | Stoner | Ducati Marlboro Team | 106 |
| 4 | Dovizioso | Repsol Honda Team | 69 |
| 5 | Pedrosa | Repsol Honda Team | 67 |
| 6 | Edwards | Monster Yamaha Tech 3 | 54 |
| 7 | Melandri | Hayate Racing Team | 50 |
| 8 | Capirossi | Rizla Suzuki MotoGP | 49 |
| 9 | De Puniet | LCR Honda MotoGP | 42 |
| 10 | Vermeulen | Rizla Suzuki MotoGP | 42 |
| 11 | Toseland | Monster Yamaha Tech 3 | 29 |
| 12 | Kallio | Pramac Racing | 26 |
| 13 | De Angelis | San Carlo Honda Gresini | 25 |
| 14 | Elias | San Carlo Honda Gresini | 23 |
| 15 | Hayden | Ducati Marlboro Team | 19 |
| 16 | Canepa | Pramac Racing | 10 |
| 17 | Gibernau | Grupo Francisco Hernando | 9 |
| 18 | Takahashi | Scot Racing Team MotoGP | 8 |

the bike turned. A bad start didn't help, but at least seventh promoted him to sixth in the points table.

**8 RANDY DE PUNIET** Another solid result. Got a stunning start to be fourth at the end of the first lap but was then passed by the factory bikes on the straight. Sat in Edwards' slipstream for the last ten laps but couldn't make an attack. Happy to be first satellite bike home.

**9 MIKA KALLIO** Like Hayden, benefited from the new electronics package and work done at Mugello after the Italian GP. Cautious with the full tank, made a small mistake on the first lap, then passed Elias and Melandri. A welcome return to form after a run of disappointing races.

**10 NICKY HAYDEN** Signs of progress at last! New electronics and what looked like a very different set-up restored enough confidence for him to be sixth fastest on Friday and then get his first top-ten finish of the year. 'It's not a spectacular result but it's definitely a step forward.'

**11 CHRIS VERMEULEN** Never happy with his rhythm, lacked confidence in the front end, and his new motor blew on the final run out of the last corner.

**12 ALEX DE ANGELIS** Complained, like every Honda rider, about lack of edge grip under acceleration at high lean angles. That's a problem that hurts in Catalunya's long corners. Had a dice with Hayden early on but couldn't stay with the Ducati.

**13 JAMES TOSELAND** Wasted his best qualifying of the season so far with a terrible start that lost him six places. Had rear grip problems towards the flag but said afterwards the real problem was that start, which was his own fault.

**14 MARCO MELANDRI** Always knew he'd be in trouble on a track where there's no making up for a lack of power. Had fun getting into the top ten in the early laps but then started sliding all over the place. Not disappointed because he knew what to expect.

**15 SETE GIBERNAU** Returned from the collarbone injury sustained at Le Mans but wasn't fully fit. Did a good professional job, as expected, to bag the last point.

**16 NICCOLO CANEPA** Like several others, he struggled with the effects on tyre grip of the elevated track temperature. A difficult first GP at Catalunya.

**17 GABOR TALMACSI** Brought his sponsor's cash to the hard-up Scot team and sat on his RC212V for the first time on Saturday morning. Was pleasantly surprised to be closer to the front men than he expected in both practice and the race.

**TONI ELIAS** Desperate to redeem his season at his home race. Looked to be on course when he qualified fifth but was down in eleventh when he lost the front at the left-hander at the end of the back straight.

**YUKI TAKAHASHI** Crashed out after tagging Vermeulen on the first lap. Broke the little finger on his right hand.

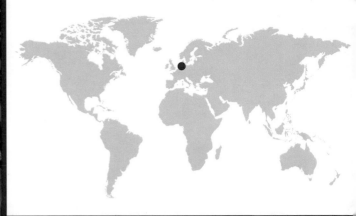

# THE CENTURION

**Another Fiat Yamaha one–two, but this time Rossi was never threatened on his way to his 100th Grand Prix win**

Even second-place man Jorge Lorenzo had no trouble admitting it: 'The big hero of the day is Vale, because 100 is a big, big number.' Indeed it is. Valentino Rossi's majestic win made him only the second racer in the 60-year history of the World Championships to rack up a century of wins. Only the most successful motorcycle racer ever, Giacomo Agostini, has won more races, with an astonishing 122 victories. Somehow it was fitting that Valentino passed his milestone on the Assen circuit, a place he referred to as 'the university' and where his father Graziano won his first Grand Prix, the 250cc race of 1979.

Valentino dominated the weekend, but the race didn't feature the close combat of his previous thrilling encounter with Jorge in Barcelona. Rossi started from pole for only the second time in the season and took the lead from Stoner on the second lap. The other two 'Aliens' went with them – Pedrosa after getting the holeshot, Lorenzo after messing up the start and having to get past a fast-starting Vermeulen. (Chris was using the old-spec Suzuki motor after blowing the new one at the Barcelona test.) The front four steadily dropped the Suzuki rider, who then came under attack from Colin Edwards and Andrea Dovizioso.

The Repsol Honda challenge soon evaporated. Pedrosa lost the front in Turn 1 at the start of lap five and his team-mate Dovizioso had exactly the same crash in the same place at the start of lap 11. Both riders were using a new chassis, although with little testing Dani was far from sure if it was a major improvement. The good news was that neither rider was hurt, which was particularly heartening in the case of Pedrosa, who was looking and sounding a lot

**Above** The frantic dice for sixth place kept the crowd entertained

**Opposite** Stoner was again hit by fatigue, but still got on the rostrum

**Below** Capirossi was sixth until Elias's last-corner lunge

healthier than at any time since the end of the previous season.

The exit of the factory Hondas left Edwards and Vermeulen in lonely fourth and fifth places, respectively, where they would stay until the end of the race. The front three, now with Lorenzo in second and Stoner in third, behind a rapidly disappearing Rossi, continued to pull away and the crowd focused on a frantic battle for sixth place, which would provide the entertainment for the rest of the race. Nicky

Hayden, continuing the improvement of Barcelona, led the group until his left handlebar worked loose at half-distance. James Toseland, having benefited from some personal attention from Yamaha top brass at the Barcelona test, took over with Capirossi, de Puniet, Kallio, de Angelis and Elias in close attendance. Nicky managed to get back with the group later in the race.

At mid-race distance it looked for a lap or two as if Lorenzo was going to be able to close the gap, getting it down to 1.5 seconds before a couple of serious scares on the fast run to the final chicane persuaded him that second place wasn't such a bad idea. Four laps later the lead was just under three seconds. Stoner, in third place, was now fading badly and drifting back towards Edwards. Unhappily, this was for the same reason as in Barcelona: Casey had not felt well all weekend and when he got to *parc fermé* his legs buckled under him and doctors had to put him on a drip. In the two weeks since the Catalan GP the Aussie had tried all manner of vitamins and dietary supplements, but nothing seemed to be having an effect. He said he was grateful to his team for 'putting a fantastic bike underneath me today' and enabling him to hold on to his rostrum position, but while it was obvious that he had a problem, no-one yet realised just how serious it was.

All of the 96,000 fans in the stands – the crowd was actually up on the previous season – knew that the group fight for sixth place would be decided at the last chicane. Sure enough, there was action and controversy. Mika Kallio crashed out on the run to the final corner and the pack was led by that old devil, Loris Capirossi. It looked as if experience would tell, but

Toni Elias got into the corner way too hot and ran wide and on to the grass, forcing Loris into evasive action. That let James Toseland through for a season's best sixth place. Elias got across the line in eighth but Race Direction saw fit to hit him with a 20-second penalty, which relegated him to 12th.

Naturally, Valentino had a post-race stunt ready to celebrate his century of victories. He stopped on the slow-down lap and, with the help of the fan club, unfurled a 25-metre banner with pictures of every one of those 100 victories emblazoned on it. 'When I arrive at 70 I say no, 100 is impossible, but step-by-step I arrive. I pass through a difficult time, like 2006 and 2007, but from 2008 I come back very strong mentally and physically.' As for this race, he joked that 'Another battle like in Barcelona is too much for my grandmother's heart.' Jorge responded by saying, 'For the health of Vale's grandmother I close the throttle in the middle of the race.'

In truth, that was when Jorge found out that Valentino and his crew had set up the number 46 Yamaha to go even faster on race day than it had in qualifying, despite the significantly higher temperatures. In *parc fermé* after Barcelona, when Rossi congratulated him, Jorge's words were 'Hasta la proxima', which translates loosely as 'wait for next time'. The young Spaniard was quick, but again it was the experience of Rossi and his crew that told. It's not often that Valentino gets the full set over a weekend – pole position, the race win and fastest lap – but this was one of those rare occasions, and as a bonus he went clear at the top of the championship table. Only Giacomo Agostini's achievements remain to be surpassed.

## 'THE BIG HERO OF THE DAY IS VALE, BECAUSE 100 IS A BIG, BIG NUMBER'
### JORGE LORENZO

**Above** Colin Edwards on his way to a splendid fourth place

**Below** Even Lorenzo had to admit that there was no way to beat Rossi

**Opposite** Every race is a home race for Valentino Rossi

# TON UP

Assen 2009 was Valentino Rossi's 100th Grand Prix victory. Here are some of the landmarks along the way:

**#1** *Brno 1996:* His first pole and his first 125cc victory made him the third-youngest GP winner ever.

**#13** *Assen 1998:* First win on a 250, to become the third-youngest winner in that class.

**#26** *Rio 1999:* His ninth win of the year made him the youngest-ever 250cc World Champion, at 20.

**#27** *Donington Park 2000:* The first win on a 500 in his ninth start in the class.

**#30** *Welkom 2001:* A first pole in 500s, a win and the fastest lap gave him the full set for the first time.

**#39** *Rio 2001:* Won the last 500cc GP.

**#40** *Suzuka 2002:* Won the first MotoGP race.

**#49** *Rio 2002:* Secured the first MotoGP crown.

**#59** *Valencia 2003:* Won on his last ride for Honda.

**#60** *Welkom 2004:* Won on his first ride for Yamaha to become the first man to win back-to-back races on different makes of bike.

**#67** *Phillip Island 2004:* Won the MotoGP title for Yamaha for the first time to become only the second rider to win back-to-back titles on different makes of bike.

**#76** *Sachsenring 2005:* Equalled Mike Hailwood's career total of wins.

**#90** *Le Mans 2008:* Equalled Angel Nieto's career total of wins.

**#94** *Misano 2008:* His 68th win in the premier class equalled Agostini's record.

# DUTCH TT
## TT CIRCUIT ASSEN
### ROUND 7
June 27

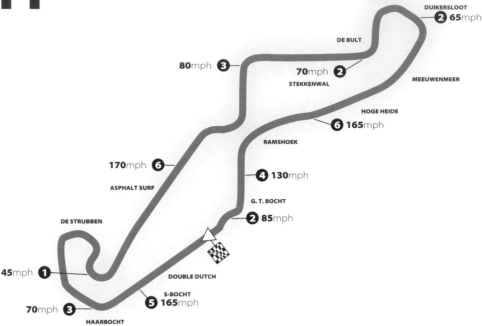

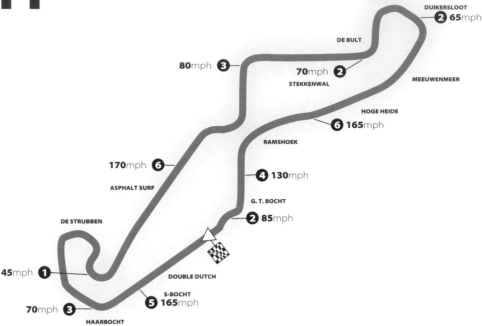

**BRIDGESTONE**
TYRE OPTIONS
FRONT SOFT (S) / MEDIUM (M)
REAR SOFT (S) / MEDIUM (M)

**MotoGP** **TISSOT** SWISS WATCHES SINCE 1853
OFFICIAL TIMEKEEPER

## RACE RESULTS

**CIRCUIT LENGTH** 2.830 miles
**NO. OF LAPS** 26
**RACE DISTANCE** 73.592 miles
**WEATHER** Dry, 24°C
**TRACK TEMPERATURE** 30°C
**WINNER** Valentino Rossi
**FASTEST LAP** 1m 36.558s, 105.524mph, Valentino Rossi (record)
**PREVIOUS LAP RECORD** 1m 36.738s, 105.328mph, Casey Stoner, 2008

## QUALIFYING

| | Rider | Nationality | Team | Qualifying | Pole + | Gap |
|---|---|---|---|---|---|---|
| 1 | Rossi | ITA | Fiat Yamaha Team | 1m 36.025s | | |
| 2 | Pedrosa | SPA | Repsol Honda Team | 1m 36.110s | 0.085s | 0.085s |
| 3 | Lorenzo | SPA | Fiat Yamaha Team | 1m 36.393s | 0.368s | 0.283s |
| 4 | Stoner | AUS | Ducati Marlboro Team | 1m 36.633s | 0.608s | 0.240s |
| 5 | Edwards | USA | Monster Yamaha Tech 3 | 1m 36.760s | 0.735s | 0.127s |
| 6 | Capirossi | ITA | Rizla Suzuki MotoGP | 1m 36.953s | 0.928s | 0.193s |
| 7 | Vermeulen | AUS | Rizla Suzuki MotoGP | 1m 37.194s | 1.169s | 0.241s |
| 8 | Dovizioso | ITA | Repsol Honda Team | 1m 37.237s | 1.212s | 0.043s |
| 9 | Toseland | GBR | Monster Yamaha Tech 3 | 1m 37.323s | 1.298s | 0.086s |
| 10 | De Puniet | FRA | LCR Honda MotoGP | 1m 37.473s | 1.448s | 0.150s |
| 11 | De Angelis | RSM | San Carlo Honda Gresini | 1m 37.637s | 1.612s | 0.164s |
| 12 | Kallio | FIN | Pramac Racing | 1m 37.749s | 1.724s | 0.112s |
| 13 | Hayden | USA | Ducati Marlboro Team | 1m 37.759s | 1.734s | 0.010s |
| 14 | Melandri | ITA | Hayate Racing Team | 1m 37.948s | 1.923s | 0.189s |
| 15 | Elias | SPA | San Carlo Honda Gresini | 1m 38.136s | 2.111s | 0.188s |
| 16 | Gibernau | SPA | Grupo Francisco Hernando | 1m 38.453s | 2.428s | 0.317s |
| 17 | Canepa | ITA | Pramac Racing | 1m 38.605s | 2.580s | 0.152s |
| 18 | Takahashi | JPN | Scot Racing Team MotoGP | 1m 38.619s | 2.594s | 0.014s |
| 19 | Talmacsi | HUN | Scot Racing Team MotoGP | 1m 39.407s | 3.382s | 0.788s |

## FINISHERS

**1 VALENTINO ROSSI** No repeat of the Catalunya duel: got a near-perfect set-up, started from pole, took the lead on lap two and was never headed. The win came 30 years after father Graziano won the 250cc race here and was the 100th GP victory of Valentino's 13-year career. Celebrated by unveiling a 25-metre banner with pictures of all 100 wins.

**2 JORGE LORENZO** Probably the only man who could have given Rossi a race, but made a mess of the start. Took five laps to get up to second, by which time Vale was 1.5s ahead. Pressed to close the gap, then felt the front trying to tuck and decided second would do. His 50th rostrum in GPs.

**3 CASEY STONER** The sickness that had affected him at Barcelona made its presence felt again. Casey faded after half-distance and looked pale and sick in parc fermé, so a rostrum was a near achievement. Not happy about being off the front row for the first time this season.

**4 COLIN EDWARDS** A good weekend, with the longer-wheelbase set-up helping him take advantage of his fifth on the grid and get a good start. Dovizioso came past then crashed, so held station in what turned out to be a lonely race to equal his best finish of the season so far.

**5 CHRIS VERMEULEN** Didn't use the new Suzuki engine, but the team continued to improve chassis settings. Got an even better start than Edwards and was fourth after the first lap, but once the Yamaha came past and the Hondas had crashed it was a solitary race, though his best finish of the season so far.

**6 JAMES TOSELAND** A vast improvement thanks to special attention at the recent test, and at Assen from Mr Nakajima, the Yamaha team manager. James reported the bike now felt less comfortable but was faster; more importantly, his old confidence seemed to reappear. Led a spectacular fight for sixth for most of the race. A timely return to form.

**7 RANDY DE PUNIET** First Honda home despite fraught qualifying due to electrical glitches and a crash. Took risks

Track map labels: MANDEVEEN, DUIKERSLOOT 2 65mph, DE BULT, 80mph 3, 70mph 2, STEKKENWAL, MEEUWENMEER, HOGE HEIDE, 6 165mph, RAMSHOEK, 170mph 6, 4 130mph, ASPHALT SURF, G. T. BOCHT, 2 85mph, DE STRUBBEN, 45mph 1, DOUBLE DUTCH, S-BOCHT, 5 165mph, 70mph 3, HAARBOCHT

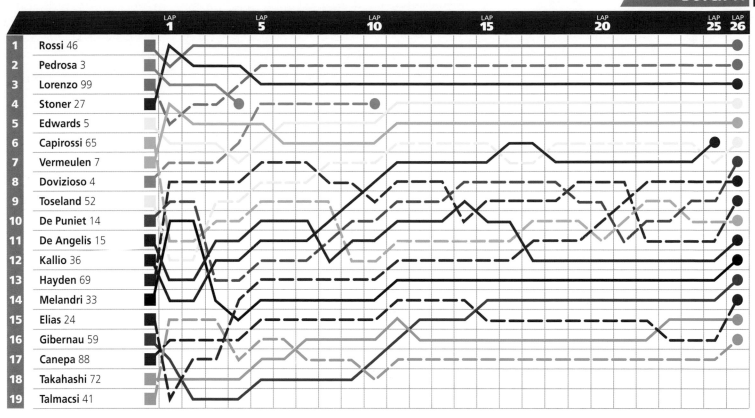

|  | | LAP 1 | LAP 5 | LAP 10 | LAP 15 | LAP 20 | LAP 25 | LAP 26 |
|---|---|---|---|---|---|---|---|---|
| 1 | Rossi 46 | | | | | | | |
| 2 | Pedrosa 3 | | | | | | | |
| 3 | Lorenzo 99 | | | | | | | |
| 4 | Stoner 27 | | | | | | | |
| 5 | Edwards 5 | | | | | | | |
| 6 | Capirossi 65 | | | | | | | |
| 7 | Vermeulen 7 | | | | | | | |
| 8 | Dovizioso 4 | | | | | | | |
| 9 | Toseland 52 | | | | | | | |
| 10 | De Puniet 14 | | | | | | | |
| 11 | De Angelis 15 | | | | | | | |
| 12 | Kallio 36 | | | | | | | |
| 13 | Hayden 69 | | | | | | | |
| 14 | Melandri 33 | | | | | | | |
| 15 | Elias 24 | | | | | | | |
| 16 | Gibernau 59 | | | | | | | |
| 17 | Canepa 88 | | | | | | | |
| 18 | Takahashi 72 | | | | | | | |
| 19 | Talmacsi 41 | | | | | | | |

## RACE

|  | Rider | Motorcycle | Race Time | Time + | Fastest Lap | Av Speed | Ｂ |
|---|---|---|---|---|---|---|---|
| 1 | Rossi | Yamaha | 42m 14.611s | | 1m 36.558s | 104.525mph | M/M |
| 2 | Lorenzo | Yamaha | 42m 19.979s | 5.368s | 1m 36.755s | 104.304mph | M/M |
| 3 | Stoner | Ducati | 42m 37.724s | 23.113s | 1m 36.903s | 103.581mph | M/M |
| 4 | Edwards | Yamaha | 42m 43.725s | 29.114s | 1m 37.375s | 103.339mph | M/M |
| 5 | Vermeulen | Suzuki | 42m 48.216s | 33.605s | 1m 37.613s | 103.157mph | M/M |
| 6 | Toseland | Yamaha | 42m 53.958s | 39.347s | 1m 37.934s | 102.928mph | M/M |
| 7 | De Puniet | Honda | 42m 54.154s | 39.543s | 1m 37.883s | 102.919mph | M/M |
| 8 | Hayden | Ducati | 42m 54.434s | 39.823s | 1m 38.200s | 102.908mph | M/M |
| 9 | Capirossi | Suzuki | 42m 55.284s | 40.673s | 1m 37.941s | 102.874mph | M/M |
| 10 | De Angelis | Honda | 43m 00.621s | 46.010s | 1m 37.904s | 102.662mph | M/M |
| 11 | Melandri | Kawasaki | 43m 12.388s | 57.777s | 1m 38.487s | 102.196mph | M/M |
| 12 | Elias | Honda | 43m 14.385s | 59.774s | 1m 37.955s | 102.910mph | M/s |
| 13 | Gibernau | Ducati | 43m 19.977s | 1m 05.366s | 1m 39.120s | 101.897mph | M/M |
| 14 | Canepa | Ducati | 43m 24.508s | 1m 09.897s | 1m 38.873s | 101.720mph | s/s |
| 15 | Takahashi | Honda | 43m 24.541s | 1m 09.930s | 1m 39.126s | 101.719mph | M/M |
| 16 | Talmacsi | Honda | 43m 39.710s | 1m 25.099s | 1m 39.318s | 101.130mph | M/s |
| 17 | Kallio | Ducati | 41m 14.211s | 1 lap | 1m 37.909s | 102.959mph | M/s |
| 18 | Dovizioso | Honda | 16m 24.548s | 16 laps | 1m 37.262s | 103.496mph | M/M |
| 19 | Pedrosa | Honda | 6m 36.388s | 22 laps | 1m 36.918s | 102.825mph | M/M |

## CHAMPIONSHIP

|  | Rider | Team | Points |
|---|---|---|---|
| 1 | Rossi | Fiat Yamaha Team | 131 |
| 2 | Lorenzo | Fiat Yamaha Team | 126 |
| 3 | Stoner | Ducati Marlboro Team | 122 |
| 4 | Dovizioso | Repsol Honda Team | 69 |
| 5 | Pedrosa | Repsol Honda Team | 67 |
| 6 | Edwards | Monster Yamaha Tech 3 | 67 |
| 7 | Capirossi | Rizla Suzuki MotoGP | 56 |
| 8 | Melandri | Hayate Racing Team | 55 |
| 9 | Vermeulen | Rizla Suzuki MotoGP | 53 |
| 10 | De Puniet | LCR Honda MotoGP | 51 |
| 11 | Toseland | Monster Yamaha Tech 3 | 39 |
| 12 | De Angelis | San Carlo Honda Gresini | 31 |
| 13 | Hayden | Ducati Marlboro Team | 27 |
| 14 | Elias | San Carlo Honda Gresini | 27 |
| 15 | Kallio | Pramac Racing | 26 |
| 16 | Canepa | Pramac Racing | 12 |
| 17 | Gibernau | Grupo Francisco Hernando | 12 |
| 18 | Takahashi | Scot Racing Team MotoGP | 9 |

on the first lap after a bad start. Had his progress interrupted by both Toseland and Elias banging fairings with him – not surprisingly, he described the race as 'thrilling and stressful'.

**8 NICKY HAYDEN** The signs of improvement seen at Barcelona were definitely stronger, despite qualifying a disappointing 13th. Embroiled in the battle for sixth, ran off track at one point, but was able to get back with the group. A loose left handlebar hampered progress but still said the bike was the best it had been all season.

**9 LORIS CAPIROSSI** An uncharacteristically bad start meant a lot of work to get with the big group, and then a run-on meant he had to do it all again.

Overtook three riders on the last lap to go sixth, only to be punted off track by Elias at the final chicane.

**10 ALEX DE ANGELIS** The rear traction problems that had dogged him seemed to have been cured, and for most of the race he was battling for sixth. After half-distance the front started tucking, so concentrated on staying upright. Still, a weekend that saw some significant progress.

**11 MARCO MELANDRI** Handicapped by a broken bone in his right hand after an accident at the end of testing. Also growing a little disenchanted with his bike's erratic behaviour – the old Kawasaki problems of engine braking going into a corner and lack of grip under acceleration coming out.

**12 TONI ELIAS** Crossed the line in eighth, after a wild move at the last chicane put him on the grass, and took Capirossi along too. Race Direction hit him with a 20s penalty, so classified as 12th, but the team not too bothered as points meant less at this stage than good performance.

**13 SETE GIBERNAU** Much nearer to full fitness than he was in Catalunya, and certain his team were finding the right direction with the Ducati. Still troubled, however, by front-wheel chatter.

**14 NICCOLO CANEPA** Arrived at the event with a nasty dose of 'flu and struggled all weekend. Passed Takahashi on the last corner to end a difficult race on a high note.

**15 YUKI TAKAHASHI** Got to the finish despite pain from the finger he broke at Catalunya and an early incident that pushed him wide and lost him a lot of time.

**16 GABOR TALMACSI** Happy with his first full weekend as a MotoGP rider. Used the softer tyres and was able to race with a group for the first ten laps, leading team-mate Takahashi, and Gibernau, before fading.

## NON-FINISHERS

**MIKA KALLIO** Part of the fabulous fight for sixth place until the last lap, but crashed in the ultra-fast left before the final chicane, doing some serious damage to his left-hand ring finger. Returned to Finland to see his

doctor and was unlikely to make it to the next round at Laguna Seca.

**ANDREA DOVIZIOSO** Lost the front in Turn 1 on lap 11 – the same crash as his team-mate, again with no warning when at maximum lean. Like Pedrosa, he'd started well and was also fourth when he fell.

**DANI PEDROSA** Lost the front in Turn 1 on the fifth lap. The good news was that he didn't damage himself any further in the crash. He'd led from the start after qualifying second and seemed to be in better health than at the previous round.

# LOOK WHO'S BACK

**Just when it seemed safe to write off Dani Pedrosa's season, he led the US GP from flag to flag**

**D**ani Pedrosa hadn't won a race for over a year. He was badly injured in the first pre-season test and a succession of further incidents appeared to have reduced him to an also-ran. The Honda man had been on painkillers for six months, and had only started to wean himself off them at Assen. Crucially, Dani's knee injury had prevented him from training properly so he was far from race fit. He could qualify well, he started races better than anyone, but he was usually passed early and had made only three rostrum appearances before the MotoGP circus arrived in California. When Pedrosa qualified in fourth place on the grid no-one took too much notice. After all, he hadn't actually raced at Laguna for two years, because in 2008 Dani missed the US GP after a big crash the previous week at the Sachsenring. Things didn't look any more hopeful when the Fiat Yamaha team-mates qualified first and second with Casey Stoner third.

However, the final stages of qualifying were notable for the return of the highside, with Jorge Lorenzo, Casey Stoner and Chris Vermeulen all suffering big off-throttle crashes going into corners. The finger of blame was aimed at Bridgestone, who hadn't brought dual-compound tyres to this heavily left-handed circuit. Only four tracks had been scheduled to see dual-compounds and Laguna wasn't one of them; the riders on the Safety Commission politely requested that a few more circuits be added to the list. Stoner got away with his crash, but Lorenzo was hurt. He broke a bone in his right foot, separated his right collarbone badly enough to need to wear a sling and was taken to the front-row press conference in a wheelchair.

Not surprisingly, Jorge didn't make a good start on

**Above** 'The Aliens' – Pedrosa, Lorenzo, Rossi and Stoner – lead the charge to turn one

**Opposite** Colin Edwards didn't have a happy time at his home GP, but at least the race marked his 100th points-scoring finish

race day. He was shuffled back to eighth in the first few corners but worked his way back up to fifth by the end of the first lap. To no-one's surprise Pedrosa got the holeshot, but this time he didn't slip backwards. Quite the reverse. Rossi lost second place to Stoner on lap three as his set-up troubles continued, and he couldn't ride at the maximum until about half-distance, by which time Dani had a three-second advantage and Stoner was starting to fade. Worryingly, Casey had not shaken off whatever had been afflicting him in Barcelona and at Assen, and he was scheduled to go to San Francisco for some intensive tests straight after the GP. This time the Aussie reported that he wasn't so tired at the end of the race, but he'd suffered from arm pump, perhaps as a result of restricted movement in the wrist he'd had repaired over winter and the fact that Laguna was the first left-handed track he'd been to since the operation. Once Lorenzo got past him, Stoner was consigned to a lonely fourth place.

'I'D LIKE TO THANK THE DOCTORS WHO HAVE TREATED ME, BECAUSE THERE HAVE BEEN QUITE A FEW OF THEM!'
**DANI PEDROSA**

To everyone's surprise, Lorenzo then proceeded to close down on his team-mate, moving into third on lap 21, just over 1.5 seconds behind Rossi. Six laps later he was right on Valentino's tail as they came down to the last corner. Jorge tried an outbraking move on the left but only managed to tie the bike in knots. Somehow he avoided both ramming his team-mate and running off track. That should have been it, but he then managed to get back to within a second of Valentino as they started the last lap. The gaps between these top three riders weren't large, but there seemed no likelihood of a change in the rostrum positions and they continued in their order right round to the top of the Corkscrew. Then, suddenly, Rossi started closing on Pedrosa, charging down the hill 'like a crazy man'. Coming to the final corner he was close enough to try a foot-waving lunge on the brakes, but he just wasn't quite near enough. The gap at the line was a mere third of a second.

Why was Pedrosa so slow on the last lap? Was it the bike's electronics reacting to dangerously low fuel? No, said Dani. His pit board had told him he had a cushion of nearly two seconds as he started the last lap and he'd simply relaxed too much. Fortunately he heard Rossi's bike as they went into the final corner. 'Lucky it was the last lap,' said Dani with a grin, ignoring the less-than-rapturous reception from the American crowd, who have yet to forgive him for knocking Nicky Hayden down at Estoril in 2006. Nicky posted his best result of the season so far with fifth but was anxious not 'to sound like a fool'; then he admitted to being pretty happy. His chances of getting up with the front men disappeared when he took time to pass Elias, who ended up with an encouraging finish in sixth place, also a season's best.

**Right** Toni Elias finally started to come good, with sixth place his best result of the season so far

**Opposite** Suzuki had a tough weekend. A battered Chris Vermeulen managed only eighth on a circuit where he normally shines

**Below** Nicky Hayden was delighted with his fifth place and the special livery for his Ducati

All three men on the rostrum had plenty to be happy about. Pedrosa's victory was as emphatic as they come and ended a winless period for both himself and Honda. (Their last victory had been at Barcelona over 12 months previously.) As usual, Rossi seemed nearly as pleased for Dani as when he wins himself – and of course Vale had extended his championship lead. He also expressed some surprise at Pedrosa's pace, admitting he couldn't match it in the first part of the race, although the gap stayed constant after half-distance. But then he'd had to cope with Lorenzo's

attack over the last ten laps, too, before that last-lap charge up to the Honda rider.

Lorenzo thought he'd ridden one of the best races of his career, although he did admit that that assessment didn't include his lurid attempt to pass on the brakes. Given his physical condition, which he described as 'very poor', it was difficult to argue with that analysis. Jorge got a bad start, fought through past some good racers and challenged his team-mate on a very physical circuit – not bad for someone with a dislocated collarbone and further proof that the kid could be a real contender.

## SCOT FREE

The Scot Honda satellite team started the season with one rider, Yuki Takahashi. The class rookie didn't have an easy start and his progress wasn't helped by the team running so short of cash there were rumours they wouldn't be able to finish the season. At Barcelona they fielded a second rider, the 2007 125cc World Champion Gabor Talmacsi. The Hungarian had fallen out with Aspar Martinez's 250 team and was available. More importantly, he had some serious financial backing from the Hungarian state oil company, MOL. They wanted to support one of the country's highest-profile sportsmen, but they were only interested in MotoGP, not the smaller classes.

So for the Catalan GP and the Dutch TT the team had fielded both men, although rumours continued to circulate about Takahashi being eased out. Nevertheless, Yuki travelled to Laguna Seca only to discover that the team had announced he was unfit to ride thanks to a back injury that would require an operation.

The Japanese man was not amused. 'I haven't got a problem with my back. The problem is the team cannot continue with two riders and just two bikes, and there isn't the money to obtain more bikes.' That seemed an honest assessment, and given those facts of financial life it was no surprise that Talmacsi found himself the sole

Scot Honda rider for the rest of the season.

The departure of Takahashi meant that Honda didn't have a Japanese rider in the top class for the first time in many years. Takazumi Katayama arrived on the scene in 1982 as part of the factory team running the new NS500 triples, and since then the likes of Tadahiko Taira, Shinichi Itoh, Norick Abe, Tadayuki Okada, the Aoki brothers, Makoto Tamada, Shinya Nakano and Daijiro Kato have all added their magic to the Championships.

**BRIDGESTONE**
TYRE OPTIONS
FRONT MEDIUM (M) / HARD (H)
REAR MEDIUM (M) / HARD (H)

motoGP | **TISSOT** SWISS WATCHES SINCE 1853
OFFICIAL TIMEKEEPER

# UNITED STATES GP
## LAGUNA SECA

### ROUND 8
July 5

# RACE RESULTS

**CIRCUIT LENGTH** 2.243 miles
**NO. OF LAPS** 32
**RACE DISTANCE** 71.776 miles
**WEATHER** Dry, 22°C
**TRACK TEMPERATURE** 42°C
**WINNER** Dani Pedrosa
**FASTEST LAP** 1m 21.928s, 98.566mph, Dani Pedrosa
**LAP RECORD** 1m 21.488s, 99.098mph, Casey Stoner, 2008

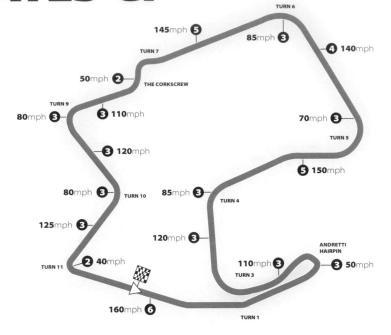

## QUALIFYING

| | Rider | Nationality | Team | Qualifying | Pole + | Gap |
|---|---|---|---|---|---|---|
| 1 | Lorenzo | SPA | Fiat Yamaha Team | 1m 21.678s | | |
| 2 | Rossi | ITA | Fiat Yamaha Team | 1m 21.845s | 0.167s | 0.167s |
| 3 | Stoner | AUS | Ducati Team | 1m 21.910s | 0.232s | 0.065s |
| 4 | Pedrosa | SPA | Repsol Honda Team | 1m 22.113s | 0.435s | 0.203s |
| 5 | Dovizioso | ITA | Repsol Honda Team | 1m 22.135s | 0.457s | 0.022s |
| 6 | Elias | SPA | San Carlo Honda Gresini | 1m 22.146s | 0.468s | 0.011s |
| 7 | Edwards | USA | Monster Yamaha Tech 3 | 1m 22.490s | 0.812s | 0.344s |
| 8 | Hayden | USA | Ducati Team | 1m 22.540s | 0.862s | 0.050s |
| 9 | Vermeulen | AUS | Rizla Suzuki MotoGP | 1m 22.633s | 0.955s | 0.093s |
| 10 | Capirossi | ITA | Rizla Suzuki MotoGP | 1m 22.662s | 0.984s | 0.029s |
| 11 | Melandri | ITA | Hayate Racing Team | 1m 22.842s | 1.164s | 0.180s |
| 12 | De Angelis | RSM | San Carlo Honda Gresini | 1m 23.004s | 1.326s | 0.162s |
| 13 | Gibernau | SPA | Grupo Francisco Hernando | 1m 23.106s | 1.428s | 0.102s |
| 14 | De Puniet | FRA | LCR Honda MotoGP | 1m 23.147s | 1.469s | 0.041s |
| 15 | Toseland | GBR | Monster Yamaha Tech 3 | 1m 23.390s | 1.712s | 0.243s |
| 16 | Canepa | ITA | Pramac Racing | 1m 23.912s | 2.234s | 0.522s |
| 17 | Talmacsi | HUN | Scot Racing Team MotoGP | 1m 24.528s | 2.850s | 0.616s |

## FINISHERS

**1 DANI PEDROSA** Nearly pain-free but far from fit. Managed his trademark cannonball start and kept the momentum, though nearly handed Rossi the win on the last lap. Dani's (and Honda's) first victory in over a year was a reminder that, but for his injuries, there'd have been a four-way title fight.

**2 VALENTINO ROSSI** Never happy with the set-up of his front fork in practice and qualifying, things only improving when the fuel load lightened in the race. By then Dani had disappeared; also had to fend off his very aggressive team-mate. Not disappointed by the result and fulsome in his congratulations to Pedrosa.

**3 JORGE LORENZO** Suffered his first big crash of the season at the end of qualifying and raced with a broken metatarsal and a separation of the right collarbone from the shoulder, but still caught his team-mate and tried a pass on the brakes that nearly brought them both down. Without that mistake felt he could have been second, and possibly first!

**4 CASEY STONER** Still dogged by illness, and made things worse with a big crash in qualifying that damaged his ribs. Unhappy with fourth, however good it seemed under the circumstances. Went to San Francisco after the race to Dr Art Ting's clinic to try for a definitive diagnosis.

**5 NICKY HAYDEN** Best qualifying and result of the season so far, reassuring the team they'd found a direction to work in. Even said this seemed as good as his two wins at Laguna. Wore a special stars-and-stripes colour scheme for race day, echoing the limited-edition 848 being sold by Ducati in the USA.

**6 TONI ELIAS** Competitive from the first session and best finish of the year to date, right behind Hayden, with whom he diced for most of the race. Replicated his pace in practice despite a crash in warm-up. 'Much better than previous races but we still want more,' said both rider and team-owner.

**7 COLIN EDWARDS** Disappointed with the result and tired because he struggled all race to get the M1 to turn. Lots of

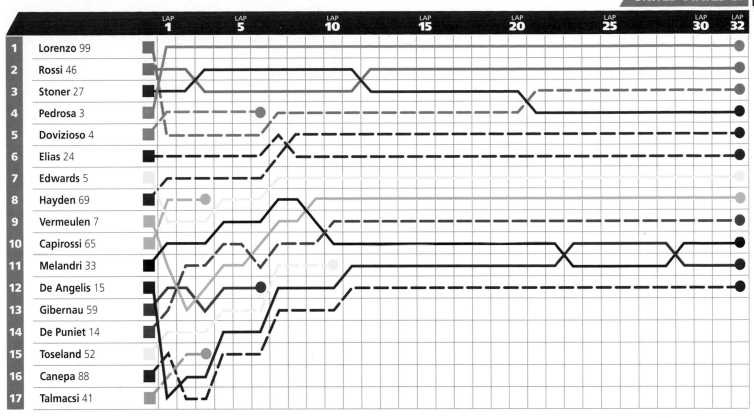

| | | LAP 1 | LAP 5 | LAP 10 | LAP 15 | LAP 20 | LAP 25 | LAP 30 | LAP 32 |
|---|---|---|---|---|---|---|---|---|---|
| 1 | Lorenzo 99 | | | | | | | | |
| 2 | Rossi 46 | | | | | | | | |
| 3 | Stoner 27 | | | | | | | | |
| 4 | Pedrosa 3 | | | | | | | | |
| 5 | Dovizioso 4 | | | | | | | | |
| 6 | Elias 24 | | | | | | | | |
| 7 | Edwards 5 | | | | | | | | |
| 8 | Hayden 69 | | | | | | | | |
| 9 | Vermeulen 7 | | | | | | | | |
| 10 | Capirossi 65 | | | | | | | | |
| 11 | Melandri 33 | | | | | | | | |
| 12 | De Angelis 15 | | | | | | | | |
| 13 | Gibernau 59 | | | | | | | | |
| 14 | De Puniet 14 | | | | | | | | |
| 15 | Toseland 52 | | | | | | | | |
| 16 | Canepa 88 | | | | | | | | |
| 17 | Talmacsi 41 | | | | | | | | |

## RACE

| | Rider | Motorcycle | Race Time | Time + | Fastest Lap | Av Speed | 🅱 |
|---|---|---|---|---|---|---|---|
| 1 | Pedrosa | Honda | 44m 01.580s | | 1m 21.928s | 97.828mph | H/H |
| 2 | Rossi | Yamaha | 44m 01.924s | 0.344s | 1m 21.944s | 97.815mph | H/H |
| 3 | Lorenzo | Yamaha | 44m 03.506s | 1.926s | 1m 21.951s | 97.757mph | H/H |
| 4 | Stoner | Ducati | 44m 14.012s | 12.432s | 1m 22.083s | 97.370mph | H/H |
| 5 | Hayden | Ducati | 44m 23.243s | 21.663s | 1m 22.703s | 97.032mph | M/H |
| 6 | Elias | Honda | 44m 23.621s | 22.041s | 1m 22.665s | 97.019mph | M/M |
| 7 | Edwards | Yamaha | 44m 31.781s | 30.201s | 1m 22.878s | 96.722mph | M/H |
| 8 | Vermeulen | Suzuki | 44m 34.437s | 32.857s | 1m 22.796s | 96.626mph | H/H |
| 9 | De Puniet | Honda | 44m 41.905s | 40.325s | 1m 22.981s | 96.357mph | H/M |
| 10 | Melandri | Kawasaki | 44m 49.608s | 48.028s | 1m 23.242s | 96.081mph | H/H |
| 11 | De Angelis | Honda | 44m 50.390s | 48.810s | 1m 23.024s | 96.053mph | M/M |
| 12 | Canepa | Ducati | 45m 20.111s | 1m 18.531s | 1m 24.192s | 95.003mph | H/M |
| | Dovisioso | Honda | 8m 23.703s | 26 laps | 1m 22.179s | 96.195mph | H/H |
| | Gibernau | Ducati | 8m 32.190s | 26 laps | 1m 23.342s | 94.601mph | H/H |
| | Capirossi | Suzuki | 4m 19.395s | 29 laps | 1m 23.756s | 93.398mph | H/H |
| | Talmacsi | Honda | 4m 22.278s | 29 laps | 1m 24.301s | 92.371mph | H/H |

## CHAMPIONSHIP

| | Rider | Team | Points |
|---|---|---|---|
| 1 | Rossi | Fiat Yamaha Team | 151 |
| 2 | Lorenzo | Fiat Yamaha Team | 142 |
| 3 | Stoner | Ducati Team | 135 |
| 4 | Pedrosa | Repsol Honda Team | 92 |
| 5 | Edwards | Monster Yamaha Tech 3 | 76 |
| 6 | Dovizioso | Repsol Honda Team | 69 |
| 7 | Melandri | Hayate Racing Team | 61 |
| 8 | Vermeulen | Rizla Suzuki MotoGP | 61 |
| 9 | De Puniet | LCR Honda MotoGP | 58 |
| 10 | Capirossi | Rizla Suzuki MotoGP | 56 |
| 11 | Toseland | Monster Yamaha Tech 3 | 39 |
| 12 | Hayden | Ducati Team | 38 |
| 13 | Elias | San Carlo Honda Gresini | 37 |
| 14 | De Angelis | San Carlo Honda Gresini | 36 |
| 15 | Kallio | Pramac Racing | 26 |
| 16 | Canepa | Pramac Racing | 16 |
| 17 | Gibernau | Grupo Francisco Hernando | 12 |
| 18 | Takahashi | Scot Racing Team MotoGP | 9 |

problems with the front end – and Colin relies completely on a good feeling with the front. Became the 14th rider in GP history to finish in the points 100 times.

**8 CHRIS VERMEULEN** Crashed twice in practice, got boxed in at Turn 1, then tangled with his team-mate and Edwards, putting him back to 14th. Again struggled to get any heat into the tyres in the opening laps. Pace in the second half was the same as the Hayden–Elias dice for fifth.

**9 RANDY DE PUNIET** Used the softer tyre in the race so suffered in the last ten laps, but made up for a dreadful practice and qualifying with another solid top-ten finish that maintained his 100 per cent record, despite a machine he was never happy with.

**10 MARCO MELANDRI** A promising start to the weekend was ruined by a crash in warm-up. 'We tried to repair the bike and use the same one but it was a big mistake because the settings were completely different to the morning. I had a completely different feeling on left and right corners and the throttle wasn't smooth, so it was tough.'

**11 ALEX DE ANGELIS** Changes made after qualifying didn't have the desired effect and he couldn't replicate his practice lap times in the race. The early laps were his problem, and once things felt better the chance of a decent finish was long gone.

**12 NICCOLO CANEPA** Another who had no front grip early on, and when he saw riders crash in front of him he decided that discretion was the better part of valour. A tough debut at the Dry Lake.

### NON-FINISHERS

**ANDREA DOVIZIOSO** Clipped one of the plastic posts that delineate the pit exit while shadowing Rossi and bent his clutch lever, making it difficult to change down and manage the Honda's engine braking, then lost the front. Disappointed his error wasted the chance of a good result.

**SETE GIBERNAU** Crashed uninjured on lap seven while lying in 12th place. Subsequent events made it likely that this was Gibernau's final Grand Prix.

**LORIS CAPIROSSI** Had the same lack of front grip as his team-mate, but Loris's aggression saw him lose the front end at the frighteningly fast Turn 6 on lap four after a big warning at the same place the previous time round.

**GABOR TALMACSI** Less than three seconds off pole on his first visit to the track, but lost the front and crashed three laps into the race.

### EXCLUDED

**JAMES TOSELAND** Jumped the start but didn't see his pit board telling him to take a ride-through penalty and so was black-flagged.

### NON-STARTERS

**MIKA KALLIO** Unable to race as he had to have a skin graft on the ring finger of his left hand following his crash at Assen the previous weekend.

# GERMAN GP
## SACHSENRING CIRCUIT

**ROUND 9**
**July 19**

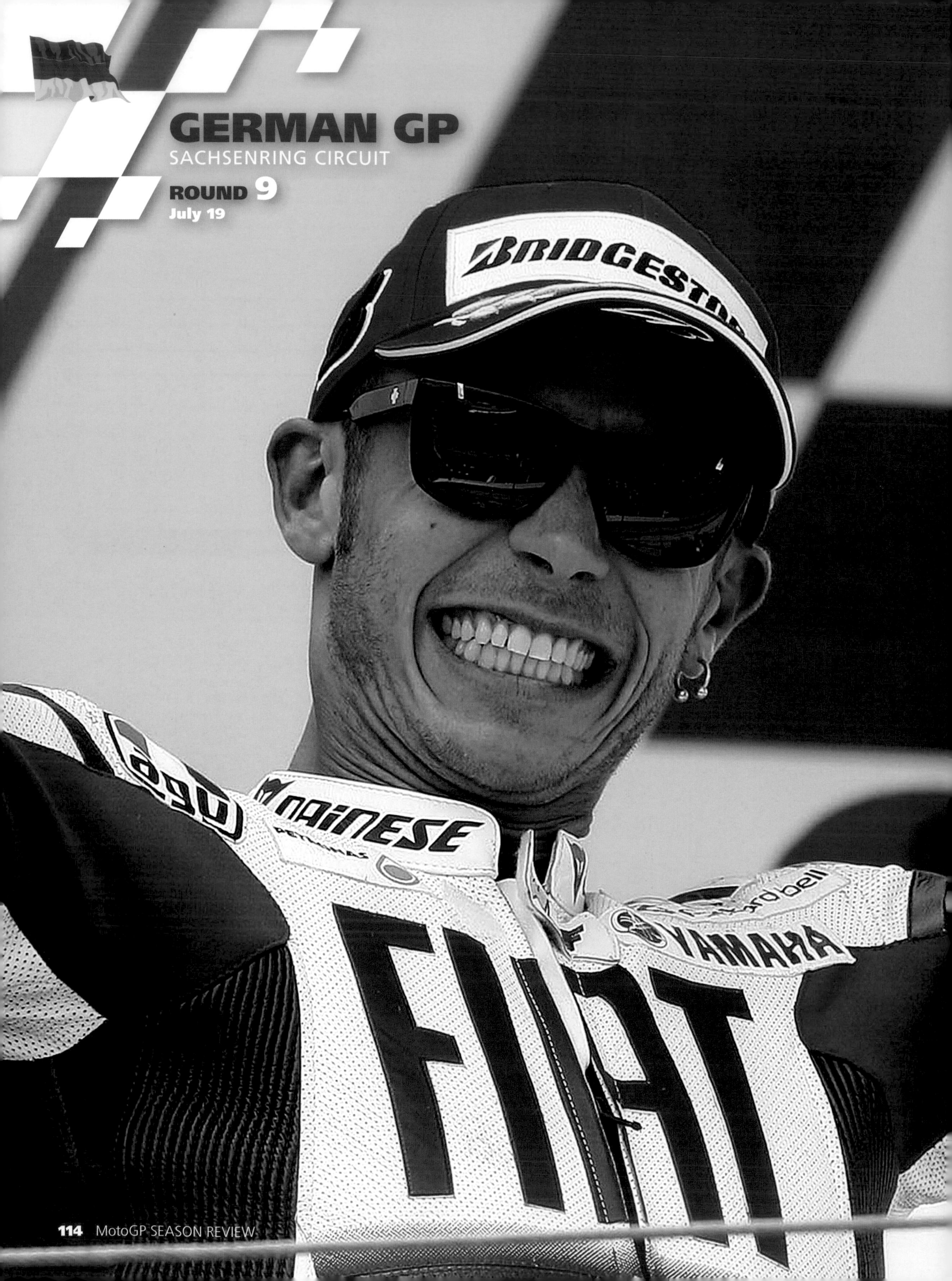

# ROSSI GETS SERIOUS

**Another confrontation between the Fiat Yamaha team-mates; another win for Valentino Rossi**

If it weren't for the stellar race at Catalunya, the German GP would have been remembered as one of the great battles of the year. It was certainly highly entertaining, with another fight between Valentino Rossi and Jorge Lorenzo, but also the reassuring sight of Casey Stoner leading for ten laps. As well as winning on track, Rossi also started to aim some well-chosen words at his young team-mate. The paddock was preoccupied with a rumour that Lorenzo was on the brink of signing for the factory Honda team for 2010. Jorge insisted it wasn't about money but about being valued. Masao Furusawa took a hard line, pointing out that Jorge had yet to prove he could develop a motorcycle and refusing to get into a bidding war. Rossi had a similar opinion: 'I am number one at Yamaha. I arrived here when they were at the bottom of a hole, and it was me who developed this bike.' He would later say that he liked the idea of Lorenzo going to Honda and became increasingly irritated with Yamaha for having two of the top four riders in the world in one team.

Most of that was for the future, however. The first priority at the tight German track was a front-row start. Despite some of the worst conditions imaginable, and also some spectacular crashes, notably from Nicky Hayden, Valentino duly qualified on pole, with Lorenzo and Stoner alongside him on the front row.

Thankfully the weather relented for race day and the usual sell-out crowd was treated to the four 'Aliens' at the front for nearly the whole race, with three of them taking turns to lead. Dani Pedrosa never actually headed the race, but he came very close in Turn 1 thanks to his usual lightning start – from the third row! Dani and team-mate Dovizioso had new engines with less

aggressive mid-range response. Andrea and Randy de Puniet got among the top four, but the Frenchman made a very early exit when he asked too much of his cold rear tyre, and Dovi later wrecked his front tyre – on-board TV pictures clearly showed excessive wear. Pedrosa even noticed this on a giant trackside screen and had a moment of panic until he realised the pictures were from his team-mate's bike rather than his own.

Of the top men, only Lorenzo had gone for the harder tyre option, so he took his time, disputing fourth place with Dovizioso for the opening half-dozen laps and giving himself a lot of work in order to get into the top three. It only took a couple more laps before the usual four suspects were together at the front, well in front of Alex de Angelis, who had been brutal in Turn 1,

with Hayden as prime victim, before having a lonely ride to fifth.

Pedrosa was the first of the main men to hit trouble. A big moment at the final corner dropped him off the back of the group just as Stoner went to the front. Casey then set the pace, with Valentino in close attendance, and then two laps later Lorenzo took Pedrosa to go third. The second Fiat Yamaha pilot didn't close the gap to the leaders until Stoner had been leading for ten laps. It looked as if the Australian's stamina problem was kicking in as Pedrosa again made it a four-man group at the front. Rossi sensed the threat and went past at the bottom of the hill, two corners from the end of the lap, his favoured Sachsenring passing place. Two corners later Lorenzo pushed through

**Above** Only a big moment stopped Dani Pedrosa from disputing the win

**Opposite** Casey Stoner leads the 'Aliens' through the Waterfall corner; he led for ten laps

**Below** Once again the race came down to a confrontation between the Fiat Yamaha team-mates

'ALL FOUR LEADING RIDERS OF THE CHAMPIONSHIP WERE FIGHTING CLOSELY AND ALL IN STRONG FORM'
**VALENTINO ROSSI**

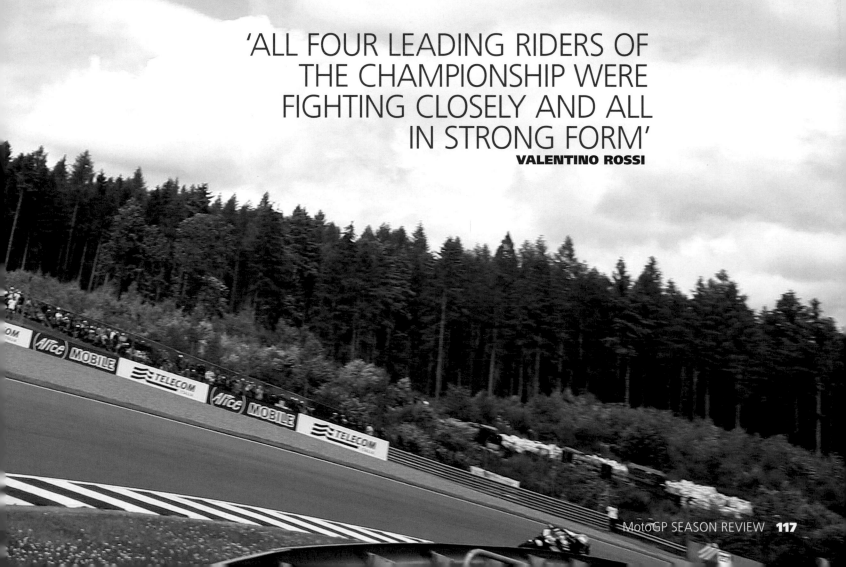

Above Marco Melandri leads Toni Elias, but the Spaniard got past to equal his season's best finish so far

Below Casey Stoner didn't seem as badly affected by his fatigue problem as in previous races

and the team-mates crossed swords again. Stoner did his best to hang on to them but fell victim to Pedrosa five laps from home. That was also when Lorenzo went to the front, having looked comfortable shadowing number 46. Maybe his harder rear tyre would give him an advantage in the final laps…

Rossi, as usual, had other ideas. He also had a plan. He retook the lead two laps from home, this time with an outbraking move at Turn 1, where Lorenzo had

looked faster all race. Valentino then gave a perfect exhibition of defensive riding, and although the gap at the flag was tiny, less than a tenth of a second, the result never looked in doubt. Jorge considered he'd made two tactical errors. The first was not to attack earlier when he felt comfortable with the pace; the second was that he thought there were more laps left when he did go to the front. Rossi thought that Lorenzo was faster on the flowing parts of the track but, as usual, knew he had the bike set up for the places that mattered: 'I made sure I was fast in the crucial parts – I was very good on the brakes.'

Pedrosa was nearly as pleased with his third place, regarding it as a continuation of his return to form. It was more difficult to know what to make of Casey Stoner's race. He ran at the front for the first time since his illness had struck, and he finished only ten seconds behind the winner. However, although fatigue set in later than at Barcelona or Assen, the Sachsenring track is less demanding physically and the conditions were considerably cooler. Casey felt much better than after the previous three races but when he got off the bike his legs gave way again. And after he'd lost touch with the leaders, because of a moment at the bottom of the fast hill, he'd given up hope of winning, and that's when it hit him: 'I realised it was adrenaline that had been keeping me going.'

Yet again Valentino Rossi underlined the point he first made on the last bend at Barcelona. For the past four races he hadn't let Jorge Lorenzo finish in front of him, and there were those first hints of discontent from the other side of the garage. The Doctor was at work again.

# SETE'S SWANSONG

The Grupo Francisco Hernando team withdrew from MotoGP before the German GP. The blame was laid on the credit crunch, obviously, for this is a company that derives most of its income from construction, and that industry was suffering more than most – and in Spain unemployment was heading for 20 per cent. Well, yes, except for the fact that Senor Hernando has a personal fortune estimated at between 400 and 500 million Euros and the bikes had been paid for up front before the season started. One would have thought that the cash necessary to finish the season would have been small change for such an outfit. As recently as Le Mans, Bologna people were even dropping hints about there being two bikes in the team next year.

So why pull out? The most likely reason was that Hernando had been given to understand that his team would be competitive enough to fight for rostrums almost from the off. Patently this hadn't been the case, and there were no real signs that the situation would improve. Senor Hernando isn't noted for his patience. He's a self-made man from an extremely poor background who has made a lot of money, and has also been embroiled in considerable controversy along the way. There was little sympathy for the Nietos who ran the team. Spanish opinion seemed, rather unfairly, to be that they were a couple of over-privileged kids who'd never had to do a day's work in their lives, so it was they who took the flak rather than the sponsor and team owner.

The great shame of the team's withdrawal was that Sete

Gibernau's GP career would surely now be at an end. After Rossi, Sete is far and away the most successful rider of the 990 era. He came back this year after a two-season lay-off and immediately picked up the sort of shoulder injury that brought about his first retirement. It may well be that his seventh-lap crash at Laguna Seca was his last act in bike racing.

The sport will miss him. What won't be missed, though, is the link with the dictator of Equatorial Guinea – Grupo Hernando have plans to build a vacation complex in the Spanish-speaking African country – and certainly no-one will mourn the departure of the posse of bodyguards who hung around outside the team's paddock hospitality.

**Below** Gabor Talmacsi, here leading Niccolo Canepa, scored his first championship point in the MotoGP class

# GERMAN GP
## SACHSENRING CIRCUIT

### ROUND 9
July 19

# RACE RESULTS

**CIRCUIT LENGTH** 2.281 miles
**NO. OF LAPS** 30
**RACE DISTANCE** 68.430 miles
**WEATHER** Dry, 19°C
**TRACK TEMPERATURE** 27°C
**WINNER** Valentino Rossi
**FASTEST LAP** 1m 22.126s, 99.990mph, Dani Pedrosa (record)
**PREVIOUS LAP RECORD** 1m 23.082s, 98.839mph, Dani Pedrosa, 2007

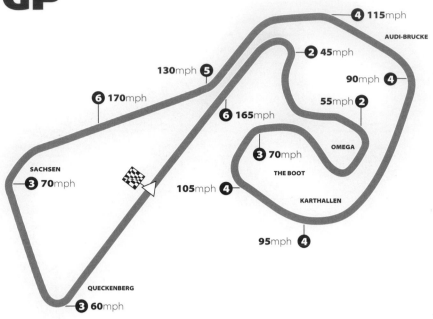

## QUALIFYING

| | Rider | Nationality | Team | Qualifying | Pole + | Gap |
|---|---|---|---|---|---|---|
| 1 | Rossi | ITA | Fiat Yamaha Team | 1m 32.520s | | |
| 2 | Lorenzo | SPA | Fiat Yamaha Team | 1m 33.160s | 0.640s | 0.640s |
| 3 | Stoner | AUS | Ducati Marlboro Team | 1m 33.759s | 1.239s | 0.599s |
| 4 | Hayden | USA | Ducati Marlboro Team | 1m 34.404s | 1.884s | 0.645s |
| 5 | De Angelis | RSM | San Carlo Honda Gresini | 1m 34.490s | 1.970s | 0.086s |
| 6 | De Puniet | FRA | LCR Honda MotoGP | 1m 34.564s | 2.044s | 0.074s |
| 7 | Edwards | USA | Monster Yamaha Tech 3 | 1m 34.607s | 2.087s | 0.043s |
| 8 | Pedrosa | SPA | Repsol Honda Team | 1m 34.725s | 2.205s | 0.118s |
| 9 | Capirossi | ITA | Rizla Suzuki MotoGP | 1m 34.741s | 2.221s | 0.016s |
| 10 | Kallio | FIN | Pramac Racing | 1m 34.771s | 2.251s | 0.030s |
| 11 | Dovizioso | ITA | Repsol Honda Team | 1m 34.892s | 2.372s | 0.121s |
| 12 | Vermeulen | AUS | Rizla Suzuki MotoGP | 1m 34.937s | 2.417s | 0.045s |
| 13 | Melandri | ITA | Hayate Racing Team | 1m 34.938s | 2.418s | 0.001s |
| 14 | Toseland | GBR | Monster Yamaha Tech 3 | 1m 35.005s | 2.485s | 0.067s |
| 15 | Canepa | ITA | Pramac Racing | 1m 36.012s | 3.492s | 1.007s |
| 16 | Talmacsi | HUN | Scot Racing Team MotoGP | 1m 36.055s | 3.535s | 0.043s |
| 17 | Elias | SPA | San Carlo Honda Gresini | 1m 36.531s | 4.011s | 0.476s |

## FINISHERS

**1 VALENTINO ROSSI** Another narrow win over his team-mate, but his experience and racecraft shone through again – as did the expertise of Burgess and the crew, who made sure the bike worked perfectly in the areas that made a difference and left the rider to sort out the rest.

**2 JORGE LORENZO** Professed himself happy with yet another second place behind Rossi but was quick to identify how he made life slightly easier for his team-mate by attacking too late. Worked hard after a bad start though still suffering the effects of that big US crash.

**3 DANI PEDROSA** The new engine, he said, made a small difference, and after a difficult qualifying ran a good race interrupted only by a big moment at the final corner that put him back to fourth. Got past Stoner five laps from home for a comfortable third place.

**4 CASEY STONER** Looked good while leading for a dozen laps, then hit front-tyre problems until the fuel load lightened. Relaxed after a big scare at the bottom of the hill, but his strength had gone. Post-race, didn't look as ill as before, but felt his legs buckle under him when he got off the bike.

**5 ALEX DE ANGELIS** By far his best weekend of the year so far on a circuit where he usually goes well; fast in wet qualifying, then fast in the dry race. Ran with the top four but gradually lost contact for a lonely but well-deserved best result to date.

**6 TONI ELIAS** Equalled his season's best result in a great weekend for San Carlo Gresini, but had a far more eventful and mixed time than his team-mate. Stomach cramps, then last in qualifying after a big crash, got up to eighth, then made his final pass on Melandri with four laps to go.

**7 MARCO MELANDRI** Back in the top ten after four difficult races and up to sixth in the table. Could have been even better, but first-corner bumping put him to the back of the field despite a good start. Lost some concentration towards the end when a large bug hit his visor and Elias got past.

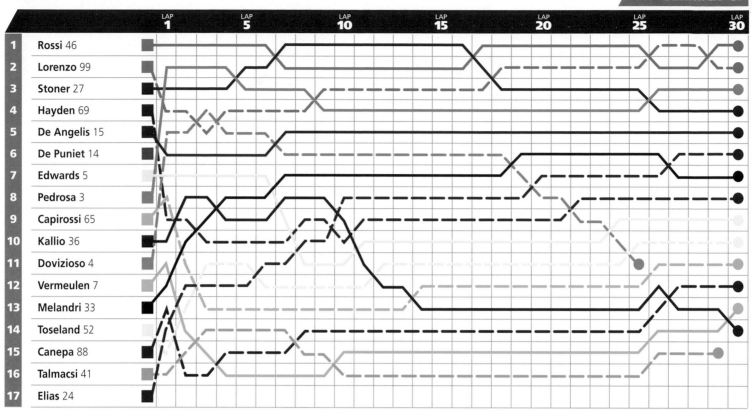

| | | LAP 1 | LAP 5 | LAP 10 | LAP 15 | LAP 20 | LAP 25 | LAP 30 |
|---|---|---|---|---|---|---|---|---|
| 1 | Rossi 46 | | | | | | | |
| 2 | Lorenzo 99 | | | | | | | |
| 3 | Stoner 27 | | | | | | | |
| 4 | Hayden 69 | | | | | | | |
| 5 | De Angelis 15 | | | | | | | |
| 6 | De Puniet 14 | | | | | | | |
| 7 | Edwards 5 | | | | | | | |
| 8 | Pedrosa 3 | | | | | | | |
| 9 | Capirossi 65 | | | | | | | |
| 10 | Kallio 36 | | | | | | | |
| 11 | Dovizioso 4 | | | | | | | |
| 12 | Vermeulen 7 | | | | | | | |
| 13 | Melandri 33 | | | | | | | |
| 14 | Toseland 52 | | | | | | | |
| 15 | Canepa 88 | | | | | | | |
| 16 | Talmacsi 41 | | | | | | | |
| 17 | Elias 24 | | | | | | | |

## RACE

| | Rider | Motorcycle | Race Time | Time + | Fastest Lap | Av Speed | B |
|---|---|---|---|---|---|---|---|
| 1 | Rossi | Yamaha | 41m 21.769s | | 1m 22.231s | 99.269mph | H/H |
| 2 | Lorenzo | Yamaha | 41m 21.868s | 0.099s | 1m 22.209s | 99.265mph | H/XH |
| 3 | Pedrosa | Honda | 41m 24.668s | 2.899s | 1m 22.126s | 99.153mph | H/XH |
| 4 | Stoner | Ducati | 41m 31.995s | 10.226s | 1m 22.272s | 98.862mph | XH/X |
| 5 | De Angelis | Honda | 41m 43.291s | 21.522s | 1m 22.711s | 98.416mph | H/H |
| 6 | Elias | Honda | 41m 52.621s | 30.852s | 1m 22.989s | 98.050mph | H/H |
| 7 | Melandri | Kawasaki | 41m 53.070s | 31.301s | 1m 23.052s | 98.033mph | H/XH |
| 8 | Hayden | Ducati | 41m 53.495s | 31.726s | 1m 23.093s | 98.016mph | H/H |
| 9 | Edwards | Yamaha | 41m 54.634s | 32.865s | 1m 23.034s | 97.972mph | H/H |
| 10 | Toseland | Yamaha | 42m 05.695s | 43.926s | 1m 23.591s | 97.543mph | H/XH |
| 11 | Capirossi | Suzuki | 42m 19.144s | 57.375s | 1m 23.772s | 97.026mph | X/XH |
| 12 | Canepa | Ducati | 42m 22.308s | 1m 00.539s | 1m 24.023s | 97.527mph | H/H |
| 13 | Vermeulen | Suzuki | 42m 25.414s | 1m 03.645s | 1m 24.068s | 96.787mph | H/XH |
| 14 | Kallio | Ducati | 42m 25.924s | 1m 04.155s | 1m 23.083s | 96.768mph | H/H |
| 15 | Talmacsi | Honda | 41m 22.338s | 1 lap | 1m 24.235s | 95.938mph | H/H |
| | Dovizioso | Honda | 35m 10.150s | 5 laps | 1m 22.790s | 97.293mph | H/XH |

## CHAMPIONSHIP

| | Rider | Team | Points |
|---|---|---|---|
| 1 | Rossi | Fiat Yamaha Team | 176 |
| 2 | Lorenzo | Fiat Yamaha Team | 162 |
| 3 | Stoner | Ducati Marlboro Team | 148 |
| 4 | Pedrosa | Repsol Honda Team | 108 |
| 5 | Edwards | Monster Yamaha Tech 3 | 83 |
| 6 | Melandri | Hayate Racing Team | 70 |
| 7 | Dovizioso | Repsol Honda Team | 69 |
| 8 | Vermeulen | Rizla Suzuki MotoGP | 64 |
| 9 | Capirossi | Rizla Suzuki MotoGP | 61 |
| 10 | De Puniet | LCR Honda MotoGP | 58 |
| 11 | De Angelis | San Carlo Honda Gresini | 47 |
| 12 | Elias | San Carlo Honda Gresini | 47 |
| 13 | Hayden | Ducati Marlboro Team | 46 |
| 14 | Toseland | Monster Yamaha Tech 3 | 45 |
| 15 | Kallio | Pramac Racing | 28 |
| 16 | Canepa | Pramac Racing | 20 |
| 17 | Gibernau | Grupo Francisco Hernando | 12 |
| 18 | Takahashi | Scot Racing Team MotoGP | 9 |
| 19 | Talmacsi | Scot Racing Team MotoGP | 1 |

**8 NICKY HAYDEN** By far his best qualifying, despite a massive crash which flicked him off his bike and into Canepa's Ducati; the luckless Italian came off worse. Another crash in warm-up, then got into the first turn too hot and shuffled to the back, but a much-improved showing.

**9 COLIN EDWARDS** Benefited from a new electronic anti-wheelie system that should help with starts, but problems came from the rear pushing the front early in the race. Things eased as the tyre wore in and he was able to turn the bike as he wanted, recovering a couple of places.

**10 JAMES TOSELAND** Like his team-mate, James was impressed with the new anti-wheelie system at the start, but his problems were with the front tyre. Happier after half-distance and thought his harder rear tyre would give him an advantage, but that didn't turn out to be the case.

**11 LORIS CAPIROSSI** Another dismal weekend for Suzuki on a tight and twisty track. Gambled on the harder tyre despite not having tried it in practice, then found he couldn't get any heat into it. Destroyed one bike on Saturday and struggled on race day to get any feedback from the GSV.

**12 NICCOLO CANEPA** Was doubtful for the race after being taken off his bike by a flying Hayden in qualifying, but the Clinica Mobile got him to the grid, despite a very sore left ankle. Got stuck behind Talmacsi for too long to catch the group in front.

**13 CHRIS VERMEULEN** Followed his Laguna Seca crash with another big highside on Friday, losing a lot of track time. Lack of braking performance after a good start, then ran off track at Turn 1 and spent the rest of the race chasing the Pramac Ducatis.

**14 MIKA KALLIO** Back after missing a race thanks to his Assen crash, and got up to eighth, despite pain from his injured finger, before his front tyre's grip dropped precipitously. Reckoned he could have raced with Melandri and Elias.

**15 GABOR TALMACSI** Scored his first points in MotoGP despite his front tyre going off mid-race. Lapped last time round by the Fiat Yamahas.

## NON-FINISHERS

**ANDREA DOVIZIOSO** Retired with what the team said was an electrical problem, but not before on-board footage showed a dramatic degradation of his front tyre's left side. In fourth when the front started tucking early on, then it was a matter of survival – until the electrical problem.

**RANDY DE PUNIET** A crash on the first lap ended his 100 per cent finishing record. Got a little too excited after a good start from sixth on the grid took him up to third – gave it too much gas coming out of a right-hander.

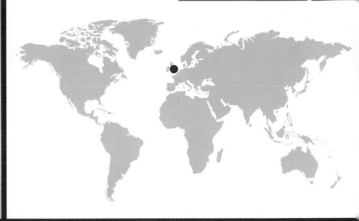

# GOODBYE TO ALL THIS

**Donington Park's last GP threw up a debut winner in Andrea Dovizioso, and the first rostrum of the season for Edwards and de Puniet**

It hasn't always been easy to love Donington Park. Working conditions for press and paddock are cramped, spectators have to endure primitive facilities and appalling traffic, and the track surface has been variable, to say the least. Nicky Hayden was quite surprised on his Thursday cycle round the track to see muddy kerbs being painted without anyone bothering to clear the mud off first.

But Donington has always had one great redeeming feature for which it could be forgiven almost anything: the stretch of tarmac from the first corner, Redgate, round to the double-apex right-hander of Coppice that leads on to the back straight. From Valentino Rossi down to the youngest 125 rider, there was almost universal regret that one of the great bike circuits was to be lost to MotoGP and, despite the weather, a massive crowd turned up to see Donington's last hurrah. However, Silverstone staff were on hand to assure all and sundry that they were working hard for their 2010 event and understood the differences between a Formula 1 car race and a bike race.

Let's hope they can arrange for the weather to be an improvement on the mixed bag that afflicted this event. Friday started wet then dried, Saturday was dry, race day was neither one thing nor the other. As usual, the track surface came in for a great deal of criticism, and Bridgestone were politely asked why they hadn't brought a dual-compound tyre. It's doubtful if any rubber would have been able to cope with conditions on Sunday, which was damp and misty with occasional flurries of light rain – just what no-one enjoys at any circuit, and a nightmare at Donington where the surface has always been inconsistent, at best. Rider

after rider said later that they didn't know from lap to lap whether they were going to make it round any given corner. A lot didn't, and some even gambled on changing to their wet bikes. And that didn't work either. It seemed that the left side of the front was a particular problem for many riders.

Everyone, apart from the factory Ducati riders (see inset story), started on slicks. First man down was Toni Elias, who had led for two laps and was in the front group when he touched a white line on the outside of Schwantz's; he was lucky to walk away. Jorge Lorenzo then took the lead from Andrea Dovizioso and he lasted four laps before touching a white line on the entry to Foggy's Esses; the bike was too damaged for Jorge to continue.

That left Valentino Rossi in the lead, trailed by the impressive Dovizioso. For ten laps they pulled clear, first of Pedrosa, who eventually slid downfield when he lost the heat from his tyres, to be replaced in third by Randy de Puniet, who had resisted the temptation to swap to his wet bike, and Alex de Angelis who, as he'd done in Germany, was riding another controlled race. Almost unnoticed, Colin Edwards was stealthily climbing through the field from 15th place.

Then Rossi crashed at Foggy's, although he was able to remount. He later said he'd made a serious tactical error in showing Dovi the way round for so long. In wet conditions the leader – the fastest guy – is always the one taking the most risks, and Donington's ultra-slick surface only magnified those risks. Andrea had been happy to follow and said that he didn't see Valentino do anything different from

previous laps to cause the crash. The Honda man had ten laps to go on his own, with a nine-second cushion over the rest. For three laps he increased his lead, but by then Edwards had got to grips with the softer front tyre and he and de Puniet closed right up on Dovizioso. Andrea steeled himself, upped the pace and kept over a second between himself and the pair fighting for second. Edwards and de Puniet swapped places twice on the final lap, but the American was ahead on the last corner.

It was an unfamiliar-looking rostrum. None of the three had been on the podium so far this season, and

**Above** Dani Pedrosa, his race engineer Mike Leitner and his tyre man Klaus Nohles worry on the grid – with reason, it transpired

**Below** This is the bit of Donington everyone will miss: the charge down Craner Curves in front of a full house

# 'I RACE TO WIN, EVEN AFTER THE CRASH OF LORENZO. WITH THIS APPROACH I WON 101 RACES; THIS IS THE PRICE TO PAY SOMETIMES'

**VALENTINO ROSSI**

none of them had previously won a race (the first time that had happened since Assen in 1980). It was also the first time there had been two Honda riders on the rostrum since Sepang last year, and the first time since the introduction of the 800cc limit in 2007 that two riders from satellite teams had finished in the top three places.

Edwards' description of the race as '48 minutes of pure bullshit that I wouldn't have wished on my worst enemy' didn't seem out of place. He and de Puniet reported that they were on the limit, and over it, in the final laps. One would have expected two riders who'd never won a MotoGP race to be depressed or angry about coming so close to victory and not grasping the opportunity, but not a bit of it: the predominant emotion was relief. Ducati's wet-tyre gamble failed in the biggest possible way. Stoner and Hayden were the last two finishers and both suffered the indignity of being lapped.

Rossi made it home in fifth place, after a last-lap ding-dong with James Toseland, to extend his championship lead. He told Italian TV that not letting Dovi through was a bad mistake but that it was still a good weekend 'because I was the fastest guy out there'. Should he have settled for second? 'I race to win, even after the crash of Lorenzo. With this approach I won 101 races; this is the price to pay sometimes.'

Vale congratulated Dovizioso on the slow-down lap and told Andrea he owed him €10 for the guided tour. That estimate was later revised upwards by a considerable amount.

# THE TYRE GAMBLE

There are precedents for the gamble the factory Ducati riders took at Donington, not least Ralf Waldmann's 250cc race at the same track in 2000. He qualified downfield, gambled on wets and despite nearly being lapped early on charged through to the most theatrical of victories when it rained. It was the reverse of that most famous of tyre gambles, Eddie Lawson's 1992 victory in Hungary, and Cagiva's first 500cc win. Eddie qualified seventh and knew he couldn't win, so when the race started wet he fitted slicks. He wasn't in the running for the championship, so he was not obliged to hedge his bets. The rain stopped, the track dried, and Eddie carved through the field to an historic victory.

The situation in which Nicky Hayden found himself at the British GP was entirely analogous. He was down the grid and way down the points table, so why not gamble on wets? Casey Stoner's circumstances were totally different. He was on the second row of the grid and a close third in the World Championship. In that combination of circumstances there was only one thing to do: exactly the same as the other championship contenders. And all of them were on slicks. Subsequent events showed exactly why Casey should have been too.

Both Stoner and Hayden maintained that it had been their own tyre choice, not that of the team. Jeremy McWilliams described Casey's decision as the assessment of a rider who had lost interest in racing. The Aussie said he'd been influenced by his physical condition, and that the gamble came within 'a fingernail' of working. What we didn't know

at the time was that he would be missing the next three races in order to sort out his health.

With hindsight it looked like a disaster for Ducati, but one shower of rain could have made it look like a stroke of genius. Ask Ralf Waldmann. The race before that astonishing Donington win, the German rider had been on pole, at Assen, but he chose intermediates for a race that demanded full wets – and he didn't score a point. As he said after his British win: 'The line between hero and idiot is very small.'

**Opposite top** The factory Ducatis circulate together at the back of the field

**Opposite left** The regrettable but inevitable track invasion

**Right** The fight for second place: Colin Edwards leads Randy de Puniet

**BRIDGESTONE**
TYRE OPTIONS
SOFT (S) / MEDIUM (M)
SOFT (S) / MEDIUM (M)

**TISSOT**
OFFICIAL TIMEKEEPER

# BRITISH GP
## DONINGTON PARK
### ROUND 10
July 26

# RACE RESULTS

**CIRCUIT LENGTH** 2.500 miles
**NO. OF LAPS** 30
**RACE DISTANCE** 75.000 miles
**WEATHER** Wet, 18°C
**TRACK TEMPERATURE** 21°C
**WINNER** Andrea Dovizioso
**FASTEST LAP** 1m 31.554s, 98.293mph, Jorge Lorenzo
**LAP RECORD** 1m 28.174s, 101.440mph, Dani Pedrosa, 2006

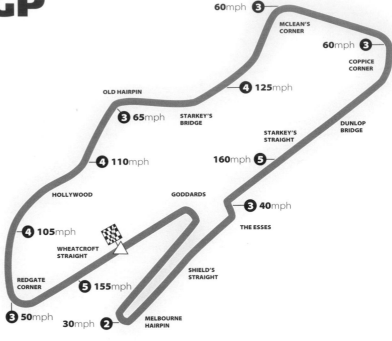

## QUALIFYING

| | Rider | Nationality | Team | Qualifying | Pole + | Gap |
|---|---|---|---|---|---|---|
| 1 | Rossi | ITA | Fiat Yamaha Team | 1m 28.116s | | |
| 2 | Pedrosa | SPA | Repsol Honda Team | 1m 28.211s | 0.095s | 0.095s |
| 3 | Lorenzo | SPA | Fiat Yamaha Team | 1m 28.402s | 0.286s | 0.191s |
| 4 | Stoner | AUS | Ducati Marlboro Team | 1m 28.446s | 0.330s | 0.044s |
| 5 | Dovizioso | ITA | Repsol Honda Team | 1m 28.778s | 0.662s | 0.332s |
| 6 | Edwards | USA | Monster Yamaha Tech 3 | 1m 28.865s | 0.749s | 0.087s |
| 7 | Melandri | ITA | Hayate Racing Team | 1m 29.065s | 0.949s | 0.200s |
| 8 | Elias | SPA | San Carlo Honda Gresini | 1m 29.175s | 1.059s | 0.110s |
| 9 | Toseland | GBR | Monster Yamaha Tech 3 | 1m 29.270s | 1.154s | 0.095s |
| 10 | De Puniet | FRA | LCR Honda MotoGP | 1m 29.434s | 1.318s | 0.164s |
| 11 | Kallio | FIN | Pramac Racing | 1m 29.599s | 1.483s | 0.165s |
| 12 | De Angelis | RSM | San Carlo Honda Gresini | 1m 29.600s | 1.484s | 0.001s |
| 13 | Vermeulen | AUS | Rizla Suzuki MotoGP | 1m 30.098s | 1.982s | 0.498s |
| 14 | Capirossi | ITA | Rizla Suzuki MotoGP | 1m 30.153s | 2.037s | 0.055s |
| 15 | Hayden | USA | Ducati Marlboro Team | 1m 30.268s | 2.152s | 0.115s |
| 16 | Canepa | ITA | Pramac Racing | 1m 30.572s | 2.456s | 0.304s |
| 17 | Talmacsi | HUN | Scot Racing Team MotoGP | 1m 31.193s | 3.077s | 0.621s |

## FINISHERS

**1 ANDREA DOVIZIOSO** Did everything right to take his first MotoGP win: shadowed Rossi, slowed when he crashed out, then pushed again when challenged in the closing laps. Quick to point out, though, that he wouldn't have been able to race the top men under 'normal conditions'. Has now won at Donington in all three classes.

**2 COLIN EDWARDS** A brilliant ride from 'lollygagging about' in 15th and 30s behind the leaders to come within an ace of his first GP win. Used the soft-compound Bridgestone front despite not trying it in practice, moving through the

field after he worked it out, then diced with de Puniet until the last corner.

**3 RANDY DE PUNIET** One of only four riders to go with the medium-compound front tyre, making his race even more impressive. A model of consistency all weekend, as he'd been for most of the season, and didn't surrender second without a fight. His and the team's first rostrum under the 800cc formula.

**4 ALEX DE ANGELIS** Equalled his best result but described it as 'the toughest race of my whole career'. Rider and team keen to emphasise that with the chance of a rostrum he might have gone into his previous win-it-or-bin-it mode; this was evidence of a new, thinking Alex.

**5 VALENTINO ROSSI** Crashed while leading but without damaging the bike, got back on, finished fifth and extended his championship lead. Who writes this guy's scripts? Said he was 'riding to win' after Lorenzo crashed out, and with hindsight could have let Dovizioso lead for a bit.

**6 JAMES TOSELAND** Deprived of a career-best finish by Rossi's penultimate-corner move. Rode solidly all weekend and went a long way to making up for his personal nightmare of the previous GP at Donington. On the down-side, was still well beaten by his team-mate.

**7 MARCO MELANDRI** Unhappy with the result as conditions should have enabled him to be competitive.

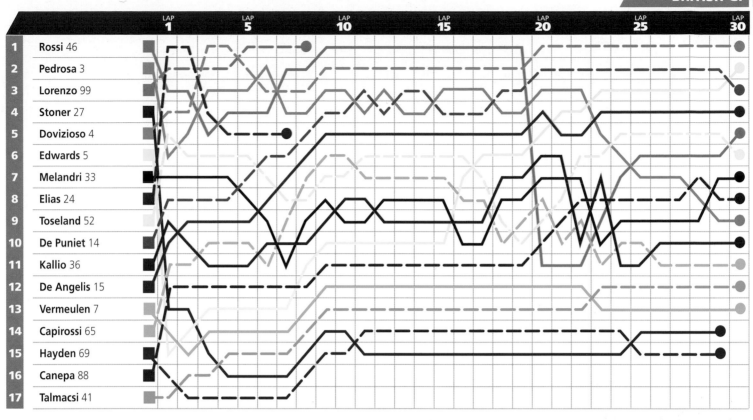

| | | LAP 1 | LAP 5 | LAP 10 | LAP 15 | LAP 20 | LAP 25 | LAP 30 |
|---|---|---|---|---|---|---|---|---|
| 1 | Rossi 46 | | | | | | | |
| 2 | Pedrosa 3 | | | | | | | |
| 3 | Lorenzo 99 | | | | | | | |
| 4 | Stoner 27 | | | | | | | |
| 5 | Dovizioso 4 | | | | | | | |
| 6 | Edwards 5 | | | | | | | |
| 7 | Melandri 33 | | | | | | | |
| 8 | Elias 24 | | | | | | | |
| 9 | Toseland 52 | | | | | | | |
| 10 | De Puniet 14 | | | | | | | |
| 11 | Kallio 36 | | | | | | | |
| 12 | De Angelis 15 | | | | | | | |
| 13 | Vermeulen 7 | | | | | | | |
| 14 | Capirossi 65 | | | | | | | |
| 15 | Hayden 69 | | | | | | | |
| 16 | Canepa 88 | | | | | | | |
| 17 | Talmacsi 41 | | | | | | | |

## RACE

| | Rider | Motorcycle | Race Time | Time + | Fastest Lap | Av Speed | B |
|---|---|---|---|---|---|---|---|
| 1 | Dovizioso | Honda | 48m 26.267s | | 1m 32.150s | 92.898mph | s/s |
| 2 | Edwards | Yamaha | 48m 27.627s | 1.360s | 1m 32.503s | 92.855mph | s/s |
| 3 | De Puniet | Honda | 48m 27.867s | 1.600s | 1m 32.553s | 92.847mph | M/S |
| 4 | De Angelis | Honda | 48m 35.225s | 8.958s | 1m 32.428s | 92.612mph | s/s |
| 5 | Rossi | Yamaha | 48m 47.889s | 21.622s | 1m 31.741s | 92.212mph | s/s |
| 6 | Toseland | Yamaha | 48m 48.732s | 22.465s | 1m 32.567s | 92.185mph | s/s |
| 7 | Melandri | Kawasaki | 49m 01.551s | 35.284s | 1m 32.981s | 91.783mph | s/s |
| 8 | Canepa | Ducati | 49m 05.036s | 38.769s | 1m 33.505s | 91.675mph | M/S |
| 9 | Pedrosa | Honda | 49m 08.379s | 42.112s | 1m 31.742s | 91.368mph | M/S |
| 10 | Kallio | Ducati | 49m 12.112s | 45.845s | 1m 32.642s | 91.455mph | s/s |
| 11 | Capirossi | Suzuki | 49m 19.457s | 53.190s | 1m 32.769s | 91.228mph | s/s |
| 12 | Talmacsi | Honda | 49m 38.582s | 1m 12.315s | 1m 35.858s | 90.642mph | s/s |
| 13 | Vermeulen | Suzuki | 49m 46.665s | 1m 20.398s | 1m 33.903s | 90.397mph | M/S |
| 14 | Stoner | Ducati | 49m 25.241s | 1 lap | 1m 38.609s | 88.015mph | w |
| 15 | Hayden | Ducati | 49m 43.835s | 1 lap | 1m 39.547s | 87.467mph | w |
| 16 | Lorenzo | Yamaha | 12m 33.642s | 22 laps | 1m 31.554s | 95.531mph | s/s |
| 17 | Elias | Honda | 11m 02.391s | 23 laps | 1m 31.797s | 95.105mph | s/s |

## CHAMPIONSHIP

| | Rider | Team | Points |
|---|---|---|---|
| 1 | Rossi | Fiat Yamaha Team | 187 |
| 2 | Lorenzo | Fiat Yamaha Team | 162 |
| 3 | Stoner | Ducati Marlboro Team | 150 |
| 4 | Pedrosa | Repsol Honda Team | 115 |
| 5 | Edwards | Monster Yamaha Tech 3 | 103 |
| 6 | Dovizioso | Repsol Honda Team | 94 |
| 7 | Melandri | Hayate Racing Team | 79 |
| 8 | De Puniet | LCR Honda MotoGP | 74 |
| 9 | Vermeulen | Rizla Suzuki MotoGP | 67 |
| 10 | Capirossi | Rizla Suzuki MotoGP | 66 |
| 11 | De Angelis | San Carlo Honda Gresini | 60 |
| 12 | Toseland | Monster Yamaha Tech 3 | 55 |
| 13 | Hayden | Ducati Marlboro Team | 47 |
| 14 | Elias | San Carlo Honda Gresini | 47 |
| 15 | Kallio | Pramac Racing | 34 |
| 16 | Canepa | Pramac Racing | 28 |
| 17 | Gibernau | Grupo Francisco Hernando | 12 |
| 18 | Takahashi | Scot Racing Team MotoGP | 9 |
| 19 | Talmacsi | Scot Racing Team MotoGP | 5 |

Uncomfortable with the dry bike, especially 'the back pushing the front' going down the Craner Curves, so was one of the first to come in and change machines.

**8 NICCOLO CANEPA** First Ducati home for a career-best result. Made up four positions with overtakes between laps 20 and 28 but was caught by Melandri on wet tyres two laps from the flag. 'Today has finally gone well!'

**9 DANI PEDROSA** Started well on the harder of Bridgestone's compounds front and back, and ran in third early on. But when he lost heat from the tyres he also lost all confidence and dropped back through the field.

**10 MIKA KALLIO** Lying sixth and looking good when the rain worsened, so came in for his wet bike, only to see the rain stop again. When he got back home to Finland, had surgery to close the wound on his left ring finger, the legacy of his Assen crash.

**11 LORIS CAPIROSSI** The recent problems didn't go away at Donington and both rider and team had a truly miserable time. Couldn't get any heat in his tyres, especially the left side, so changed to the wet bike, only to destroy those tyres in two laps when the rain ceased.

**12 GABOR TALMACSI** Second points-scoring ride in his four races as a MotoGP rider. He was favoured by the conditions but did a good, professional job.

**13 CHRIS VERMEULEN** All the problems that afflicted his team-mate hampered Chris too, plus he ran off track after a big slide. Like Capirossi, he also changed bikes in the hope the rain would get heavier.

**14 CASEY STONER** Went to the grid with wet tyres because he knew his physical condition would cause problems if the track was dry – a gamble that didn't work and one that was difficult to understand given his grid position and third place in the table.

**15 NICKY HAYDEN** Took the same gamble as his team-mate but, as he qualified back in 15th and wasn't a championship contender, it was more understandable.

## NON-FINISHERS

**JORGE LORENZO** Leading his team-mate when he got on the white line while braking for Foggy's Esses and crashed in a straight line. His Fiat Yamaha was too badly damaged for Jorge to continue.

**TONI ELIAS** Came through from the third row of the grid to lead the first two laps, then touched a white line on the outside of Schwantz's and was lucky to walk away from the ensuing high-speed crash.

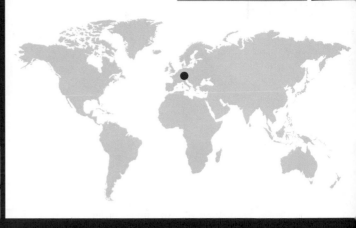

# NO LIMITS

**If proof were ever needed that Rossi and Lorenzo were competing on the limit, this race provided it**

The single tyre supplier rule that debuted for the 2009 season and the engine-life rule that came in for this race were both supposed to slow things down and help the have-nots race with the haves. If only racing were that simple. Bridgestone had put the brake on tyre development, and therefore expenditure, as well as ultimate performance, and now all riders had just five engines for the rest of the season. These engines would be sealed by the series scrutineer once they had been out on track, and using an extra, fresh motor would result in a ten-point penalty. Did that slow the riders down? No. Well, maybe for half a season.

Valentino Rossi's pole-position time broke his record from 2006, set on a 990, of course. This was the first new pole record since the introduction of the single-tyre rule. In the race, Jorge Lorenzo bettered the absent Casey Stoner's lap record by a third of a second. However, it was only the two Fiat Yamahas that were going at that sort of pace. With Ducati's top man on sick leave, the picture was even clearer than usual. Rossi and Lorenzo waged a private war at lap-record pace for the entire weekend, with Dani Pedrosa chasing in a somewhat lonely third in front of entertaining battles for the minor placings.

This was racing at an astonishingly high level – not always enthralling for the spectators, but riveting for the connoisseur. It's rare to get a head-to-head battle between the two best riders in the world without extraneous factors such as the weather, injury or machinery problems confusing the issue. Group battles are always thrilling to watch but there's usually the feeling that luck plays too big a part on a crowded track; it's too easy for a rider to get boxed in or pushed

**Opposite top** Another round of the Rossi-versus-Lorenzo title fight; another win on points for Valentino

**Opposite below** Dani Pedrosa had another quietly efficient weekend on his way to second place

**Below** Randy de Puniet rests his recently screwed and plated ankle as he confers with Christophe 'Beefy' Bourginon

wide. This was different. And for the third time in six races it looked like a fight to the finish.

Right up until Sunday morning it seemed as if Lorenzo was ahead on points. He'd been fastest in every session except qualifying, when he was caught in traffic on his last run. Rossi had fallen when asking too much of a well-used front tyre, but it was obvious that on the harder race rubber Jorge was quicker by a significant margin.

Valentino wasn't happy with his tyres – he had understeer and was 'looking for a better feeling'. He didn't much like the new long-life motors either: 'Is worse, a little more tired.' He also let slip that he would like to see Jorge go to Honda: 'I think Yamaha would be very happy; great motivation.' Lorenzo got his own back by suggesting that the two were now on equal bikes for the first time. Warm-up didn't improve Rossi's frame of mind because, for once, the modifications thrown at the bike by Jerry Burgess and the crew didn't solve enough of the problems. So they threw some more at it for the race.

This forced Rossi to go as hard as he could off the start – not his preferred tactic. 'I was very nervous. To understand if the modification work, I have to push.' He put a lot of emphasis on the last word. And he certainly did push, with Lorenzo right in his wheel tracks. The gap stayed around 0.3–0.4s as they pulled away from Pedrosa at over a second a lap. Rossi was at the limit – he used the Italian gesture of putting the tip of the thumb to his chin to illustrate his point – and he knew Jorge was on the limit as

# 'I WAS VERY NERVOUS. TO UNDERSTAND IF THE MODIFICATION WORK, I HAVE TO PUSH'
**VALENTINO ROSSI**

him and thought, 'If he can make the corner from there, I am in trouble.' But Jorge was out of the race, and Rossi cruised to the flag 'like a tourist' to beat Agostini's career record of podium finishes.

Lorenzo's crash gave Toni Elias 'a present' of third place, and he used the post-race interviews to vent his frustration at not having a ride for the following season. 'When I think, I become angry. There are riders who never get podiums who get bikes, good bikes! I was as fast as Dovizioso all race.' He then did his employment chances no good by complaining he hadn't received help from Honda all year.

Loris Capirossi's fighting fifth place showed that Suzuki's long-life engine was at least as powerful as the old one. The team had a new chassis to test on the Monday, when the Repsol Honda riders would get the chance to try Ohlins suspension. That HRC would cast aside their decades-long relationship with Showa demonstrated just how desperately they were trying to catch the Yamahas.

Jorge Lorenzo was unrepentant afterwards. 'I had to take risks because second today was not…' He didn't complete the sentence, but everyone knew what he meant. 'I have passed worse situations in my career, we are learning.' Then he repeated what had become his mantra, another reference to Rossi's experience: 'It is not our sixth year.' Indeed it is not. The modification that Burgess and the crew made after warm-up, to cope with the conditions, enabled Valentino to run the same sort of times as he had earlier in the weekend. As Jorge noted, 'Every other rider was slower.' You can't beat experience, on or off the bike.

**Above** Toni Elias got his and Team Gresini's first rostrum of the year

**Below** To make it even more enjoyable, Elias held off the factory Honda of Dovizioso to take third

well because the gap hardly fluctuated. 'I guard my 0.4s like treasure!'

Lorenzo had to set a new lap record to close the gap and next time round he went past. Rossi – and everyone else – prepared themselves for five laps of high tension. 'I give him hard work. I expected a hard last five laps.' It didn't happen. Three corners into the next lap Lorenzo went in far too deep and lost the front. Valentino saw

CINZANO CINZ

## CASEY'S STRANGE CASE

*Everyone who had seen Casey Stoner at any of the races since Barcelona had no doubts. The lad was ill. No-one knew exactly what the problem was, and therefore what to do about it. Nevertheless, the decision to miss three races – Brno, Indianapolis and Misano – shocked the paddock and raised some serious questions.*

*The schedule after Barcelona, with two pairs of back-to-back races, hadn't helped in trying to get a diagnosis, so Casey felt he had no option but to take time out. The tentative consensus was that the Aussie had been hit by a virus at Barcelona and never had time to recover, so the result was post-viral fatigue syndrome, a little-understood condition with no specific definition or cure. Was stress a contributory factor? Most people thought so, although they had to admit that Casey had seemed much more at ease in his dealings with the media this season, thanks in part to the influence of Nicky Hayden on the other side of the garage.*

*Paddock gossips brought up the subject of Freddie Spencer and his frighteningly similar fall from grace, as well as the more recent case of Manuel Poggiali. Looking at other sports, it was difficult to find a sportsman who'd gone through this sort of episode and come back at their old level.*

*Casey's absence put Ducati in an impossible situation. More than any other manufacturer, the*

*Bologna factory's commercial success is directly related to their racetrack performance. They professed, as they had to, total belief in Stoner's return at Estoril, but also knew they had to make sure they had one of the top four riders for next season. They immediately offered Jorge Lorenzo a massive salary, several times greater than those of their current riders. In truth there was nothing else they could do, but it wasn't a move that would have gone down well back in Australia.*

*In the meantime Ducati moved Mika Kallio up to the factory team, put World Superbike star Michel Fabrizio on the Finn's Pramac satellite-team bike, and went back to praying for the health of Casey Stoner.*

**Above** Casey looks tense and drawn on the grid despite the presence of wife Adriana

**Top** Michel Fabrizio was drafted in from Ducati's World Superbike team to ride the satellite bike

**BRIDGESTONE**
TYRE OPTIONS
FRONT HARD (H) / EXTRA HARD (XH)
REAR MEDIUM (M) / HARD (H)

motoGP
T+ TISSOT
SWISS WATCHES SINCE 1853
OFFICIAL TIMEKEEPER

# CZECH REPUBLIC GP
## AUTOMOTODROM BRNO

### ROUND 11
**August 16**

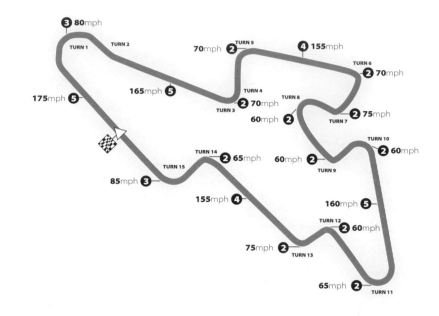

## RACE RESULTS

**CIRCUIT LENGTH** 3.357miles
**NO. OF LAPS** 22
**RACE DISTANCE** 73.854 miles
**WEATHER** Dry, 29°C
**TRACK TEMPERATURE** 45°C
**WINNER** Valentino Rossi
**FASTEST LAP** 1m 56.670s,
103.592mph, Jorge Lorenzo (record)
**PREVIOUS LAP RECORD** 1m 57.199s,
103.125mph, Casey Stoner, 2008

## QUALIFYING

| | Rider | Nationality | Team | Qualifying | Pole + | Gap |
|---|---|---|---|---|---|---|
| 1 | Rossi | ITA | Fiat Yamaha Team | 1m 56.145s | | |
| 2 | Lorenzo | SPA | Fiat Yamaha Team | 1m 56.195s | 0.050s | 0.050s |
| 3 | Pedrosa | SPA | Repsol Honda Team | 1m 56.528s | 0.383s | 0.333s |
| 4 | Elias | SPA | San Carlo Honda Gresini | 1m 56.817s | 0.672s | 0.289s |
| 5 | Edwards | USA | Monster Yamaha Tech 3 | 1m 56.954s | 0.809s | 0.137s |
| 6 | Dovizioso | ITA | Repsol Honda Team | 1m 57.108s | 0.963s | 0.154s |
| 7 | De Angelis | RSM | San Carlo Honda Gresini | 1m 57.775s | 1.630s | 0.667s |
| 8 | Hayden | USA | Ducati Marlboro Team | 1m 57.803s | 1.658s | 0.028s |
| 9 | Capirossi | ITA | Rizla Suzuki MotoGP | 1m 57.811s | 1.666s | 0.008s |
| 10 | Kallio | FIN | Ducati Marlboro Team | 1m 57.994s | 1.849s | 0.183s |
| 11 | Vermeulen | AUS | Rizla Suzuki MotoGP | 1m 58.087s | 1.942s | 0.093s |
| 12 | Canepa | ITA | Pramac Racing | 1m 58.208s | 2.063s | 0.121s |
| 13 | De Puniet | FRA | LCR Honda MotoGP | 1m 58.298s | 1.253s | 0.090s |
| 14 | Toseland | GBR | Monster Yamaha Tech 3 | 1m 58.331s | 2.186s | 0.033s |
| 15 | Melandri | ITA | Hayate Racing Team | 1m 58.477s | 2.332s | 0.146s |
| 16 | Fabrizio | ITA | Pramac Racing | 1m 58.680s | 2.535s | 0.203s |
| 17 | Talmacsi | HUN | Scot Racing Team MotoGP | 1m 58.749s | 2.604s | 0.069s |

## FINISHERS

**1 VALENTINO ROSSI** Unhappy with the feel from the front right up until the race, but some new settings coped with the higher track temperature, something no-one else managed. Cruised to a 50-point lead once Lorenzo crashed, and claimed his 160th podium, a new record.

**2 DANI PEDROSA** A solid second place didn't seem to excite him too much, no doubt because he couldn't get near the pace of the factory Yamahas, but obviously delighted to finish a race at such a hot and demanding track in good physical condition.

**3 TONI ELIAS** On the pace all weekend, qualified higher than he'd done all year and always in the fight for the final podium, though he called it 'a present' from Lorenzo. Complained at the press conference about others getting good rides when his future was uncertain.

**4 ANDREA DOVIZIOSO** Attacked Elias continuously in the closing stages but couldn't make a pass stick. Disappointed not to be on the rostrum, but race day was an improvement on his qualifying position.

**5 LORIS CAPIROSSI** Again felt he had a podium chance: qualifying not stunning but good pace on race tyres all weekend. A demon first lap saw him up to sixth, shadowed the third-place dice all race, and attacked on the last lap when a rostrum position was up for grabs.

**6 NICKY HAYDEN** Thought he could have been with the group fighting for third if de Angelis hadn't 'turned right in front of me' off the start. Won the fight for sixth after a tussle with Edwards. Given how awful the bike looked on Friday, this must be counted as an encouraging result.

**7 COLIN EDWARDS** Up with the third-place group early on but reported his engine felt flat all weekend so he had to push the front hard in corners. Ended up overheating the right side of his front Bridgestone. Brno hasn't been kind to him: he's never had a top-six finish there.

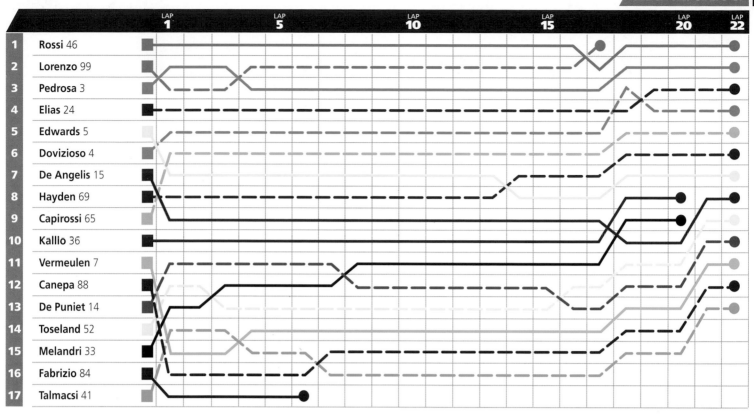

| | | LAP 1 | LAP 5 | LAP 10 | LAP 15 | LAP 20 | LAP 22 |
|---|---|---|---|---|---|---|---|
| 1 | Rossi 46 | | | | | | |
| 2 | Lorenzo 99 | | | | | | |
| 3 | Pedrosa 3 | | | | | | |
| 4 | Elias 24 | | | | | | |
| 5 | Edwards 5 | | | | | | |
| 6 | Dovizioso 4 | | | | | | |
| 7 | De Angelis 15 | | | | | | |
| 8 | Hayden 69 | | | | | | |
| 9 | Capirossi 65 | | | | | | |
| 10 | Kalllo 36 | | | | | | |
| 11 | Vermeulen 7 | | | | | | |
| 12 | Canepa 88 | | | | | | |
| 13 | De Puniet 14 | | | | | | |
| 14 | Toseland 52 | | | | | | |
| 15 | Melandri 33 | | | | | | |
| 16 | Fabrizio 84 | | | | | | |
| 17 | Talmacsi 41 | | | | | | |

## RACE

| | Rider | Motorcycle | Race Time | Time + | Fastest Lap | Av Speed | B |
|---|---|---|---|---|---|---|---|
| 1 | Rossi | Yamaha | 43m 08.991s | | 1m 56.694s | 102.706mph | XH/H |
| 2 | Pedrosa | Honda | 43m 20.757s | 11.766s | 1m 57.228s | 102.242mph | XH/H |
| 3 | Elias | Honda | 43m 29.747s | 20.756s | 1m 57.949s | 101.889mph | XH/H |
| 4 | Dovizioso | Honda | 43m 30.409s | 21.418s | 1m 57.994s | 101.864mph | XH/H |
| 5 | Capirossi | Suzuki | 43m 30.529s | 21.538s | 1m 57.964s | 101.859mph | XH/H |
| 6 | Hayden | Ducati | 43m 34.535s | 25.544s | 1m 58.110s | 101.703mph | XH/H |
| 7 | Edwards | Yamaha | 43m 34.667s | 25.676s | 1m 58.140s | 101.698mph | XH/H |
| 8 | De Angelis | Honda | 43m 43.100s | 34.109s | 1m 58.056s | 101.371mph | XH/H |
| 9 | Toseland | Yamaha | 43m 44.608s | 35.617s | 1m 58.493s | 101.313mph | XH/H |
| 10 | De Puniet | Honda | 43m 48.815s | 39.824s | 1m 58.471s | 101.150mph | XH/H |
| 11 | Vermeulen | Suzuki | 43m 49.767s | 40.776s | 1m 58.775s | 101.114mph | XH/M |
| 12 | Canepa | Ducati | 43m 59.652s | 50.661s | 1m 58.835s | 100.735mph | XH/H |
| 13 | Talmacsi | Honda | 44m 08.179s | 59.188s | 1m 59.020s | 100.411mph | XH/H |
| | Kallio | Ducati | 39m 38.278s | 2 laps | 1m 58.105s | 101.642mph | XH/H |
| | Melandri | Kawasaki | 39m 38.518s | 2 laps | 1m 58.153s | 101.631mph | XH/H |
| | Lorenzo | Yamaha | 33m 15.284s | 5 laps | 1m 56.670s | 102.979mph | XH/H |
| | Fabrizio | Ducati | 12m 13.902s | 16 laps | 1m 59.147s | 98.814mph | XH/H |

## CHAMPIONSHIP

| | Rider | Team | Points |
|---|---|---|---|
| 1 | Rossi | Fiat Yamaha Team | 212 |
| 2 | Lorenzo | Fiat Yamaha Team | 162 |
| 3 | Stoner | Ducati Marlboro Team | 150 |
| 4 | Pedrosa | Repsol Honda Team | 135 |
| 5 | Edwards | Monster Yamaha Tech 3 | 112 |
| 6 | Dovizioso | Repsol Honda Team | 107 |
| 7 | De Puniet | LCR Honda MotoGP | 80 |
| 8 | Melandri | Hayate Racing Team | 79 |
| 9 | Capirossi | Rizla Suzuki MotoGP | 77 |
| 10 | Vermeulen | Rizla Suzuki MotoGP | 72 |
| 11 | De Angelis | San Carlo Honda Gresini | 68 |
| 12 | Elias | San Carlo Honda Gresini | 63 |
| 13 | Toseland | Monster Yamaha Tech 3 | 62 |
| 14 | Hayden | Ducati Marlboro Team | 57 |
| 15 | Kallio | Ducati Marlboro Team | 34 |
| 16 | Canepa | Pramac Racing | 32 |
| 17 | Gibernau | Grupo Francisco Hernando | 12 |
| 18 | Takahashi | Scot Racing Team MotoGP | 9 |
| 19 | Talmacsi | Scot Racing Team MotoGP | 8 |

**8 ALEX DE ANGELIS** There may have been stranger reasons for slowing down but no-one can remember them … a butterfly got into his crash helmet five laps from the flag and he was passed by Kallio and Melandri. They promptly crashed and gave him the places back again.

**9 JAMES TOSELAND** Called the result 'a lucky top ten': his big problem was serious chatter in the race's first half, the bike 'hopping' at the front and killing corner speed. Two laps from the flag, did a lap only a tenth slower than his qualifying time – good enough for the top six.

**10 RANDY DE PUNIET** A top-ten finish with seven screws in an ankle broken just over two weeks previously has

to be considered heroic. Randy described it both as 'the hardest race of my life' and 'a miracle'.

**11 CHRIS VERMEULEN** Brno has always been a tricky track for him and this year was no different. Qualified on the fourth row, got blocked in at Turn 1 and was then pushed wide later in the first lap, putting him down to 15th. Scored useful points, but it wasn't a happy weekend.

**12 NICCOLO CANEPA** Like several others, didn't cope well with the change in conditions from qualifying and had problems with rear grip later in the race.

**13 GABOR TALMACSI** Happy at the start when he overtook three riders, but

once the rear grip went he had trouble holding his line out of corners.

## NON-FINISHERS

**MIKA KALLIO** A good solid weekend in his first ride on the factory Ducati came to a messy end in the gravel trap after Melandri tried to pass 'where it was impossible', according to Mika. Spent most of the race 1.5s behind Hayden and was closing when the crash happened.

**MARCO MELANDRI** Was having a brilliant race, through from 13th after the first lap and challenging for eighth when he came together with Kallio. Appeared to offer an apology to the Finn in the gravel trap.

**JORGE LORENZO** Looked a likely winner until Sunday afternoon when Rossi's crew found the answer to the elevated track temperature. Pushed hard to stay with his team-mate, passed him at the first chance but went too wide and deep into Turn 3, losing the front as Rossi retook the lead.

**MICHEL FABRIZIO** The MotoGP Ducati had no mercy on Michel's injury from Friday, a few laps at race pace turning a sore right shoulder into a torn muscle. He pulled in with 'a golf ball under the skin'.

## NON-STARTERS

**CASEY STONER** This was the first of three races he was scheduled to miss as he recuperated from the mystery illness that had afflicted him since the Catalunya round.

# INDIANAPOLIS GP

## INDIANAPOLIS MOTOR SPEEDWAY

**ROUND 12**

**August 30**

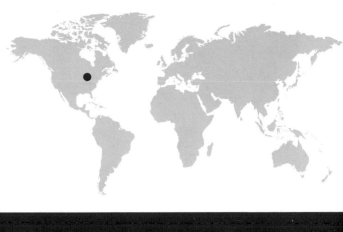

# THE LEAGUE OF SUPERHEROES

Captain America, aka Jorge
Lorenzo, defeated them all.
And Kevin Schwantz and Kenny
Roberts turned back time

**J**orge Lorenzo couldn't quite make up his mind which comic-book superhero he wanted to be. His crash helmet and the shield he picked up on his victory lap said 'Captain America' (the Marvel version, not Peter Fonda's *Easy Rider* one), then he climbed the wire 'like Spiderman' to celebrate with the fans. Actually, he said *Speederman*, which was even better. His whole weekend was a superhuman performance in which he dominated the race, saw his championship rivals crash and halved Valentino Rossi's championship lead. He also re-signed for the Fiat Yamaha team despite a big-money offer from Ducati. All in all, not a bad way to bounce back from two consecutive crashes.

In the continuing absence of Casey Stoner, Mika Kallio continued on the factory Ducati and was replaced in the Pramac team by the older of the two Espargaro brothers, Aleix. Rumours about Casey's health and the causes of his three-race sabbatical scaled the heights of fantasy at Indy. Even team manager Livio Suppo's radical haircut sparked new speculation. Thankfully the performances of Nicky Hayden and Espargaro moved the focus of attention back on the track. Espargaro, who became the youngest Spaniard to ride in the MotoGP class, acquitted himself well in all sessions but was the instigator of a Turn 2 domino effect that put both Suzukis and his friend Toni Elias on to the grass. For once, it wasn't the surface at Turn 2, or the even bigger bumps at Turn 6, that caused the problem, just youthful exuberance. Contrary to expectations, no work had been done to the track since the inaugural event 12 months previously.

As expected, qualifying and practice had been dominated by Dani Pedrosa and the Fiat Yamahas. The

Above There's an awful lot of room on the Indianapolis Motor Speedway

Opposite Aleix Espargaro on the grid for his first MotoGP race; his younger brother Pol, winner of the 125 race, lends his support

Below The field rounds turn one, where they leave the oval and get on to the newer tarmac in front of the Ducati stand

Honda rider took pole by the astonishing margin of over half a second, and he had also been quickest in both practice sessions, but Valentino Rossi and his crew seemed more worried about Lorenzo. Hayden showed how much things had improved for him by being quick in every session, particularly the first, when he was second fastest by the slim margin of a tenth of a second. Nicky usually spent Fridays riding what looked like an out-of-control mechanical bucking bronco. Now, at last, he appeared to have something like a workable base setting for the Ducati. Sixth in qualifying was not earth-shattering, but Hayden was able to run with the second group and his overtake on Colin Edwards in the race, displaying big lean angle and lots of corner speed, showed a new-found confidence.

Once the dust had settled after the second-corner

incident, the race looked to be settling into a predictable pattern, but then came two strange crashes. First Pedrosa lost the front at the final corner on lap four. He was leading at the time, but not by the margin many expected; he was only around half a second ahead. Race day was a little cooler than the rest of the weekend and, under these circumstances, Dani may have been asking too much of the front tyre. Whatever the cause, when he tried to pull the bike up from full right lean the front simply let go. That allowed Rossi through into the lead, with Lorenzo right in his wheel tracks. The pair already had the best part of five seconds on the next group. The two Fiat Yamahas pulled away steadily for the next four laps, by which time surprise package Alex de Angelis was up to third in front of a fading Edwards, with Hayden closing in. Pedrosa, meanwhile, did manage to

Turn 2. He later said that he'd been 1.5 metres off line on the dirty part of the circuit, but there was a further suggestion that he'd been a victim of the track surface. At first it looked as if the Rossi luck was holding – he got the bike back on track – but two laps later he was in the pits with a sticking throttle. Lorenzo was now in the lead by over nine seconds, and he just had to concentrate, despite getting a 'little bit bored'. He passed the time planning a giant wheelie down the front straight on the last lap and coming to the conclusion that 'My pass in Brno was better.'

The crashes left de Angelis in a safe second place. This was no fluke result, because he'd been fast all weekend and was the quickest man out there in morning warm-up. For the second race running one of Team Gresini's soon-to-be-unemployed riders got to stand on the rostrum. 'The trick is to do it every week,' said the watching Wayne Rainey with his usual precision. The crowd, posted as smaller than last year's despite the infinitely better weather, were hoping that de Angelis wouldn't become the first rider from San Marino to step on to a premier-class podium, because Hayden was less than a second behind him until lap 18 of the 28. But Nicky couldn't press home the challenge and had to worry about an attack from Dovizioso in the closing laps: 'I gave myself a pep talk out there – don't give it to him!' He didn't, and claimed the third rostrum place.

It was a good weekend for the 2006 World Champion, but a better one for the Spaniard who wanted to emulate the American's success. Before the race Jorge Lorenzo had said that the title was 'impossible'. Now it was merely 'difficult'.

**Above** Kenny Roberts rolls back the years at Indy Mile on the legendary TZ-powered dirt-tracker. He was simply amazing

**Opposite** Nicky Hayden held off Andrea Dovizioso for a very popular rostrum in front of his home crowd

**Below** Valentino Rossi's exit isn't very elegant

pick his bike up, with considerable effort, and his charge back through the pack to a top-ten finish was impressive.

Lorenzo went to the front on lap nine, and immediately pulled out a significant advantage. It looked like Rossi's crew were right in their analysis. Then Valentino ran wide at the first corner of lap ten and, trying to get back on line, he lost the front going into

# 'THE CHAMPIONSHIP WAS ALMOST GONE BUT IN ONE DAY THINGS HAVE CHANGED A LOT'
**JORGE LORENZO**

# ENGINE NOISES

*The joint Dorna–IRTA suggestion for modified 1,000cc production motors to be allowed in MotoGP had the desired effect on the MSMA. IRTA President Hervé Poncharal described the idea, with modest understatement, as 'a bit provocative' – not least, one assumes, to the rights holders of the World Superbike Championship.*

*The factories came back at Indianapolis with a proposal to make lease engines available for the 2011 season. That, said Poncharal, could see the MotoGP grid expand to '22 or 23' bikes and involve a 'significant cost reduction'. He estimated that as much as 30 per cent might be possible. Not everyone was so sure. Livio Suppo, Ducati team manager, pointed to the costs of building and developing a chassis, engine management electronics, buying in suspension, etc., and could not see a significant saving. Suppo also observed that this was the route taken by Kenny Roberts' team, and it hadn't helped them. The Italian wanted teams to talk about increasing revenues rather than letting engineers fiddle with the rules all the time.*

*Agreeing to supply engines was all very well in principle, but now the hard detail had to be hammered out, not least quantities and costs. In the meantime, the new long-life engine rule that came in at Brno continued to cause waves. Valentino Rossi sat out for 20 minutes of the Friday session to preserve one of his engines, and afterwards suggested we would be seeing plenty of riders spending lots of time in the pits. And as for the 2010 allocation of six engines for the whole year, Valentino wanted to see two or three more motors. But, as he acknowledged, this was a decision made by the manufacturers and there was very little the riders could do about it.*

**Above** Yamaha engineers keep their secrets under cover during engine changes

BRIDGESTONE
TYRE OPTIONS
FRONT MEDIUM (M) / HARD (H)
REAR HARD (H) / EXTRA HARD (XH)

OFFICIAL TIMEKEEPER

# INDIANAPOLIS GP
## INDIANAPOLIS MOTOR SPEEDWAY

### ROUND 12
**August 30**

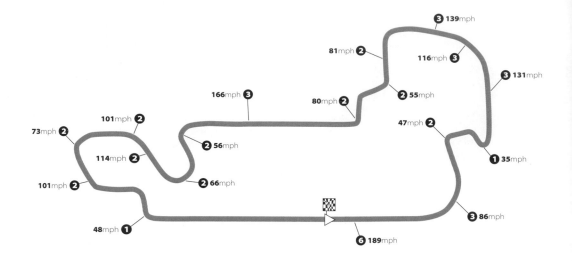

# RACE RESULTS

**CIRCUIT LENGTH** 2.620 miles
**NO. OF LAPS** 28
**RACE DISTANCE** 73.360 miles
**WEATHER** Dry, 20°C
**TRACK TEMPERATURE** 27°C
**WINNER** Jorge Lorenzo
**FASTEST LAP** 1m 40.152s, 94.166mph, Jorge Lorenzo (record)
**PREVIOUS LAP RECORD** 1m 49.668s, 85.995mph, Valentino Rossi, 2008

## QUALIFYING

| | Rider | Nationality | Team | Qualifying | Pole + | Gap |
|---|---|---|---|---|---|---|
| 1 | Pedrosa | SPA | Repsol Honda Team | 1m 39.730s | | |
| 2 | Lorenzo | SPA | Fiat Yamaha Team | 1m 40.236s | 0.506s | 0.506s |
| 3 | Rossi | ITA | Fiat Yamaha Team | 1m 40.609s | 0.879s | 0.373s |
| 4 | De Angelis | RSM | San Carlo Honda Gresini | 1m 40.620s | 0.890s | 0.011s |
| 5 | Edwards | USA | Monster Yamaha Tech 3 | 1m 40.961s | 1.231s | 0.341s |
| 6 | Hayden | USA | Ducati Team | 1m 41.067s | 1.337s | 0.106s |
| 7 | Elias | SPA | San Carlo Honda Gresini | 1m 41.283s | 1.553s | 0.216s |
| 8 | Dovizioso | ITA | Repsol Honda Team | 1m 41.309s | 1.579s | 0.026s |
| 9 | Melandri | ITA | Hayate Racing Team | 1m 41.530s | 1.800s | 0.221s |
| 10 | Toseland | GBR | Monster Yamaha Tech 3 | 1m 41.620s | 1.890s | 0.090s |
| 11 | Capirossi | ITA | Rizla Suzuki MotoGP | 1m 41.742s | 2.012s | 0.122s |
| 12 | De Puniet | FRA | LCR Honda MotoGP | 1m 41.773s | 2.043s | 0.031s |
| 13 | Canepa | ITA | Pramac Racing | 1m 41.910s | 2.180s | 0.137s |
| 14 | Vermeulen | AUS | Rizla Suzuki MotoGP | 1m 42.038s | 2.308s | 0.128s |
| 15 | Kallio | FIN | Ducati Team | 1m 42.250s | 2.520s | 0.212s |
| 16 | Espargaro | SPA | Pramac Racing | 1m 42.577s | 2.847s | 0.327s |
| 17 | Talmacsi | HUN | Scot Racing Team MotoGP | 1m 42.736s | 3.006s | 0.159s |

## FINISHERS

**1 JORGE LORENZO** No doubt about the winner once Rossi had crashed: Jorge cruised home to halve the points gap at the top of the table between himself and his team-mate. Despite Pedrosa's pole position, he was the fastest man in race trim all weekend.

**2 ALEX DE ANGELIS** A debut podium in MotoGP after his best-ever qualifying in the class – and being fastest in warm-up – shows this was no fluke result. Just what he needed after finding out, only one week before his home GP, that the team wouldn't be keeping him.

**3 NICKY HAYDEN** Undoubtedly the happiest Nicky has ever been about finishing third. After an awful start to his Ducati career, this was, to put it mildly, a welcome rostrum.

**4 ANDREA DOVIZIOSO** Competitive thanks to a radical set-up modification after the warm-up. Looked set to deprive Hayden of third place on the last lap, but a big moment allowed the American to escape.

**5 COLIN EDWARDS** Couldn't put any load on the rear and disappointed the race wasn't as much fun as he thought it was going to be. Chose the same tyre as the winner, so acknowledged that the problem had to come from set-up or riding style.

**6 JAMES TOSELAND** A good start from an average grid position and a combative race with Melandri by a much happier James. Worried after warm-up because the crew softened the bike, but still able to keep his pace from qualifying.

**7 LORIS CAPIROSSI** A better result than his grid position suggested. Didn't feel comfortable at Indianapolis first time round and hadn't changed his opinion but, despite being involved in the Turn 2 coming-together, he was his old battling self in the race.

**8 MIKA KALLIO** A major victim of the first-lap domino effect, which only added to problems caused by poor qualifying. Getting up to eighth from 13th has to

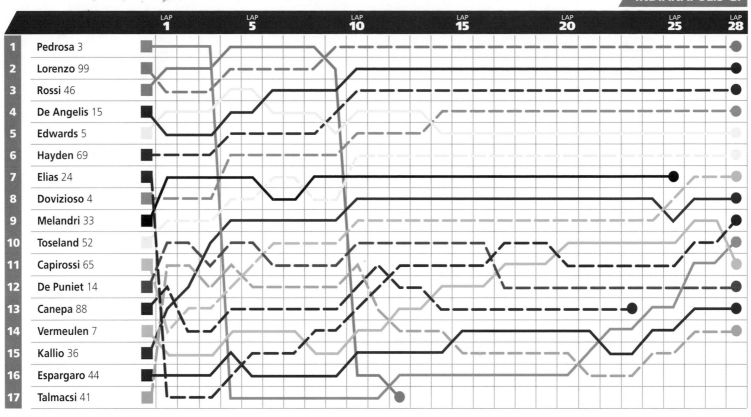

| | | LAP 1 | LAP 5 | LAP 10 | LAP 15 | LAP 20 | LAP 25 | LAP 28 |
|---|---|---|---|---|---|---|---|---|
| 1 | Pedrosa 3 | | | | | | | |
| 2 | Lorenzo 99 | | | | | | | |
| 3 | Rossi 46 | | | | | | | |
| 4 | De Angelis 15 | | | | | | | |
| 5 | Edwards 5 | | | | | | | |
| 6 | Hayden 69 | | | | | | | |
| 7 | Elias 24 | | | | | | | |
| 8 | Dovizioso 4 | | | | | | | |
| 9 | Melandri 33 | | | | | | | |
| 10 | Toseland 52 | | | | | | | |
| 11 | Capirossi 65 | | | | | | | |
| 12 | De Puniet 14 | | | | | | | |
| 13 | Canepa 88 | | | | | | | |
| 14 | Vermeulen 7 | | | | | | | |
| 15 | Kallio 36 | | | | | | | |
| 16 | Espargaro 44 | | | | | | | |
| 17 | Talmacsi 41 | | | | | | | |

## RACE

| | Rider | Motorcycle | Race Time | Time + | Fastest Lap | Av Speed | 🅱 |
|---|---|---|---|---|---|---|---|
| 1 | Lorenzo | Yamaha | 47m 13.592s | | 1m 40.152s | 93.195mph | H/H |
| 2 | De Angelis | Honda | 47m 23.027s | 9.435s | 1m 40.862s | 92.885mph | H/H |
| 3 | Hayden | Ducati | 47m 26.539s | 12.947s | 1m 41.041s | 92.771mph | M/H |
| 4 | Dovizioso | Honda | 47m 27.070s | 13.478s | 1m 41.106s | 92.753mph | H/H |
| 5 | Edwards | Yamaha | 47m 39.846s | 26.254s | 1m 41.256s | 92.339mph | H/H |
| 6 | Toseland | Yamaha | 47m 46.000s | 32.408s | 1m 41.576s | 92.141mph | H/H |
| 7 | Capirossi | Suzuki | 47m 47.992s | 34.400s | 1m 41.576s | 92.077mph | H/H |
| 8 | Kallio | Ducati | 47m 48.448s | 34.856s | 1m 41.664s | 92.062mph | M/H |
| 9 | Elias | Honda | 47m 58.597s | 45.005s | 1m 41.573s | 91.737mph | H/H |
| 10 | Pedrosa | Honda | 47m 58.969s | 45.377s | 1m 40.200s | 91.726mph | H/H |
| 11 | Vermeulen | Suzuki | 47m 59.070s | 45.478s | 1m 41.840s | 91.722mph | H/H |
| 12 | De Puniet | Honda | 48m 05.886s | 52.294s | 1m 41.983s | 91.506mph | H/XH |
| 13 | Espargaro | Ducati | 48m 17.144s | 1m 03.552s | 1m 42.138s | 91.150mph | H/H |
| 14 | Talmacsi | Honda | 48m 28.678s | 1m 15.086s | 1m 42.317s | 90.789mph | H/H |
| | Melandri | Kawasaki | 42m 36.675s | 3 laps | 1m 41.490s | 92.222mph | H/H |
| | Canepa | Ducati | 39m 29.440s | 5 laps | 1m 42.087s | 91.548mph | H/H |
| | Rossi | Yamaha | 21m 16.362s | 16 laps | 1m 40.287s | 88.670mph | H/H |

## CHAMPIONSHIP

| | Rider | Team | Points |
|---|---|---|---|
| 1 | Rossi | Fiat Yamaha Team | 212 |
| 2 | Lorenzo | Fiat Yamaha Team | 187 |
| 3 | Stoner | Ducati Marlboro Team | 150 |
| 4 | Pedrosa | Repsol Honda Team | 141 |
| 5 | Edwards | Monster Yamaha Tech 3 | 123 |
| 6 | Dovizioso | Repsol Honda Team | 120 |
| 7 | De Angelis | San Carlo Honda Gresini | 88 |
| 8 | Capirossi | Rizla Suzuki MotoGP | 86 |
| 9 | De Puniet | LCR Honda MotoGP | 84 |
| 10 | Melandri | Hayate Racing Team | 79 |
| 11 | Vermeulen | Rizla Suzuki MotoGP | 77 |
| 12 | Hayden | Ducati Team | 73 |
| 13 | Toseland | Monster Yamaha Tech 3 | 72 |
| 14 | Elias | San Carlo Honda Gresini | 70 |
| 15 | Kallio | Ducati Team | 42 |
| 16 | Canepa | Pramac Racing | 32 |
| 17 | Gibernau | Grupo Francisco Hernando | 12 |
| 18 | Talmacsi | Scot Racing Team MotoGP | 10 |
| 19 | Takahashi | Scot Racing Team MotoGP | 9 |
| 20 | Espargaro | Pramac Racing | 3 |

be counted as a good race, although he refused to get excited about it.

**9 TONI ELIAS** Pushed off the track at the second corner so did well to get a top-ten finish. Felt he would have got in the top five, at the very least, after a weekend when he started badly but improved markedly in every session.

**10 DANI PEDROSA** Fell out of the lead when he lost the front at the end of lap four, then mounted a spirited fight-back, passing Vermeulen on the run to the flag. Fastest man on track in the second part of the race despite a twisted handlebar, no rear brake pedal and only half a right footrest.

**11 CHRIS VERMEULEN** Started well but was hit by Kallio in the second turn and ran off track. His pace from then on was better than he'd shown in practice, and he got up to ninth before a mistake on the last lap sent him backwards.

**12 RANDY DE PUNIET** The left ankle broken only a month before suffered badly on a course that features many more left-hand corners than rights. Choosing to go with the harder rear tyre didn't help either; Randy never had the grip he expected on the left side.

**13 ALEIX ESPARGARO** An impressive MotoGP debut in both qualifying and the race. Was the instigator of the first-lap domino effect that put him and his friend

Elias off track. After that he was alone for most of the race, which he felt was 'like a test'.

**14 GABOR TALMACSI** Went well at the start, getting as high as 11th, but the bike's set-up made it very heavy in changes of direction. Also had problems with wheelies, all of which took a toll on his upper body strength, and he lost touch with the group.

### NON-FINISHERS

**MARCO MELANDRI** Fought throughout with Toseland despite a 'total lack of grip and traction on the rear tyre'. Made up ground on the brakes, which stressed the front tyre, so when he attacked at the end he made a

small mistake and lost the front: 'That's going to happen.'

**NICCOLO CANEPA** The bike stopped on lap 24 when the engine management electronics detected a problem. Niccolo was lying in 13th place at the time.

**VALENTINO ROSSI** Ran wide in the first corner, just after Lorenzo took the lead off him, then crashed on the brakes going into Turn 2. He either hit one of the big bumps or was off-line on the very dirty part of the track. Got the bike going again but a sticking throttle forced him out.

# SAN MARINO GP

MISANO WORLD CIRCUIT

**ROUND 13**

**September 6**

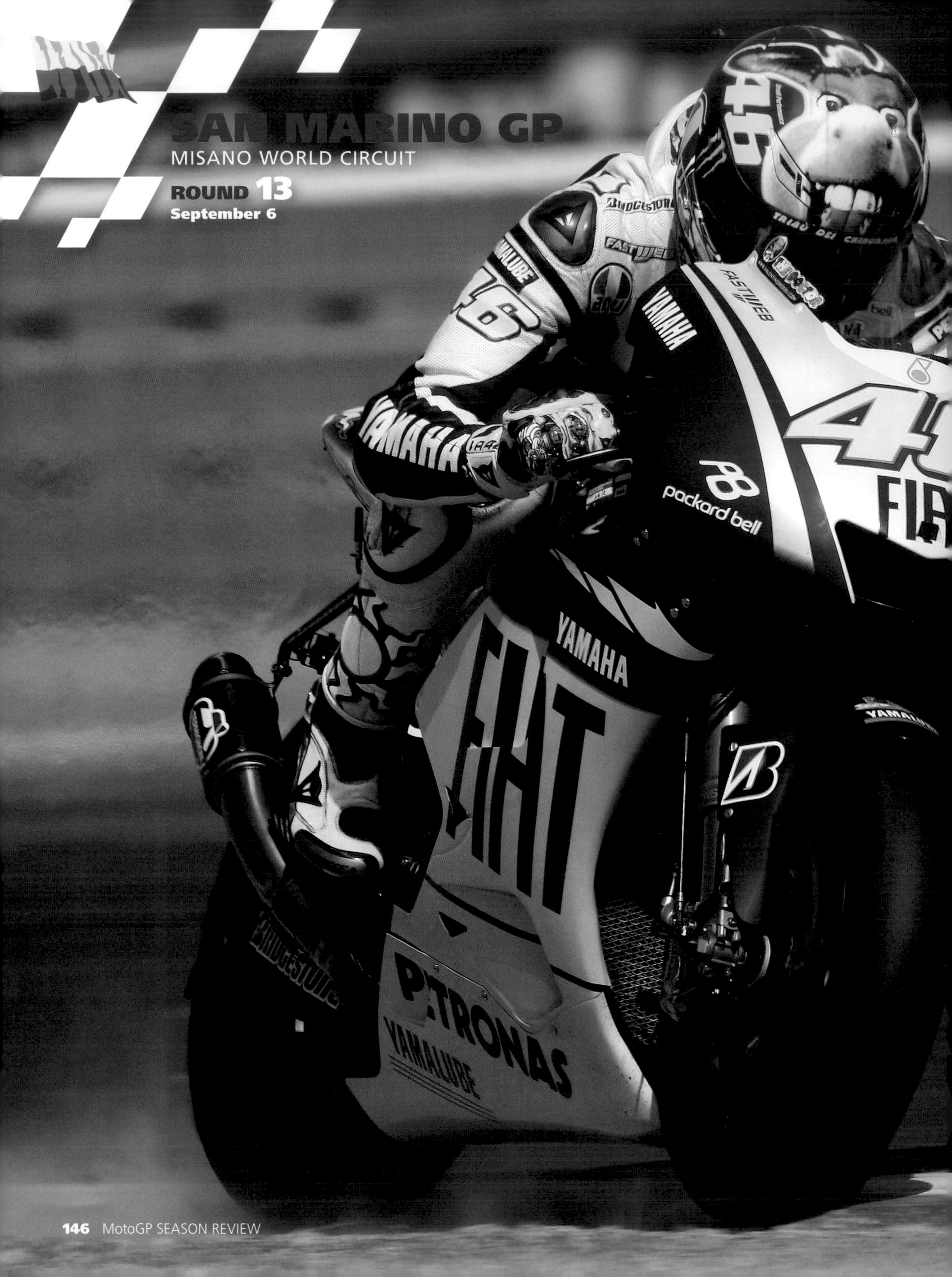

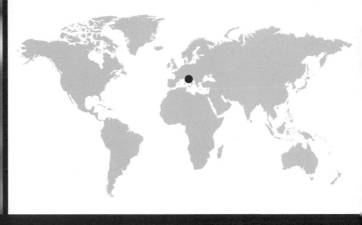

# DONKEY SANCTUARY

**Valentino Rossi made up for the disaster of Indianapolis with a faultless weekend at a track that is all of five miles from his home town**

**V**alentino Rossi can always be relied upon for a good quote – it's one of the reasons why the media love him so much. Barry Sheene had the same gift. When asked why the special crash helmet for his home race featured a picture of Donkey from *Shrek*, he replied that when he was sliding across the grass at Indianapolis his first thought had been 'I am a donkey!' (as in ass). Back home he rang his designer, Aldo Drudi, and said: 'We lose 25 points but find the right idea for Misano.'

So the hero arrived as a penitent in front of the faithful, and lost no time in redeeming himself. Valentino was fastest in every session and once he'd got over the problems caused by a full fuel tank he went to the front on lap eight of 28 and never looked in danger. In a complete reversal of the situation a week earlier at Indianapolis, Lorenzo was never able to run at Rossi's pace and cut a slightly forlorn figure for the whole weekend. Nevertheless, even an imperfectly set-up Fiat Yamaha was good enough for Jorge to finish a comfortable second. He did go past Valentino on the first lap, but he was soon re-passed and then got stuck behind the Hondas of Toni Elias and Dani Pedrosa for too long while his team-mate opened up a winning lead.

Pedrosa and Elias were both early leaders, and both had problems. Dani reported misfiring, although it wasn't visible from the side of the track. He also ran out of petrol on the slow-down lap. As the engine of his RCV looked significantly different from any other Honda, there was again the suspicion that HRC were fielding more new equipment and pushing their fuelling calculations to the limit in search of competitiveness with the Yamahas. Pedrosa certainly didn't give Honda a vote of confidence with his off-track pronouncements. After

**Above** Colin Edwards tumbles through the gravel trap after being scooped up by Alex de Angelis's Honda. Nicky Hayden was the other victim

**Below** Things you thought you'd never see: a factory Honda rider using Ohlins, not Showa, suspension. Andrea Dovizioso consults his technician

**Opposite** Being from San Marino, Alex de Angelis featured in all the event publicity. Unfortunately he didn't make it past the second corner

the HRC president's statement at Brno that both Dani and Andrea Dovizioso would be re-signing for the factory team on two-year contracts, it was announced on race-day morning that the Spanish rider had indeed signed up – but only for one year. Dovi had also agreed to stay for another year but with an option for another season. And after the race Pedrosa made it very clear to Italian TV that he would have preferred to be on a Yamaha in 2010. The message was clear: give me a better bike or I'm off.

In the continuing absence of Casey Stoner, expected back at the next race, Ducati announced the re-signing of Nicky Hayden, who looked and sounded like his old relaxed self. 'I've said it's been the worst year of my life but it ain't so bad. You've only got to watch the news to see there are a lot of people out there having a lot worse time than me.' He gave every impression of enjoying the responsibility of carrying the Ducati banner in front of the company's top brass, employees and customers, and he put in his best dry-weather qualifying of the season so far. Nicky even set a fastest sector time, something he hadn't previously achieved in the dry. Crucially, he didn't appear to spend Friday trying to get the Desmosedici to act like a normal motorcycle. It looked as if he'd be able to run in the top six at least.

However, Nicky also said on Saturday that 'the first two or three turns are going to be harsh'. He wasn't wrong. It's in the nature of the Misano track to string the pack out over the first half-lap, so anyone not on the front two rows has to get a good start. Hayden didn't mention any names, but a disappointed Alex de Angelis headed the third row. He had the pace to be higher up but couldn't make use of the softer tyre. The previous week he'd been

**Right** James Toseland was one of several riders who lost time avoiding the first-lap mêlée

**Below** Valentino Rossi leads the usual suspects through Buccine in front of a full house

**Opposite below** Mika Kallio had his season's best result, seventh, in his last ride for the Ducati factory team

## PENALTY

*The first-lap crash initiated by Alex de Angelis reopened the debate on what penalties should and should not be handed down by Race Direction for incidents that happen in a race. Most riders weren't in favour of the idea of penalties in such cases, although Rossi did feel moved to remark that 'sometimes de Angelis is a little bit aggressive in the first corner' – which could be the understatement of the season. Other riders would say that the problems always came from the same people.*

*There was an incident in the 125 race which illustrated how most racers think about these matters. Andrea Iannone tried an optimistic last-corner pass on Pol Espargaro that resulted in both crashing. That could have been regarded as a purely racing incident, but unfortunately Iannone followed it up by head-butting the Spaniard and making some borderline-racist remarks in a TV interview. The head-butt cost him a $5,000 fine, and his team later lost two sponsors. Valentino Rossi and other MotoGP riders agreed that the penalty was correctly applied and that the crash, while regrettable, was the sort of thing that happens – especially in 125 racing.*

*However, Jorge Lorenzo and some others were much more exercised about problems in qualifying and practice, such as riders going slow on the racing line, getting in the way of guys on a fast lap and other such 'misdemeanours'. It seemed that being followed on a quick lap was just about the most annoying thing for the top men, with de Angelis and Toni Elias coming in for some criticism. Valentino Rossi even suggested that he'd send an invoice to Team Gresini at the end of the season for all the work he'd done for them during the year!*

*As regards the Turn 2 crash, Alex de Angelis was called up to Race Direction to explain himself but escaped without a penalty.*

on the rostrum for the first time; now he was at his home race and riding for a job.

The first corner, the Park Chicane, is a tight second-gear right/left. De Angelis charged up the inside of the left-hand section and lost the front. His bike scooped up Colin Edwards, whose bike then brought down Hayden. Lorenzo was lucky to survive, Chris Vermeulen was baulked and Randy de Puniet had to go off the track to avoid the carnage. The Americans were furious, Hayden especially so. Was it just a racing incident? Nicky was adamant: 'He was never going to make that corner; on the left of the front tyre you have to be careful for two laps.' He put a lot of emphasis on the words 'two laps'.

De Angelis's rush of blood may have had further consequences. Before the race it looked as if he was in line for a ride with the satellite Pramac Ducati team in 2010, but after Alex had snuffed out Ducati's best chance of putting on a good show at home – and, assuming Nicky had run with the Dovizioso/Capirossi dice for fourth, of collecting a lot of significant data – no-one could now imagine the Bologna factory signing him.

All this was a sideshow to Rossi's untroubled progress to another win. He continued the donkey theme on the rostrum with a giant pair of comedy floppy ears. He even made his mechanics wear sets in *parc fermé* – they didn't look entirely amused. Needless to say, Jerry Burgess wasn't seen in such undignified apparel. The helmet design may have been a rush job, but the legendary Rossi attention to detail was there. See the diamond stud in Donkey's front tooth? It's a Yamaha logo. All of which slightly overshadowed the fact that this was Yamaha's 50th win under the MotoGP formula, just four short of Honda's record.

## 'HE WAS NEVER GOING TO MAKE THAT CORNER; ON THE LEFT OF THE FRONT TYRE YOU HAVE TO BE CAREFUL FOR TWO LAPS'
**NICKY HAYDEN**

**BRIDGESTONE**
TYRE OPTIONS
FRONT MEDIUM (M) / HARD (H)
REAR MEDIUM (M) / HARD (H)

**MotoGP** **TISSOT** SWISS WATCHES SINCE 1853
OFFICIAL TIMEKEEPER

# SAN MARINO GP
## MISANO WORLD CIRCUIT

### ROUND 13
September 6

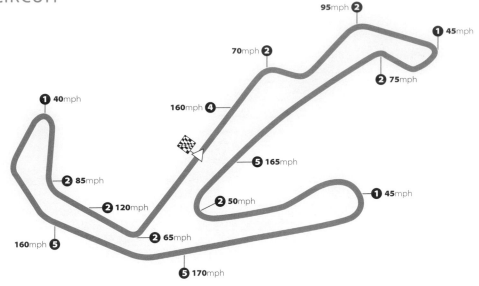

# RACE RESULTS

**CIRCUIT LENGTH** 2.626 miles
**NO. OF LAPS** 28
**RACE DISTANCE** 73.529 miles
**WEATHER** Dry, 24°C
**TRACK TEMPERATURE** 41°C
**WINNER** Valentino Rossi
**FASTEST LAP** 1m 34.746s, 99.575mph, Valentino Rossi (record)
**PREVIOUS LAP RECORD** 1m 34.904s, 99.609mph, Valentino Rossi, 2008

## QUALIFYING

| | Rider | Nationality | Team | Qualifying | Pole + | Gap |
|---|---|---|---|---|---|---|
| 1 | Rossi | ITA | Fiat Yamaha Team | 1m 34.338s | | |
| 2 | Pedrosa | SPA | Repsol Honda Team | 1m 34.560s | 0.222s | 0.222s |
| 3 | Lorenzo | SPA | Fiat Yamaha Team | 1m 34.808s | 0.470s | 0.248s |
| 4 | Elias | SPA | San Carlo Honda Gresini | 1m 34.907s | 0.569s | 0.099s |
| 5 | Edwards | USA | Monster Yamaha Tech 3 | 1m 35.184s | 0.846s | 0.277s |
| 6 | Hayden | USA | Ducati Marlboro Team | 1m 35.223s | 0.885s | 0.039s |
| 7 | De Angelis | RSM | San Carlo Honda Gresini | 1m 35.343s | 1.005s | 0.120s |
| 8 | Dovizioso | ITA | Repsol Honda Team | 1m 35.492s | 1.154s | 0.149s |
| 9 | De Puniet | FRA | LCR Honda MotoGP | 1m 35.554s | 1.216s | 0.062s |
| 10 | Capirossi | ITA | Rizla Suzuki MotoGP | 1m 35.561s | 1.223s | 0.007s |
| 11 | Kallio | FIN | Ducati Marlboro Team | 1m 35.601s | 1.263s | 0.040s |
| 12 | Melandri | ITA | Hayate Racing Team | 1m 35.785s | 1.447s | 0.184s |
| 13 | Vermeulen | AUS | Rizla Suzuki MotoGP | 1m 35.790s | 1.452s | 0.005s |
| 14 | Toseland | GBR | Monster Yamaha Tech 3 | 1m 36.070s | 1.732s | 0.280s |
| 15 | Espargaro | SPA | Pramac Racing | 1m 36.228s | 1.890s | 0.158s |
| 16 | Canepa | ITA | Pramac Racing | 1m 36.264s | 1.926s | 0.036s |
| 17 | Talmacsi | HUN | Scot Racing Team MotoGP | 1m 37.091s | 2.753s | 0.827s |

## FINISHERS

**1 VALENTINO ROSSI** A perfect weekend redeemed the Indy disaster. Fastest in every session, sixth pole of the season – the most he's had on a Yamaha – and what turned into an easy win. Took the lead on lap eight after a cautious start with a full fuel load and was never in danger.

**2 JORGE LORENZO** Lucky to survive the first lap, then took too long to get past Pedrosa and Elias to be a threat to Rossi. But, as Jorge himself admitted, he struggled all weekend to find the right settings and had no option but to settle for second.

**3 DANI PEDROSA** First rostrum at Misano, led early on after another superb start, but complained the bike was cutting out during the race. Said the Yamahas could brake harder and get through corners better. Ran out of petrol on the slow-down lap, indicating HRC were cutting it fine.

**4 ANDREA DOVIZIOSO** Raced with Ohlins suspension for the first time after a successful test at Brno. Lost touch with the leaders when he made a mistake at the last of the three fast right-handers on the back straight on lap seven. Did well to retake fourth on the last lap.

**5 LORIS CAPIROSSI** Faster through the weekend as the team continued to work well with the new chassis, but it took

time – hence the tenth grid place. Spent the first ten laps jumping a big gap to Elias, then got Dovi four laps from home, only to be retaken on the last lap.

**6 TONI ELIAS** Started the weekend with a terrible practice on Friday, then got quicker with every session. Led for a while but lost performance in the second part of the race. Not long ago sixth would have been a great result; this time he had very mixed feelings.

**7 MIKA KALLIO** A season's best result in his final ride for the works team before returning to the satellite squad. Slowed by the first-lap incident, then had to get past Talmacsi and Melandri, so there was a 4s gap to the group ahead. Spent the rest of the race fighting off Melandri.

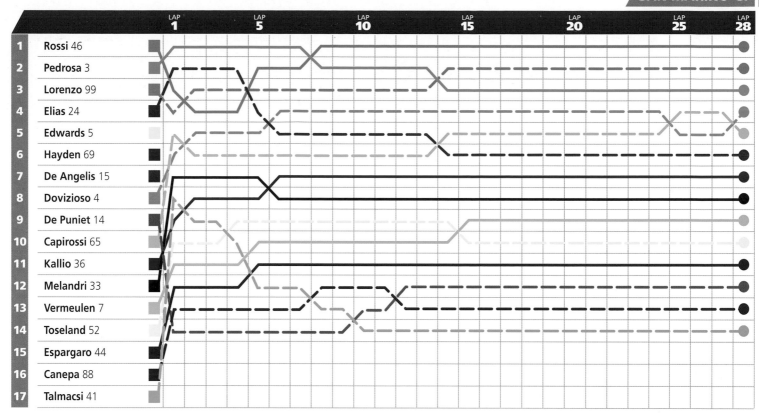

| | | | LAP 1 | LAP 5 | LAP 10 | LAP 15 | LAP 20 | LAP 25 | LAP 28 |
|---|---|---|---|---|---|---|---|---|---|
| 1 | Rossi 46 | | | | | | | | |
| 2 | Pedrosa 3 | | | | | | | | |
| 3 | Lorenzo 99 | | | | | | | | |
| 4 | Elias 24 | | | | | | | | |
| 5 | Edwards 5 | | | | | | | | |
| 6 | Hayden 69 | | | | | | | | |
| 7 | De Angelis 15 | | | | | | | | |
| 8 | Dovizioso 4 | | | | | | | | |
| 9 | De Puniet 14 | | | | | | | | |
| 10 | Capirossi 65 | | | | | | | | |
| 11 | Kallio 36 | | | | | | | | |
| 12 | Melandri 33 | | | | | | | | |
| 13 | Vermeulen 7 | | | | | | | | |
| 14 | Toseland 52 | | | | | | | | |
| 15 | Espargaro 44 | | | | | | | | |
| 16 | Canepa 88 | | | | | | | | |
| 17 | Talmacsi 41 | | | | | | | | |

## RACE

| | Rider | Motorcycle | Race Time | Time + | Fastest Lap | Av Speed | 🅱 |
|---|---|---|---|---|---|---|---|
| 1 | Rossi | Yamaha | 44m 32.882s | | 1m 34.746s | 99.033mph | H/H |
| 2 | Lorenzo | Yamaha | 44m 35.298s | 2.416s | 1m 34.823s | 98.943mph | H/H |
| 3 | Pedrosa | Honda | 44m 45.282s | 12.400s | 1m 35.115s | 98.575mph | H/H |
| 4 | Dovizioso | Honda | 44m 59.212s | 26.330s | 1m 35.435s | 98.066mph | H/H |
| 5 | Capirossi | Suzuki | 44m 59.421s | 26.539s | 1m 35.680s | 98.059mph | H/H |
| 6 | Elias | Honda | 45m 01.168s | 28.286s | 1m 35.779s | 97.996mph | H/H |
| 7 | Kallio | Ducati | 45m 03.066s | 30.184s | 1m 35.742s | 97.927mph | H/H |
| 8 | Melandri | Kawasaki | 45m 04.639s | 31.757s | 1m 35.877s | 97.870mph | H/H |
| 9 | Vermeulen | Suzuki | 45m 04.791s | 31.909s | 1m 35.703s | 97.864mph | H/H |
| 10 | Toseland | Yamaha | 45m 11.229s | 38.347s | 1m 36.026s | 97.632mph | H/H |
| 11 | Espargaro | Ducati | 45m 19.555s | 46.673s | 1m 35.673s | 97.333mph | H/H |
| 12 | De Puniet | Honda | 45m 24.923s | 52.041s | 1m 35.988s | 97.141mph | H/H |
| 13 | Canepa | Ducati | 45m 36.080s | 1m 03.198s | 1m 36.448s | 96.745mph | H/H |
| 14 | Talmacsi | Honda | 45m 55.229s | 1m 22.347s | 1m 37.019s | 96.073mph | H/H |

## CHAMPIONSHIP

| | Rider | Team | Points |
|---|---|---|---|
| 1 | Rossi | Fiat Yamaha Team | 237 |
| 2 | Lorenzo | Fiat Yamaha Team | 207 |
| 3 | Pedrosa | Repsol Honda Team | 157 |
| 4 | Stoner | Ducati Marlboro Team | 150 |
| 5 | Dovizioso | Repsol Honda Team | 133 |
| 6 | Edwards | Monster Yamaha Tech 3 | 123 |
| 7 | Capirossi | Rizla Suzuki MotoGP | 97 |
| 8 | De Angelis | San Carlo Honda Gresini | 88 |
| 9 | De Puniet | LCR Honda MotoGP | 88 |
| 10 | Melandri | Hayate Racing Team | 87 |
| 11 | Vermeulen | Rizla Suzuki MotoGP | 84 |
| 12 | Elias | San Carlo Honda Gresini | 80 |
| 13 | Toseland | Monster Yamaha Tech 3 | 78 |
| 14 | Hayden | Ducati Marlboro Team | 73 |
| 15 | Kallio | Ducati Marlboro Team | 51 |
| 16 | Canepa | Pramac Racing | 35 |
| 17 | Gibernau | Grupo Francisco Hernando | 12 |
| 18 | Talmacsi | Scot Racing Team MotoGP | 12 |
| 19 | Takahashi | Scot Racing Team MotoGP | 9 |
| 20 | Espargaro | Pramac Racing | 8 |

**8 MARCO MELANDRI** Unaffected by the big crash thanks to a good start that put him up to sixth at the end of the first lap, then spent most of the race trying to find a way to stay with and pass his old bike. As usual the Kawasaki was difficult to ride, especially on a new tyre.

**9 CHRIS VERMEULEN** A great start, but slowed by the Turn 2 crash. Found a false neutral when tried to select first gear, then ran over Edwards' front mudguard; all those he'd overtaken came back past. Top-five pace later, but the main problem was disappointing qualifying.

**10 JAMES TOSELAND** Another one who lost ground because of the crash. Went for the softer rear tyre and was able to run the same pace as the fight for fourth/fifth right up to the last five laps. Not pleased with his finishing position but happy with his lap times.

**11 ALEIX ESPARGARO** Another seriously impressive ride – his fastest lap was the fifth best of the race – and in only his second MotoGP outing. The Ducati's extra weight and power found him out, though, and he suffered severe arm pump in the later part of the race.

**12 RANDY DE PUNIET** Ran off track avoiding fallen riders at Turn 2 and rejoined over nine seconds adrift of the pack. The right-handed track was easier on his recently broken left ankle than Indianapolis, and that helped his chase.

**13 NICCOLO CANEPA** Went off track twice trying to pass Talmacsi, which both lost him time and hastened the degeneration of his rear tyre.

**14 GABOR TALMACSI** Strong at the start but his lap times dropped right off before he recovered slightly at the end of the race. Not happy.

## NON-FINISHERS

**ALEX DE ANGELIS** The instigator of the first-lap incident that caused all three retirements from the race. Charged up the inside at Turn 2, lost the front and took down the two Americans, doing his employment chances for the 2010 season no good at all.

**COLIN EDWARDS** Had no idea what happened apart from 'an Italian rider who wanted to be a hero'. After using the word 'dumb-ass' a lot, opined that it was Alex who should have been wearing the donkey ears that Rossi sported on the rostrum.

**NICKY HAYDEN** Incandescent with rage at Alex's mistake. Ruined what promised to be his best race of the year and, more importantly, his chance to run with the leaders in front of all Ducati's top brass and a stand full of the people who make and ride the red bikes from Bologna.

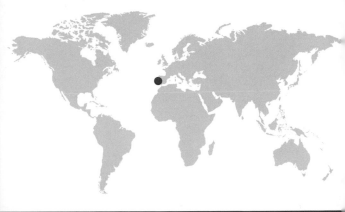

# ONE GIANT LEAP

**Jorge Lorenzo dressed up as a spaceman and was out of this world, Casey Stoner made an astonishing comeback, and Valentino Rossi had a bad weekend**

It isn't often that eight-times World Champion Valentino Rossi is overshadowed by not one but two other riders over a Grand Prix weekend, but at Estoril both Jorge Lorenzo and Casey Stoner deservedly received more airtime and column inches than the Doctor.

Lorenzo completely dominated proceedings. He was fastest in every session and in the race was only headed for two corners. Once he hit the front he never looked in any danger, and his team manager Daniele Romagnoli was moved to remark: 'Jorge rode the best he's ever ridden.' No-one was arguing. The impression was heightened by his Yamaha's one-off promotional Fiat livery which Jorge topped with an Apollo 11 tribute crash helmet. His fan club were given the full effect when Jorge did a slow-motion moonwalk through the gravel trap, in front of the stand where they were massed, to plant his 'Lorenzo's Land' flag. And Lorenzo's victory seemed even more significant because of the bad weekend suffered by his team-mate – and rival for the world title – Valentino Rossi.

Rossi was unhappy with his set-up all weekend, citing braking problems on Friday when he felt he was three-tenths off the pace. Although his Fiat Yamaha crew sorted out that problem, Vale never closed the gap on Jorge and on race day things got worse. Everyone is so used to Jerry Burgess and his mechanics throwing in some radical adjustment for Sunday morning warm-up, and maybe again before the race, that they expect a miracle every time. They usually get it, too – but not this time, maybe because warm-up was cold and misty while the race was

warm and dry. Burgess said that they 'tipped it over the top' trying to get the bike to steer more quickly, but it never had edge grip from the rear tyre, either going into or coming out of corners. Valentino, on the other hand, recalled that he'd struggled here last season as well, and wondered if there was something in the set-up that overheated the rear tyre. The end result was a lonely fourth place and a reduction of his lead in the championship from 30 to 18 points. The good news was that Fiat Yamaha secured the teams' title.

Vale's struggle, however, was merely a sideshow to both Lorenzo's dominance and a quite astonishing return to racing form by Casey Stoner. The 2007 World Champion had missed the previous three races attempting to recover from a mystery illness that had sapped his reserves of stamina by half-distance and had seen him at the point of collapse at the flag. After the British GP Casey went home to Australia, promising to come back for the Portuguese round – and it was like he'd never been away. Just a handful of laps into Friday practice, Stoner was ripping around the Estoril circuit, the Ducati Desmosedici twisting, spinning and sliding, to remind everyone just what they'd been missing. The fourth 'Alien' was back on earth. How could anyone be away from a racing motorcycle for nine weeks, having apparently not trained seriously for four months, and be that fast? It was an astonishing display. But did anyone doubt that he'd be quick? The question was surely over his stamina. We had to wait for race day to find out if the break had solved his problems.

In truth, everyone had to wait for at least half of

# 'THIS IS A GOOD TRACK FOR ME BUT I AM FAST MORE OR LESS EVERYWHERE NOW'
**JORGE LORENZO**

**Opposite** The only time Lorenzo didn't lead was for the first two corners

**Above** A vengeful Toni Elias closes in on Andrea Dovizioso's works Honda

**Below** Estoril's spectator facilities have been significantly improved over recent years

the 28 laps. Stoner slotted into second place behind Lorenzo on lap three, when Pedrosa went wide, and although a broken footrest hanger handicapped Casey on right-handers he matched the factory Honda rider's lap times right to the flag. Everyone had been watching the Aussie's lap times like a hawk. When would he hit the wall? At half-distance? But there was never any sign of fatigue. He stayed fast for the whole race, for the first time in five months, and was in the 1m 37s bracket almost throughout, only slipping into the 1m 38s range for the last six of the 28 laps. Pedrosa, finishing third, had dropped into the 1m 38s bracket one lap earlier.

Stoner looked almost shocked on the rostrum and later took delight in putting a few critics right. Kevin Schwantz received a special mention: 'I lost a lot of respect for him; it just shows experience doesn't count for anything.' Casey had had to suffer some truly fantastic stories being written and circulated about him while he was away, but his performance at Estoril totally justified his decision to take that break. No doubt his return to form was also a massive relief to Ducati, but the more his comeback is analysed, the more amazing it seems. When he went walkabout, the names Spencer and Poggiali were bandied about. And that's just from motorcycle racing. Think of other sports as well, and it's difficult to come up with a sportsman or sportswoman who has returned from an episode like this to anywhere near their previous form. The measure of Casey's achievement was that anyone who'd been on a desert island for the previous nine weeks wouldn't have noticed any change. Who'd have believed that after the debacle of Donington Park?

Dani Pedrosa led from the start, as usual, and was obviously pressing hard. An uncharacteristic mistake let Lorenzo through, and then another much bigger one – it cost him a whole second – broke the tow to Stoner. Dani proceeded to set a new lap record, by a whole half-second, midway through the race but without making any serious inroad into Stoner's advantage. Again, it emphasises just how hard the top men have been riding this season.

Behind the four front-runners, Colin Edwards again showed that he was the best of the rest, while Toni Elias won a good battle with Andrea Dovizioso to make another point about his impending unemployment. Not that anyone took too much notice of these lower-order successes – they were too busy marvelling at those dazzling performances by Lorenzo and Stoner.

**Left** Stoner's form on his return after a three-race layoff was nothing short of remarkable

**Opposite top** The battle for third. Rossi couldn't make an impression on Pedrosa

**Opposite** De Puniet was now using the same rev limit as other satellite Honda riders

## LIMITED EDITION

The new engine rules limiting teams to five motors for the final seven races of the year caused a major row at Estoril. It had nothing to do with any rider running out of engines but concerned an amendment to the regulations. Race Direction decided to alter the penalty for a rider using extra engines. Originally, any rider using an extra engine was to lose ten World Championship points. The new regulation transferred that penalty to the manufacturer's total in the Constructors' Championship, while the rider himself would have to start from the back of the grid.

The first effect of this ruling was to prevent Yamaha from wrapping up the Constructors' Championship at Estoril; they had to be content with Fiat Yamaha securing the teams' title. The most vociferous complaints, however, came from Honda for the simple reason that they field six bikes and in 2010 will compete with at least seven. Ducati will have five bikes, Yamaha four and Suzuki two. The implications are obvious: Honda are much more likely than any other manufacturer to be penalised. And in 2010 the situation will be even more delicate, with just six engines to last 18 races.

The riders are known to be anxious about the 2010 allocation, with Valentino Rossi and others publicly suggesting that at least two more motors will be needed. Technical regulations of this sort are the province of the MSMA, the manufacturers' association, though, so the riders have no direct route to lobby for a further amendment. However, the general consensus is that the allocation will be increased.

One side-effect of the endurance engines that had been in use since Brno was to give Randy de Puniet a boost. The LCR team were being used by HRC as testers for the endurance-specification motor, so the Frenchman spent several races running a lower rev limit than other satellite Honda riders. Suddenly, once the whole field was out on their long-life motors, Randy wasn't at a disadvantage any more. And the fact that his ankle was healing helped him too, of course.

**BRIDGESTONE**

TYRE OPTIONS
FRONT SOFT (S) / MEDIUM (M)
REAR MEDIUM (M) / HARD (H)

motoGP | TISSOT SWISS WATCHES SINCE 1853
OFFICIAL TIMEKEEPER

# PORTUGUESE GP
## ESTORIL
### ROUND 14
October 4

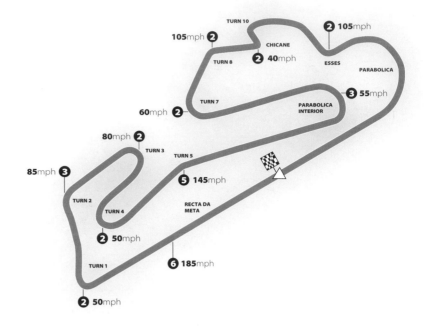

# RACE RESULTS

**CIRCUIT LENGTH** 2.599 miles
**NO. OF LAPS** 28
**RACE DISTANCE** 72.772 miles
**WEATHER** Dry, 27°C
**TRACK TEMPERATURE** 38°C
**WINNER** Jorge Lorenzo
**FASTEST LAP** 1m 36.937s, 96.505mph, Dani Pedrosa (record)
**PREVIOUS LAP RECORD** 1m 37.404s, 96.042mph, Jorge Lorenzo, 2008

## QUALIFYING

| | Rider | Nationality | Team | Qualifying | Pole + | Gap |
|---|---|---|---|---|---|---|
| 1 | Lorenzo | SPA | Fiat Yamaha Team | 1m 36.214s | | |
| 2 | Rossi | ITA | Fiat Yamaha Team | 1m 36.474s | 0.260s | 0.260s |
| 3 | Stoner | AUS | Ducati Marlboro Team | 1m 36.528s | 0.314s | 0.054s |
| 4 | Pedrosa | SPA | Repsol Honda Team | 1m 36.702s | 0.488s | 0.174s |
| 5 | Edwards | USA | Monster Yamaha Tech 3 | 1m 37.142s | 0.928s | 0.440s |
| 6 | De Puniet | FRA | LCR Honda MotoGP | 1m 37.448s | 1.234s | 0.306s |
| 7 | Capirossi | ITA | Rizla Suzuki MotoGP | 1m 37.489s | 1.275s | 0.041s |
| 8 | Dovizioso | ITA | Repsol Honda Team | 1m 37.541s | 1.327s | 0.052s |
| 9 | Hayden | USA | Ducati Marlboro Team | 1m 37.654s | 1.440s | 0.113s |
| 10 | Kallio | FIN | Pramac Racing | 1m 37.813s | 1.599s | 0.159s |
| 11 | De Angelis | RSM | San Carlo Honda Gresini | 1m 37.822s | 1.608s | 0.009s |
| 12 | Toseland | GBR | Monster Yamaha Tech 3 | 1m 37.823s | 1.609s | 0.001s |
| 13 | Elias | SPA | San Carlo Honda Gresini | 1m 37.911s | 1.697s | 0.088s |
| 14 | Canepa | ITA | Pramac Racing | 1m 38.042s | 1.828s | 0.131s |
| 15 | Vermeulen | AUS | Rizla Suzuki MotoGP | 1m 38.342s | 2.128s | 0.300s |
| 16 | Melandri | ITA | Hayate Racing Team | 1m 38.538s | 2.324s | 0.196s |
| 17 | Talmacsi | HUN | Scot Racing Team MotoGP | 1m 39.320s | 3.106s | 0.782s |

## FINISHERS

**1 JORGE LORENZO** A near-perfect weekend – fastest in every session apart from warm-up and never headed in the race bar the first couple of corners. To make things even better, his team-mate and title rival had a bad time. Put on a post-race show of which Valentino would have been proud.

**2 CASEY STONER** As fast and aggressive as ever, and minus the stamina problems that dogged him after Barcelona, totally justifying his decision to take a three-race break. Might have been even better if a footrest hanger hadn't broken, but enjoyed pointing out how wrong some people had been about him.

**3 DANI PEDROSA** Got the holeshot, as usual, but could do nothing when Lorenzo and Stoner came past. Matched Casey for pace, then had a moment on the brakes which sent him wide and broke the tow from the Aussie. Nevertheless, set the fastest lap of the race on lap 11.

**4 VALENTINO ROSSI** In trying to make the M1 turn better the mechanics loaded up the front end but 'tipped it over the top', according to Jerry Burgess. To make matters worse, team-mate Lorenzo won, closing the gap at the top of the table to just 18 points.

**5 COLIN EDWARDS** Fifth in qualifying and also in the race, confirming Colin's status as the best satellite team rider of the year. Couldn't match the pace of the four 'Aliens',

but comfortably outran the Elias/Dovizioso dice, and closed in on Andrea's fifth place in the championship table.

**6 TONI ELIAS** A great effort from 13th on the grid, despite a bad start. Had to work hard to get past Hayden and Dovizioso, and was particularly pleased to beat Dovi's factory bike and move into the top ten of the championship.

**7 ANDREA DOVIZIOSO** Not a good weekend. First came the news that crew chief Pete Benson, who took Hayden to his title, wouldn't be retained for 2010. Then there was bad qualifying followed by a race in which a mistake let Elias catch and hold him off on the run to the flag.

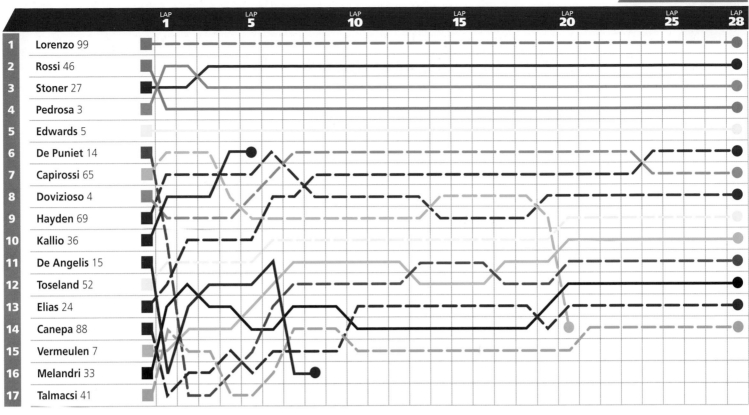

| | | LAP 1 | LAP 5 | LAP 10 | LAP 15 | LAP 20 | LAP 25 | LAP 28 |
|---|---|---|---|---|---|---|---|---|
| 1 | Lorenzo 99 | | | | | | | |
| 2 | Rossi 46 | | | | | | | |
| 3 | Stoner 27 | | | | | | | |
| 4 | Pedrosa 3 | | | | | | | |
| 5 | Edwards 5 | | | | | | | |
| 6 | De Puniet 14 | | | | | | | |
| 7 | Capirossi 65 | | | | | | | |
| 8 | Dovizioso 4 | | | | | | | |
| 9 | Hayden 69 | | | | | | | |
| 10 | Kallio 36 | | | | | | | |
| 11 | De Angelis 15 | | | | | | | |
| 12 | Toseland 52 | | | | | | | |
| 13 | Elias 24 | | | | | | | |
| 14 | Canepa 88 | | | | | | | |
| 15 | Vermeulen 7 | | | | | | | |
| 16 | Melandri 33 | | | | | | | |
| 17 | Talmacsi 41 | | | | | | | |

## RACE

| | Rider | Motorcycle | Race Time | Time + | Fastest Lap | Av Speed | |
|---|---|---|---|---|---|---|---|
| 1 | Lorenzo | Yamaha | 45m 35.522s | | 1m 36.967s | 95.757mph | M/H |
| 2 | Stoner | Ducati | 45m 41.816s | 6.294s | 1m 37.132s | 95.537mph | M/H |
| 3 | Pedrosa | Honda | 45m 45.411s | 9.889s | 1m 36.937s | 95.412mph | M/H |
| 4 | Rossi | Yamaha | 45m 58.950s | 23.428s | 1m 37.348s | 94.944mph | M/H |
| 5 | Edwards | Yamaha | 46m 08.174s | 32.652s | 1m 37.751s | 94.628mph | M/H |
| 6 | Elias | Honda | 46m 11.231s | 35.709s | 1m 38.081s | 94.523mph | M/H |
| 7 | Dovizioso | Honda | 46m 11.245s | 35.723s | 1m 38.161s | 94.523mph | M/H |
| 8 | Hayden | Ducati | 46m 14.352s | 38.830s | 1m 38.168s | 94.417mph | M/H |
| 9 | Toseland | Yamaha | 46m 19.615s | 44.093s | 1m 38.419s | 94.239mph | M/H |
| 10 | Vermeulen | Suzuki | 46m 28.385s | 52.863s | 1m 38.930s | 93.942mph | S/M |
| 11 | De Puniet | Honda | 46m 31.220s | 55.698s | 1m 38.746s | 93.846mph | M/H |
| 12 | Melandri | Kawasaki | 46m 40.037s | 1m 04.515s | 1m 39.137s | 93.551mph | S/M |
| 13 | Canepa | Ducati | 46m 40.060s | 1m 04.538s | 1m 39.186s | 93.550mph | M/H |
| 14 | Talmacsi | Honda | 47m 02.821s | 1m 27.299s | 1m 39.383s | 92.796mph | S/M |
| | Capirossi | Suzuki | 33m 23.887s | 8 laps | 1m 38.291s | 93.370mph | M/H |
| | De Angelis | Honda | 13m 44.836s | 20 laps | 1m 38.600s | 90.735mph | S/M |
| | Kallio | Ducati | 8m 18.517s | 23 laps | 1m 37.937s | 93.830mph | M/H |

## CHAMPIONSHIP

| | Rider | Team | Points |
|---|---|---|---|
| 1 | Rossi | Fiat Yamaha Team | 250 |
| 2 | Lorenzo | Fiat Yamaha Team | 232 |
| 3 | Pedrosa | Repsol Honda Team | 173 |
| 4 | Stoner | Ducati Marlboro Team | 170 |
| 5 | Dovizioso | Repsol Honda Team | 142 |
| 6 | Edwards | Monster Yamaha Tech 3 | 134 |
| 7 | Capirossi | Rizla Suzuki MotoGP | 97 |
| 8 | De Puniet | LCR Honda MotoGP | 93 |
| 9 | Melandri | Hayate Racing Team | 91 |
| 10 | Elias | San Carlo Honda Gresini | 90 |
| 11 | Vermeulen | Rizla Suzuki MotoGP | 90 |
| 12 | De Angelis | San Carlo Honda Gresini | 88 |
| 13 | Toseland | Monster Yamaha Tech 3 | 85 |
| 14 | Hayden | Ducati Marlboro Team | 81 |
| 15 | Kallio | Pramac Racing | 51 |
| 16 | Canepa | Pramac Racing | 38 |
| 17 | Talmacsi | Scot Racing Team MotoGP | 14 |
| 18 | Gibernau | Grupo Francisco Hernando | 12 |
| 19 | Takahashi | Scot Racing Team MotoGP | 9 |
| 20 | Espargaro | Pramac Racing | 8 |

**8 NICKY HAYDEN** Not happy after a good warm-up, and handicapped in the race by his disappointing qualifying and the bike feeling much looser in the warmer conditions. Also had to watch his team-mate's near-miraculous comeback.

**9 JAMES TOSELAND** Visibly trying so hard in every session despite the news that he would be moving back to World Superbikes. Enjoyed the race, though fighting a bad cold, running the same lap times as Dovizioso and Elias. Also had a good battle with Hayden and Capirossi.

**10 CHRIS VERMEULEN** Handicapped by a bad back, the result of a motocross training incident, but it did get better as the weekend went on. One of only four riders

who went for the softer rear tyre; the bike moved around a lot towards the end of the race.

**11 RANDY DE PUNIET** Managed to undo his right boot on the frame in the first corner and spent two laps trying to adjust his footwear. Got back up, in front of Vermeulen, then had a near-highside which hurt his recently injured ankle, resulting in a painful last few laps.

**12 MARCO MELANDRI** A disappointing race for Marco, given that in '08 Kawasaki had one of their best weekends of the year here at Estoril.

**13 NICCOLO CANEPA** Disappointed to make a mistake early on and lose touch with

faster riders. Spent much of the latter part of the race fighting with Melandri, losing out to him by the smallest of margins. Also found out that he wouldn't be retained for 2010.

**14 GABOR TALMACSI** Scarcely improved his lap times over the weekend, and never got the feeling he needed from the bike. Could stay with the group for five or six laps but then his times dropped.

## NON-FINISHERS

**LORIS CAPIROSSI** Started well and ran in sixth before a mistake put him back a couple of places and into a fight with Hayden. Up to eighth and closing on the two Spaniards in front of him when a gear-position sensor failed

and put the engine management system into safe mode.

**ALEX DE ANGELIS** Stopped by an electrical fault while lying 11th before ten laps had been completed.

**MIKA KALLIO** A good weekend looked like delivering a career-best result until lap six when he lost the front. The crash came at a part of the track where riders are on constant throttle so he had no explanation: 'I was doing a really good race and suddenly I found my bottom on the ground.'

# BACK FROM THE EDGE

**Casey Stoner returned in triumph to make it three in a row at home, while Lorenzo's mistake put Rossi within touching distance of the title**

**E**very time Casey Stoner hit the brakes for the Honda hairpin, the hardest braking effort on the Phillip Island circuit, he grinned to himself. He knew that his problems were over. From Barcelona until Donington Park, he'd hit a wall mid-race and faded away from the leaders. Two weeks previously, in Portugal, he'd shown he was able to be competitive over the full distance again – but that was just a warm-up for his home race. If ever there were a justification for his unprecedented decision to sit out three races, here it was. Casey started from pole and led every lap bar the first on his way to retaining his unbeaten status on an 800cc MotoGP bike at his home race.

Watching his superb performance here, it was difficult to believe that there had ever been anything wrong with the Aussie. The Ducati Desmosedici shook and shimmied for the whole race, its wheels seemingly never in line as Casey put on a show worthy of the fastest racetrack on the calendar. And it wasn't a solo exhibition; he was pursued all the way by Valentino Rossi. The pair got past the fast-starting Pedrosa on the second lap and pulled away from Dani and Alex de Angelis, who had a very impressive weekend. There were no further changes of position among the top four, but Stoner and Rossi put on a breathtaking display. The left sides of the rear Bridgestones come in for a lot of use at Phillip Island, and more often than not they were having to cope simultaneously with high speeds, high lean angles and lots of power. All the leaders were soon sliding, and by the end of the race there was some spectacular drifting over Lukey Heights and the lefts that end the lap. 'Old style racing,' Rossi called it.

Valentino was certainly trying to win, although he

was never going to take any major risks, knowing that 20 points for second place would almost guarantee him another world title. The only rival who could prevent Rossi retaining the MotoGP crown, his team-mate Jorge Lorenzo, crashed before the first corner when he cut to the left and tagged Nicky Hayden's Ducati. The American was sent on a helter-skelter cross-country ride, but Lorenzo hit the ground hard. No doubt the knowledge that his title chances were all but gone hurt far more than the loss of some skin from his nose. Nicky refused to criticise Jorge afterwards, saying it wasn't his usual style to do something like that.

Rossi stayed within a second of Stoner for the whole race, occasionally closing right up, but he was never really in a position to try to make a pass. Of course Valentino knew he mustn't make a mistake, but when he ran up the kerbing at Turn 2 after going too deep at the first corner it was obvious just how hard he was trying. His team had informed him via the pit board that Jorge was out, and although Vale was adamant that he'd tried to win he said he was all too aware of what an error could mean, and later described the race as 'the most important second place of my career'. He'd also noticed that the colour of the letter U in 'out' on the board was a different colour from the others…strange the things a racer's mind picks up at 200mph.

Dani Pedrosa was again almost apologetic about finishing third. He ruefully said that he'd done his best, and that he was pleased about the rostrum but not about the gap between himself and the leading two riders. Fourth-placed de Angelis was a lot happier. He was quick from the first session and even held on to the leaders for a few laps. Not only did it put Alex to

## 'I'D FORGOTTEN HOW GOOD THAT WINNING FEELING IS AND OF ALL MY VICTORIES THIS IS PERHAPS THE MOST SPECIAL'
**CASEY STONER**

the front of the very tight contest for seventh in the championship, it gave him more ammunition in his fight to stay in MotoGP in 2010. He nearly undid all the good with his celebratory wheelie, though, as he drifted across the front straight and came scarily close to the pit wall.

Fortunately, trackside fans also had a spectacular group dice to enjoy before Rossi and Stoner came round again. Dovizioso, Kallio, Melandri, de Puniet, Toseland, Edwards and Elias were all involved in the frantic action at one time or another. Unfortunately, neither of the Suzukis was able to play a part in the battle. The GSV has never liked the sort of long, power-on curves that abound at Phillip Island, and this time the issue was compounded by an engine problem in Loris Capirossi's bike during warm-up, which meant he had to take an extra engine above and beyond the five allocated for the last seven races of the year. For this he was demoted to the back of the grid, but as he'd only qualified on the penultimate row it wasn't really a problem. Neither was the deduction from Suzuki's points total in the Constructors' Championship, because they only had Kawasaki behind them anyway. Team manager Paul Denning thanked his riders for persevering through a terrible weekend: 'There is nothing positive to say about the performance,' was his terse summary.

The renaissance of Stoner showed just what the championship had been missing, and it was also noticeable how warmly his rivals welcomed him back. Casey managed to hide the delight he no doubt felt at making his point so forcibly, although there were, of course, some oblique references to journalistic liberties. Of more relevance to the rest of the championship, and indeed for the 2010 season, was Casey's own analysis of the race: 'I'd forgotten how good that winning feeling is and of all my victories this is perhaps the most special. I can honestly say that from a physical perspective I can't ever remember feeling this strong after a race.' Time for the other three 'Aliens' to start worrying.

# A BAD DECISION

James Toseland obviously didn't think he'd done anything wrong. When he rode steadily down pitlane to take the penalty for his jump start, he wagged his finger at the Race Director accusingly. James's team manager Herve Poncharal later described the decision as 'extremely marginal.' It was a good choice of phrase, there was a suspicious lack of TV replays as well.

Post-race, James, who already knew he was out of a job in the MotoGP paddock in 2010, was incandescent with rage. He had been in the battle for fifth place on a track where he always goes well. Remember the battle with Rossi in 2008? Here was a chance to show the MotoGP team managers and paddock that they'd made a mistake in letting him go back to World Superbike in what is effectively a job-swap with Ben Spies.

How galling, then, to get to the next race, Malaysia, and find that Race Direction were offering an apology for making a mistake over James's penalty. Maybe there's a case to be made for making the jump-start rule less draconian, because at the moment there's no leeway, and of course no redress for a wrongly penalised rider.

**Right** James Toseland was distinctly unimpressed with his jump-start penalty

**Below** The fight for fifth, before James Toseland was given his ride through penalty

# AUSTRALIAN GP
## PHILLIP ISLAND
### ROUND 15
October 18

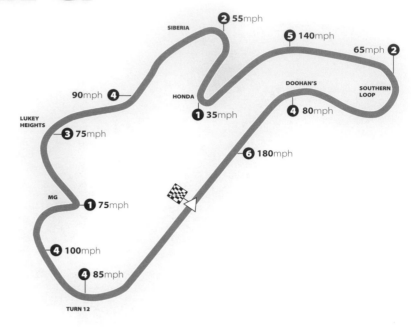

# RACE RESULTS

**CIRCUIT LENGTH** 2.760 miles
**NO. OF LAPS** 27
**RACE DISTANCE** 74.620 miles
**WEATHER** Dry, 16°C
**TRACK TEMPERATURE** 31°C
**WINNER** Casey Stoner
**FASTEST LAP** 1m 30.085s, 110.450mph, Valentino Rossi
**LAP RECORD** 1m 30.059s, 110.482mph, Nicky Hayden, 2008

## QUALIFYING

| | Rider | Nationality | Team | Qualifying | Pole + | Gap |
|---|---|---|---|---|---|---|
| 1 | Stoner | AUS | Ducati Marlboro Team | 1m 30.341s | | |
| 2 | Rossi | ITA | Fiat Yamaha Team | 1m 30.391s | 0.050s | 0.050s |
| 3 | Pedrosa | SPA | Repsol Honda Team | 1m 31.070s | 0.729s | 0.679s |
| 4 | Lorenzo | SPA | Fiat Yamaha Team | 1m 31.071s | 0.730s | 0.001s |
| 5 | Edwards | USA | Monster Yamaha Tech 3 | 1m 31.096s | 0.755s | 0.025s |
| 6 | De Angelis | RSM | San Carlo Honda Gresini | 1m 31.260s | 0.919s | 0.164s |
| 7 | Hayden | USA | Ducati Marlboro Team | 1m 31.325s | 0.984s | 0.065s |
| 8 | De Puniet | FRA | LCR Honda MotoGP | 1m 31.380s | 1.039s | 0.055s |
| 9 | Kallio | FIN | Pramac Racing | 1m 31.384s | 1.043s | 0.004s |
| 10 | Dovizioso | ITA | Repsol Honda Team | 1m 31.472s | 1.131s | 0.088s |
| 11 | Elias | SPA | San Carlo Honda Gresini | 1m 31.640s | 1.299s | 0.168s |
| 12 | Toseland | GBR | Monster Yamaha Tech 3 | 1m 31.722s | 1.381s | 0.082s |
| 13 | Capirossi | ITA | Rizla Suzuki MotoGP | 1m 31.873s | 1.532s | 0.151s |
| 14 | Melandri | ITA | Hayate Racing Team | 1m 32.190s | 1.849s | 0.317s |
| 15 | Vermeulen | ITA | Rizla Suzuki MotoGP | 1m 32.338s | 1.997s | 0.148s |
| 16 | Talmacsi | HUN | Scot Racing Team MotoGP | 1m 32.752s | 2.411s | 0.414s |
| * | Canepa | ITA | Pramac Racing | | | |

## FINISHERS

**1 CASEY STONER** This was Casey at his best, as if he'd never been away, seemingly on the ragged edge all race long in front of an ecstatic home crowd. Not surprisingly, called it the 'most special' of all his wins, but that didn't stop him mentioning his problems with traction all weekend.

**2 VALENTINO ROSSI** Pursued Stoner as hard as he dared once he knew Lorenzo was out, but had to avoid making any mistakes so decided to settle for second place and a 38-point lead. Thoroughly enjoyed an 'old style' race, with lots of sliding in the final laps.

**3 DANI PEDROSA** On the front row, but had had a big crash in qualifying. Got the holeshot, as usual, but from lap two onwards was in a lonely third place. Pushed to the maximum, but frustrated not to be able to run the pace of the leaders.

**4 ALEX DE ANGELIS** Another great result that saw him leap five places in the championship to head the fight for seventh. Fast in every session and got away with the front men, though said it had been 'an achievement' just to stick with them for a while before he was alone in fourth.

**5 COLIN EDWARDS** Another great ride, this time after a terrible start that put him back to ninth. Passed Dovizioso

on lap four and then three riders – de Puniet, Kallio and Elias – on lap five, before setting off in pursuit of de Angelis. Frustrated to be fifth again.

**6 ANDREA DOVIZIOSO** Suffered from a stomach bug (like Lorenzo) and failed to qualify well due to various set-up issues. A poor start, spent time getting ahead of the pack before pulling away, but encouraged in the second half as felt he and the bike were the best they'd been all weekend.

**7 MARCO MELANDRI** Very encouraging performance, from 14th on the grid, at a track where he'd won before. Fought with Dovi until he lost some stability on the brakes, then embroiled in a spectacular dice with de

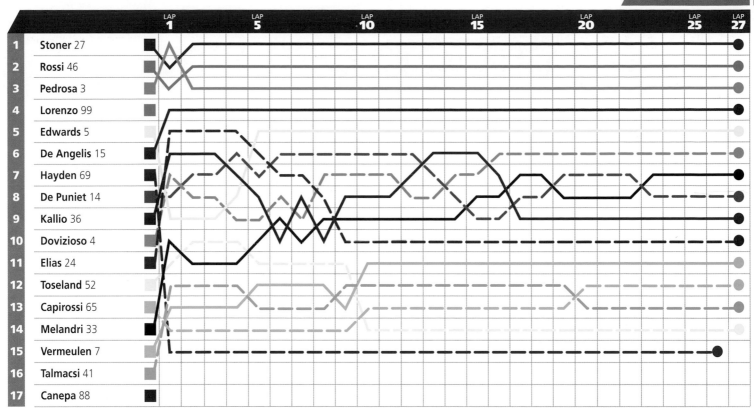

|  | | LAP 1 | LAP 5 | LAP 10 | LAP 15 | LAP 20 | LAP 25 | LAP 27 |
|---|---|---|---|---|---|---|---|---|
| 1 | Stoner 27 | | | | | | | |
| 2 | Rossi 46 | | | | | | | |
| 3 | Pedrosa 3 | | | | | | | |
| 4 | Lorenzo 99 | | | | | | | |
| 5 | Edwards 5 | | | | | | | |
| 6 | De Angelis 15 | | | | | | | |
| 7 | Hayden 69 | | | | | | | |
| 8 | De Puniet 14 | | | | | | | |
| 9 | Kallio 36 | | | | | | | |
| 10 | Dovizioso 4 | | | | | | | |
| 11 | Elias 24 | | | | | | | |
| 12 | Toseland 52 | | | | | | | |
| 13 | Capirossi 65 | | | | | | | |
| 14 | Melandri 33 | | | | | | | |
| 15 | Vermeulen 7 | | | | | | | |
| 16 | Talmacsi 41 | | | | | | | |
| 17 | Canepa 88 | | | | | | | |

## RACE

|  | Rider | Motorcycle | Race Time | Time + | Fastest Lap | Av Speed | |
|---|---|---|---|---|---|---|---|
| 1 | Stoner | Ducati | 40m 56.651s | | 1m 30.092s | 109.359mph | M/H |
| 2 | Rossi | Yamaha | 40m 58.586s | 1.935s | 1m 30.085s | 109.273mph | M/H |
| 3 | Pedrosa | Honda | 41m 19.269s | 22.618s | 1m 30.773s | 108.362mph | M/H |
| 4 | De Angelis | Honda | 41m 29.353s | 32.702s | 1m 30.826s | 107.922mph | M/H |
| 5 | Edwards | Yamaha | 41m 32.536s | 35.885s | 1m 31.273s | 107.785mph | M/H |
| 6 | Dovizioso | Honda | 41m 35.133s | 38.482s | 1m 31.570s | 107.673mph | M/H |
| 7 | Melandri | Kawasaki | 41m 41.112s | 44.461s | 1m 31.649s | 107.415mph | M/H |
| 8 | De Puniet | Honda | 41m 41.592s | 44.941s | 1m 31.443s | 107.395mph | M/H |
| 9 | Kallio | Ducati | 41m 50.996s | 54.345s | 1m 31.444s | 106.992mph | M/H |
| 10 | Elias | Honda | 41m 57.856s | 1m 01.205s | 1m 31.802s | 106.701mph | M/H |
| 11 | Vermeulen | Suzuki | 42m 02.068s | 1m 05.417s | 1m 32.815s | 106.523mph | M/XH |
| 12 | Capirossi | Suzuki | 42m 02.601s | 1m 05.950s | 1m 32.555s | 106.500mph | M/XH |
| 13 | Talmacsi | Honda | 42m 14.602s | 1m 17.951s | 1m 32.608s | 105.996mph | M/H |
| 14 | Toseland | Yamaha | 42m 14.636s | 1m 17.985s | 1m 31.666s | 105.995mph | M/H |
| 15 | Hayden | Ducati | 41m 27.127s | 1 lap | 1m 32.607s | 104.019mph | M/H |

## CHAMPIONSHIP

|  | Rider | Team | Points |
|---|---|---|---|
| 1 | Rossi | Fiat Yamaha Team | 270 |
| 2 | Lorenzo | Fiat Yamaha Team | 232 |
| 3 | Stoner | Ducati Marlboro Team | 195 |
| 4 | Pedrosa | Repsol Honda Team | 189 |
| 5 | Dovizioso | Repsol Honda Team | 152 |
| 6 | Edwards | Monster Yamaha Tech 3 | 145 |
| 7 | De Angelis | San Carlo Honda Gresini | 101 |
| 8 | De Puniet | LCR Honda MotoGP | 101 |
| 9 | Capirossi | Rizla Suzuki MotoGP | 101 |
| 10 | Melandri | Hayate Racing Team | 100 |
| 11 | Elias | San Carlo Honda Gresini | 96 |
| 12 | Vermeulen | Rizla Suzuki MotoGP | 95 |
| 13 | Toseland | Monster Yamaha Tech 3 | 87 |
| 14 | Hayden | Ducati Marlboro Team | 82 |
| 15 | Kallio | Pramac Racing | 58 |
| 16 | Canepa | Pramac Racing | 38 |
| 17 | Talmacsi | Scot Racing Team MotoGP | 17 |
| 18 | Gibernau | Grupo Francisco Hernando | 12 |
| 19 | Takahashi | Scot Racing Team MotoGP | 9 |
| 20 | Espargaro | Pramac Racing | 8 |

Puniet. A great result that keeps him in the hunt for seventh in the table.

**8 RANDY DE PUNIET** Stuck behind Elias early on, then involved in the group fight. His rear tyre started spinning and later he lost some confidence in the front, so couldn't challenge Melandri in the closing stages. Thought he should have been sixth.

**9 MIKA KALLIO** His best qualifying performance of the season so far was followed by a race of two parts. He was in the dice for sixth before he had a front-tyre problem and decided to go for the finish rather than repeat the crash of Estoril.

**10 TONI ELIAS** Knew he'd have traction problems here, and he wasn't wrong. Could only get the best out of the tyres for six or seven laps.

**11 CHRIS VERMEULEN** Suzuki had a terrible weekend – Chris fitted the harder tyre and it took time to get heat into it, and he ended up simply trying to keep his team-mate behind him.

**12 LORIS CAPIROSSI** Sent to the back of the grid because he had to use an extra engine, above and beyond the five allocated for the last seven races of the year. Had no feeling for the first six laps, then followed his team-mate home.

**13 GABOR TALMACSI** Happy with the bike in the long left that ends the lap

but still struggling with rapid changes of direction. More confident with how things were progressing than in previous races.

**14 JAMES TOSELAND** Got a drive-through penalty for a jump start, which his team manager described as 'very marginal'. James wasn't happy. On the back of the group fighting for fifth when he did the ride-through but looking strong at a track where he'd always been fast.

**15 NICKY HAYDEN** More bad luck… got his best start of the year only to be punted off by an errant Lorenzo on the way down to Turn 1. Got back on track with a damaged motorcycle and kept going, hoping for rain so he could change bikes. He was out of luck there, too.

## NON-FINISHERS

**JORGE LORENZO** First time all season he didn't get on the front row. Moved across and hit Hayden, and went down hard before the first corner. Lucky to escape serious injury, although the same cannot be said for his championship chances. Admitted the crash had been his fault.

## NON-STARTERS

**NICCOLO CANEPA** Crashed in the first session and injured his right arm, somehow suffering a serious enough abrasion to need a skin graft to the inside of his elbow. Fortunately the nerve damage that was initially diagnosed turned out to be a false alarm.

# MALAYSIAN GP
## SEPANG INTERNATIONAL CIRCUIT
### ROUND 16
**October 25**

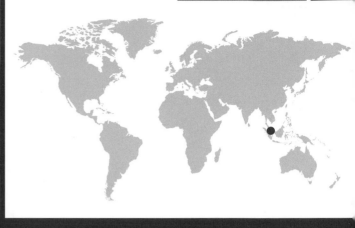

# CLOUD NINE

**Valentino Rossi duly wrapped up his ninth World Championship as Casey Stoner romped to the most dominant win of the year**

Third place was good enough for Valentino Rossi to retain his world title, although the race wasn't as simple as it might have been. Just as the MotoGP grid assembled, the heavens opened and a real tropical downpour delayed the start by over half an hour. There had been no wet practice so Rossi got in two sighting laps to try and gauge conditions. Lorenzo wanted to do the same, but had trouble with his number-one bike and was late getting out on his second machine. That put him to the back of the grid. As Jorge was the only man who could stop Rossi becoming champion again, albeit with the aid of several Acts of God, this seemed to confirm that Rossi would take the title before the race had even started.

However, nothing is ever that simple in motorcycle racing and the Malaysian round became a tale of two starts, with Lorenzo getting what must have been the best one of his career and Rossi making a complete mess of the first corner. He ran wide and was back in eighth at Turn 2. Two corners later, Lorenzo was on his back wheel. A corner later and Lorenzo was in front of his rival, with Marco Melandri now attacking Valentino. This definitely wasn't in the script.

Things were more predictable at the front of the field. Dani Pedrosa had, as is his habit, led into the first corner, but Casey Stoner went past before the end of the first lap and started to pull away at a quite astonishing rate. At one point he was lapping the best part of three seconds a lap faster than anyone else – and when he saw three seconds on his pit board he pressed even harder. In the end Rossi and Pedrosa set better fastest laps than Casey, but it was the Aussie's speed when the weather was at its worst that did the

'I KEPT PULLING OUT A SECOND A LAP AND THEN EVENTUALLY DECIDED TO BACK IT OFF AND NOT TAKE ANY RISKS'
**CASEY STONER**

damage. Stoner and the Ducati looked as perfect under monsoon conditions as they'd done a week earlier in the temperate sunshine of Phillip Island.

The Ducati isn't known as a bike that's rider-friendly in the wet, but the combination of the Desmosedici's electronics and Casey's throttle control (mainly the latter, it has to be said) was unbeatable. It wasn't just Stoner who went well on a red bike, though, because Nicky Hayden had his best weekend of the year, with the exception of the rostrum at Indianapolis. One around-the-outside overtake on Lorenzo reminded everyone of the American's talent – and for once he escaped unscathed from the barging in the first couple of bends.

It may well be that the bike with the most sophisticated electronics – the Yamaha – was at a disadvantage at the start of the race. Yamaha's mu-Learning system learns as the race goes on, but that means it starts by restricting the amount of power it lets the rider apply, gradually increasing it as the laps go by. The less sophisticated systems of the Ducati, and also the other Japanese bikes, allowed Stoner and Pedrosa to step closer to the edge and pull out significant gaps while Rossi was fighting for eighth place with Melandri and the Kawasaki. When the rain stopped the Yamaha was able to close on the Hondas, now lying in second and third places. Dovizioso was harassing Pedrosa when he crashed, and although Rossi closed on Dani he didn't press too hard once a dry line appeared in some parts of the track.

Rossi came nearest to disaster when he passed Lorenzo and immediately had a slide that flicked him out of the saddle, but Jorge couldn't take advantage.

**Opposite** Stoner was in a class of his own and at one point he led by over 20 seconds

**Above** Tension on the grid as riders prepare for the wet race that no-one had expected

**Below** Chris Vermeulen again proved that there aren't many better riders in the wet

The fact that he was as high up the order as fourth was cause for some amazement. This was the third GP at which Lorenzo had had a pre-race disaster (the others had been at Le Mans and Mugello), yet he was able to block out the mistakes and ride not just quickly but also competitively against the other 'Aliens'. No wonder Valentino said afterwards that this had been his toughest World Championship.

Casey Stoner eventually won the race by nearly 15 seconds, and it could have been even more. Pedrosa was second throughout, bar the first half-lap, to achieve what was, amazingly, his first ever MotoGP rostrum in wet conditions. He looked more relieved than pleased. Valentino achieved the minimum requirement for a World Champion, standing on the rostrum of the race

where he'd clinched the crown. But not before another crowd-pleasing stunt had taken place. The fan club was waiting for him with a real live chicken, dressed up in T-shirt and helmet. This wasn't really the return of Osvaldo the Chicken from his 250 days, but actually a reference to an Italian proverb: 'An old chicken can't lay eggs but it makes good soup' – hence the elderly chicken depicted on the T-shirts and the egg with a number nine on it. At the ripe old age of 30, Valentino was now an 'old chicken' compared to his three main rivals, but he could still lay eggs!

With the World Championship settled and Lorenzo only needing a solitary point from the final race of the year for second place in the championship, attention shifted to the battle between Pedrosa and Stoner for third, between Edwards and Dovizioso for fifth, and between most of the rest of the field for seventh. Toni Elias had a good weekend while the man who started the day in seventh, Alex de Angelis, didn't – a total reversal of the usual wet-weather form of the Team Gresini riders. The unhappiest man at the finish, however, was undoubtedly Loris Capirossi. He qualified well, in fifth, and looked to be on for a good race, but his chances were ended by the weather. It was a cruel blow for the Suzuki team, who'd looked hopeful after the disaster of Phillip Island. At least Chris Vermeulen reminded us what a good rain rider he is, even if he dislikes that label.

So Rossi got what he wanted, the title safely wrapped up before the last round at Valencia, a circuit that's never been kind to him. He was generous in his praise of the Yamaha crew – and about his team-mate. All that was left was to speculate on whether he would be around long enough to break yet more records.

**Above** Dani Pedrosa splashed his way to his first ever wet-weather podium in MotoGP

**Opposite** Old chicken Rossi proves he can still lay an egg – his ninth!

**Below** Aleix Espargaro had another impressive stand-in ride for Pramac Ducati

# RECORD BREAKER

- Rossi has now matched Mike Hailwood's and Carlo Ubbiali's records, with nine titles in all classes. Only Agostini, with 15 titles, has more.
- Rossi's win at Assen made him only the second rider in history to take 100 wins in all classes. He now has 103, 19 fewer than Agostini's all-time record of 122.
- He already held the record for all-time premier-class victories, having surpassed Agostini's tally at Indianapolis in 2008. Currently, he has 77 500cc/MotoGP wins.
- Rossi's win at Brno saw him take the all-time podium record with his 160th podium across all classes. He's also the only rider to have stood on the podium in the premier class more than 100 times. The Sepang podium was his 163rd in all classes.
- With 44 wins from 102 races since he joined the factory in 2004, Rossi is the most successful Yamaha rider of all time. He has 21 more wins than Kenny Roberts Senior, Yamaha's next most successful rider.
- His 2009 title means Valentino has now won more titles for Yamaha than for any of the other manufacturers for whom he has ridden in his career.
- The win at Misano in 2009 was his 11th win in all classes on home soil.
- Rossi is the only rider in history to have won at least one GP in 14 successive seasons.
- In 1997 Rossi became the second-youngest 125cc World Champion after scoring 321 points and 11 wins. Two years later he became the youngest-ever 250cc World Champion with nine wins.
- In 2001 Rossi joined Phil Read as one of only two riders ever to win the 125cc, 250cc and 500cc titles.
- Rossi's debut victory for Yamaha at the opening race of 2004 in South Africa made him the first rider in history to take back-to-back wins for different manufacturers.
- After winning the MotoGP World Championship three times with Honda, Rossi took his fourth premier-class title with Yamaha in 2004 and became the only rider other than Eddie Lawson to win consecutive premier-class titles for different manufacturers.
- Rossi remains the only rider to win the premier-class title on four different types of motorcycle: Honda 500cc four-cylinder two-stroke, Honda 990cc five-cylinder four-stroke, Yamaha 990cc four-cylinder four-stroke and Yamaha 800cc four-cylinder four-stroke.
- Rossi has never missed a GP since his 125cc debut in 1996. He has started 226 successive races in all classes, 166 of which have been in the premier class. Both of these are records.

# MALAYSIAN GP
## SEPANG INTERNATIONAL CIRCUIT

### ROUND 16
October 25

## RACE RESULTS

**CIRCUIT LENGTH** 3.447 miles
**NO. OF LAPS** 21
**RACE DISTANCE** 72.394 miles
**WEATHER** Wet, 27°C
**TRACK TEMPERATURE** 22°C
**WINNER** Casey Stoner
**FASTEST LAP** 2m 13.694s, 92.827mph, Valentino Rossi
**LAP RECORD** 2m 02.108s, 101.635mph, Casey Stoner, 2007

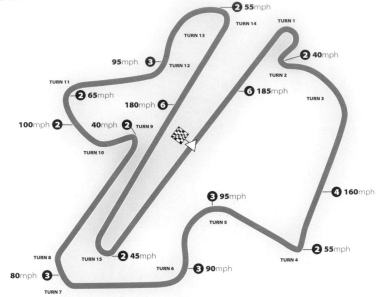

## QUALIFYING

| | Rider | Nationality | Team | Qualifying | Pole + | Gap |
|---|---|---|---|---|---|---|
| 1 | Rossi | ITA | Fiat Yamaha Team | 2m 00.518s | | |
| 2 | Lorenzo | SPA | Fiat Yamaha Team | 2m 01.087s | 0.569s | 0.569s |
| 3 | Pedrosa | SPA | Repsol Honda Team | 2m 01.254s | 0.736s | 0.167s |
| 4 | Stoner | AUS | Ducati Marlboro Team | 2m 01.455s | 0.937s | 0.201s |
| 5 | Capirossi | ITA | Rizla Suzuki MotoGP | 2m 01.716s | 1.198s | 0.261s |
| 6 | Elias | SPA | San Carlo Honda Gresini | 2m 01.918s | 1.400s | 0.202s |
| 7 | Hayden | USA | Ducati Marlboro Team | 2m 01.980s | 1.462s | 0.062s |
| 8 | De Puniet | FRA | LCR Honda MotoGP | 2m 02.098s | 1.580s | 0.118s |
| 9 | Edwards | USA | Monster Yamaha Tech 3 | 2m 02.195s | 1.677s | 0.097s |
| 10 | De Angelis | RSM | San Carlo Honda Gresini | 2m 02.274s | 1.756s | 0.079s |
| 11 | Dovizioso | ITA | Repsol Honda Team | 2m 02.362s | 1.844s | 0.088s |
| 12 | Kallio | FIN | Pramac Racing | 2m 02.435s | 1.917s | 0.073s |
| 13 | Espargaro | SPA | Pramac Racing | 2m 02.859s | 2.341s | 0.424s |
| 14 | Vermeulen | AUS | Rizla Suzuki MotoGP | 2m 03.032s | 2.514s | 0.173s |
| 15 | Melandri | ITA | Hayate Racing Team | 2m 03.088s | 2.570s | 0.056s |
| 16 | Toseland | GBR | Monster Yamaha Tech 3 | 2m 03.528s | 3.010s | 0.440s |
| 17 | Talmacsi | HUN | Scot Racing Team MotoGP | 2m 03.874s | 3.356s | 0.346s |

## FINISHERS

**1 CASEY STONER** Most dominant win of the year despite an average start from fourth on the grid. Got to the front on the first lap, then able to pull away at a second a lap, although he did back off slightly late on. His fourth victory in 2009 and the first win ever at Sepang by a rider not starting on the front row.

**2 DANI PEDROSA** His first wet-weather podium in MotoGP came from Dani's usual holeshot; only Stoner got past him. The other Repsol Honda man, Dovizioso, closed in but crashed trying to take second place off his team-mate. Was able to push late on and dissuade Rossi from attacking.

**3 VALENTINO ROSSI** Made a mess of the first corner, dropping to tenth from pole, but upped the pace later to clinch his ninth world title with a rostrum finish. Survived a massive slide as he passed Lorenzo, and decided against chasing Pedrosa as the wet tyres started to slide on the drying track.

**4 JORGE LORENZO** Another pre-race drama – as at Le Mans and Mugello – put him to the back of the grid, but got one of his best starts ever and passed 12 riders, including his team-mate, on the way to an amazing fourth-place finish. Had grip problems in the later stages, just as he had in practice and qualifying.

**5 NICKY HAYDEN** His best race apart from Indianapolis. On the pace all weekend and encouraged when it rained as he's always been quick on the Ducati in wet conditions. Got a bad start and had to fight his way up the order, and then hold off rain specialist Vermeulen.

**6 CHRIS VERMEULEN** Again suffered from lowly qualifying, so victim of pushing and shoving in the first corners, then took five laps to get any feel from his wet tyres. Underlined his wet-weather reputation with a smooth ride through the pack, but couldn't get on terms with Hayden when the track started drying.

**7 TONI ELIAS** Surprised everyone, especially himself, with a competitive wet-weather ride. Held fourth place early on and didn't lose much ground when riders started coming past. The useful points

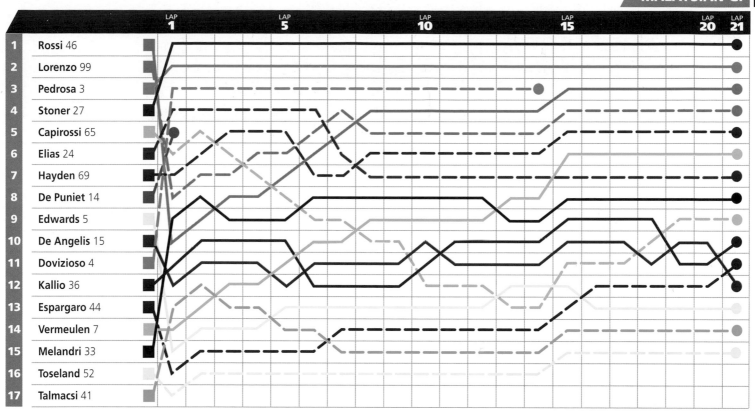

| | | LAP 1 | LAP 5 | LAP 10 | LAP 15 | LAP 20 | LAP 21 |
|---|---|---|---|---|---|---|---|
| 1 | Rossi 46 | | | | | | |
| 2 | Lorenzo 99 | | | | | | |
| 3 | Pedrosa 3 | | | | | | |
| 4 | Stoner 27 | | | | | | |
| 5 | Capirossi 65 | | | | | | |
| 6 | Elias 24 | | | | | | |
| 7 | Hayden 69 | | | | | | |
| 8 | De Puniet 14 | | | | | | |
| 9 | Edwards 5 | | | | | | |
| 10 | De Angelis 15 | | | | | | |
| 11 | Dovizioso 4 | | | | | | |
| 12 | Kallio 36 | | | | | | |
| 13 | Espargaro 44 | | | | | | |
| 14 | Vermeulen 7 | | | | | | |
| 15 | Melandri 33 | | | | | | |
| 16 | Toseland 52 | | | | | | |
| 17 | Talmacsi 41 | | | | | | |

## RACE

| | Rider | Motorcycle | Race Time | Time + | Fastest Lap | Av Speed | B |
|---|---|---|---|---|---|---|---|
| 1 | Stoner | Ducati | 47m 24.834s | | 2m 14.120s | 91.616mph | w |
| 2 | Pedrosa | Honda | 47m 39.500s | 14.666s | 2m 13.765s | 91.146mph | w |
| 3 | Rossi | Yamaha | 47m 44.219s | 19.385s | 2m 13.694s | 90.995mph | w |
| 4 | Lorenzo | Yamaha | 47m 50.684s | 25.850s | 2m 14.157s | 90.790mph | w |
| 5 | Hayden | Ducati | 48m 03.539s | 38.705s | 2m 15.258s | 90.386mph | w |
| 6 | Vermeulen | Suzuki | 48m 05.895s | 41.061s | 2m 14.820s | 90.312mph | w |
| 7 | Elias | Honda | 48m 13.389s | 48.555s | 2m 15.958s | 90.078mph | w |
| 8 | Melandri | Kawasaki | 48m 20.391s | 55.557s | 2m 15.678s | 89.861mph | w |
| 9 | Capirossi | Suzuki | 48m 25.137s | 1m 00.303s | 2m 15.854s | 89.714mph | w |
| 10 | Kallio | Ducati | 48m 25.274s | 1m 00.440s | 2m 15.894s | 89.710mph | w |
| 11 | Espargaro | Ducati | 48m 26.489s | 1m 01.655s | 2m 16.158s | 89.672mph | w |
| 12 | De Angelis | Honda | 48m 26.681s | 1m 01.847s | 2m 16.402s | 89.666mph | w |
| 13 | Edwards | Yamaha | 48m 35.612s | 1m 10.778s | 2m 16.769s | 89.392mph | w |
| 14 | Talmacsi | Honda | 48m 40.685s | 1m 15.851s | 2m 17.072s | 89.236mph | w |
| 15 | Toseland | Yamaha | 49m 15.506s | 1m 50.672s | 2m 18.824s | 88.185mph | w |
| 16 | Dovizioso | Honda | 31m 59.321s | 7 laps | 2m 14.423s | 90.529mph | w |
| 17 | De Puniet | Honda | 2m 28.718s | 20 laps | 2m 28.718s | 83.453mph | w |

## CHAMPIONSHIP

| | Rider | Team | Points |
|---|---|---|---|
| 1 | Rossi | Fiat Yamaha Team | 286 |
| 2 | Lorenzo | Fiat Yamaha Team | 245 |
| 3 | Stoner | Ducati Marlboro Team | 220 |
| 4 | Pedrosa | Repsol Honda Team | 209 |
| 5 | Dovizioso | Repsol Honda Team | 152 |
| 6 | Edwards | Monster Yamaha Tech 3 | 148 |
| 7 | Melandri | Hayate Racing Team | 108 |
| 8 | Capirossi | Rizla Suzuki MotoGP | 108 |
| 9 | De Angelis | San Carlo Honda Gresini | 105 |
| 10 | Elias | San Carlo Honda Gresini | 105 |
| 11 | Vermeulen | Rizla Suzuki MotoGP | 105 |
| 12 | De Puniet | LCR Honda MotoGP | 101 |
| 13 | Hayden | Ducati Marlboro Team | 93 |
| 14 | Toseland | Monster Yamaha Tech 3 | 88 |
| 15 | Kallio | Pramac Racing | 64 |
| 16 | Canepa | Pramac Racing | 38 |
| 17 | Talmacsi | Scot Racing Team MotoGP | 19 |
| 18 | Espargaro | Pramac Racing | 13 |
| 19 | Gibernau | Grupo Francisco Hernando | 12 |
| 20 | Takahashi | Scot Racing Team MotoGP | 9 |

haul put Toni up to equal ninth in the championship, and only three points off seventh place.

**8 MARCO MELANDRI** Competitive in the wet, as usual, exchanging places with Rossi in the early stages. However, he had more problems with the throttle twistgrip which he said prevented a much better result, even a repeat of the Le Mans rostrum.

**9 LORIS CAPIROSSI** Bitterly disappointed that the race in no way lived up to his expectations. A previous win at Sepang, and qualifying on the second row, gave him hopes of a rostrum. Got away well but took at least ten laps to get any feeling from his tyres, by which time he was way down.

**10 MIKA KALLIO** Lacked confidence in the rear under acceleration. Disappointed – felt he would have been a lot more competitive in the dry.

**11 ALEIX ESPARGARO** Another intelligent race. Spent the first five laps trying to understand the Desmosedici in the wet: 'I couldn't believe how slow I was going!' Then closed the gap on the group of four in front of him and passed two of them.

**12 ALEX DE ANGELIS** His usual wet-weather form deserted him completely. The tyre was spinning up all race so could only bring it home for a few points. Dropped two places in the table but still only three points off seventh place in the championship.

**13 COLIN EDWARDS** A seriously disappointing weekend for both Tech 3 riders, although Colin did close in on Dovizioso's fifth place in the championship thanks to the Italian's crash. Reported he could carry lean angle but couldn't load the front to make the bike turn.

**14 GABOR TALMACSI** Running the same lap times as the men in 10th and 11th places at the end, but suffered from a lack of experience with the bike in the wet.

**15 JAMES TOSELAND** Thought the rain would give him a chance of improving on his dismal qualifying, but had the same sort of rear grip problems in the wet as in the dry. Reverted to his base setting for the race, but corner entry was the problem; he just couldn't carry any corner speed.

## NON-FINISHERS

**RANDY DE PUNIET** Highsided at Turn 3 on the second lap after a good start. Lucky to avoid injury.

**ANDREA DOVIZIOSO** Was in third and closing on his team-mate when he lost the rear and crashed, without injury.

## NON-STARTERS

**NICCOLO CANEPA** Still recovering from the skin graft to his right elbow that was the result of his practice crash a week earlier in Australia.

# VALENCIAN GP

CIRCUITO RICARDO TORMO

**ROUND 17**

**November 8**

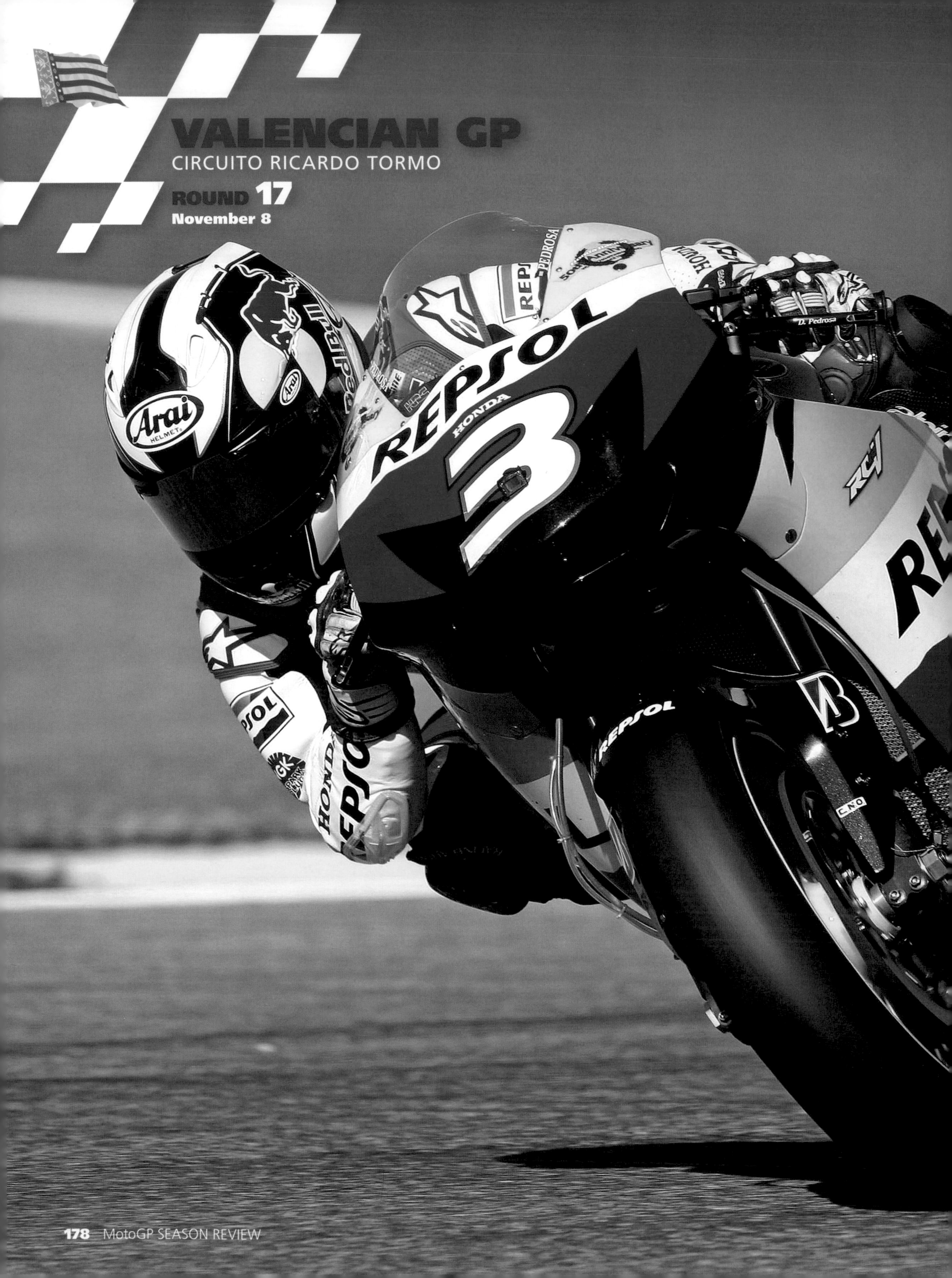

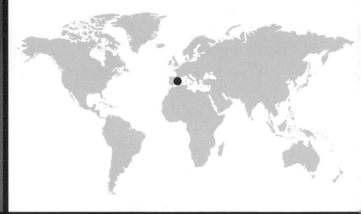

# LAST GASP

**Dani Pedrosa took his second win of the year at the final round as Casey Stoner failed to make it round the warm-up lap**

**W**ith the title already wrapped up and Jorge Lorenzo needing just one point to secure second place overall, it didn't look as if Valencia would produce anything special, though there were a few sub-plots to unravel. These included the fight between Colin Edwards and Andrea Dovizioso for fifth overall in the championship behind the four 'Aliens', the six-man fight for seventh place in the table, and the confrontation between James Toseland and Ben Spies, who would be swapping jobs over winter.

The championship might have been sorted some weeks previously, but there were plenty of scores left to settle. The arrival of the first wild card of the year, new World Superbike Champion Ben Spies on a fifth Yamaha M-1, was the real story of the weekend. The Texan was careful to downplay his chances in the run-up to the race, saying that no-one understood just how fast these guys were, that he had a very 'Superbike' riding style, that this would be the biggest learning experience of his career, and so on. The new boy's most impressive aspect was his methodical approach. No tyre or setting changes were made in the first sessions, but he did alter elements of his riding style, and the data showed he was already doing things differently – and automatically – by the end of the first hour. In among the downbeat pronouncements, Ben let one interesting opinion slip out: 'I can understand what Rossi and Lorenzo are doing with the M-1, but Casey's from a different planet.'

Not a bad assessment. Despite a strong, blustery wind and a cool racetrack, Stoner ripped to pole position by over a quarter of a second. It was normal service; no long runs, just blazing speed in short bursts. The new Ducati bodywork that debuted at Estoril helped.

'It made things consistent. I can keep the weight on the front.' By the end of qualifying it looked as if all Casey had to do on Sunday was turn up and he'd end his fractured season with a hat-trick of wins. The only man who looked as if he could be in with a chance of challenging was Dani Pedrosa. For the previous three years Dani has won two races each season, yet he came to the final round of 2009 with just one victory to his name. He'd made it very clear in the Spanish media in the run-up to Valencia that this wasn't enough. By his own admission, he had to win.

The Fiat Yamaha team was in some disarray. Lorenzo was wondering whether to ride a conservative race, make sure he didn't crash and clinch the championship runner-up spot. On the other hand, he was going well at a circuit where he has never won in any class, and he certainly didn't want to let a fellow-countryman hog the limelight. Rossi's case was different. He didn't have any rear grip, he was convinced he couldn't win the race, and he was wondering if the way he liked to set up a bike just wasn't compatible with the Valencia circuit. Once again, Jerry Burgess and his crew were going to throw in a major modification for Sunday morning warm-up. It usually worked, but the last time they'd tried to do it, at Estoril, it certainly hadn't.

Race day was just as blowy as the first two days of the GP weekend, and the wind had a completely unexpected say in the outcome of the race. Quite a few teams used windbreaks to shield their tyre warmers and help keep the Bridgestones hot. Despite the ambient temperature, all of the top four men went with the harder tyre option. For the last two

seasons, Ducati have had to conserve every last drop of fuel for the race, so Stoner has always run a slow warm-up lap. He did the same again this time, but the combination of the wind and his gentle progress caught him out. Casey highsided on his cold tyres on the warm-up lap, so he didn't even get to the start. The opposition was somewhat confused when the man with the red flag walked off the grid with no pole-position rider in place.

With Stoner missing from the race, Pedrosa was able to get his normal holeshot. Behind the rapidly disappearing Dani, Toni Elias, soon to be unemployed,

**Above** Ben Spies at work learning the track, learning the Bridgestones, learning the M-1

**Below** Pedrosa leads Elias on the first lap. Unusually, there were empty seats in the grandstands at Valencia – just the 94,000 people then

**Opposite** Casey Stoner looks on in shock as the marshals drag away his Ducati after his highside on the warm-up lap

**Left** Spies wore his World Superbike colours plus a US Air Force roundel on his crash helmet

**Opposite** Colin Edwards' splendid fourth place gave him fifth overall in the championship

'I CAN UNDERSTAND WHAT ROSSI AND LORENZO ARE DOING WITH THE M-1, BUT CASEY'S FROM A DIFFERENT PLANET'
**BEN SPIES**

came through from the third row to remind everyone yet again of his speed. It took Lorenzo three laps to get past him. Next time round, Jorge made a big mistake and Rossi was through to second. However, Valentino was now over two seconds adrift of the Repsol Honda. The order of the top three was already settled. Colin Edwards got up to fourth and was obviously not going to progress any further. His rival for fifth overall, Andrea Dovizioso, had a terrible start but when he cut through the pack to seventh his championship position looked safe. Then Edwards found an ally in his future team-mate and fellow Texan, Ben Spies, who relieved Dovi of seventh place some six laps from the flag. That move took a point away from Andrea, and Colin claimed fifth in the table to underline his status as best rider of the year after the top four. And Toni Elias won the scrap for seventh overall in the championship, his best ever finish in MotoGP.

So Dani Pedrosa took the victory and saved his season with an efficient win in front of his fellow-countrymen, as the Fiat Yamahas flew in formation behind him. Lorenzo made a late attack but couldn't quite get on terms. The real interest was in those sub-plots back in the pack. Ben Spies refused to get excited by seventh place, saying he was more interested in the lap times than his finishing position, but he did let slip another interesting line: 'It feels like winning a Superbike race.' Mick Doohan said on Saturday that he fully expected Spies to be well up in the top ten. Five times champions are usually right. Mick thinks Ben will win a race next year.

# FIGHTBACK

*More evidence of the Honda Racing Company's aggressive new approach to rediscovering competitiveness came to light at Valencia. The paddock already knew that data technicians and mechanics from Jorge Lorenzo's side of the Fiat Yamaha garage were on their way to HRC for 2010, but the announcement that Livio Suppo, project manager for Ducati's MotoGP effort since its inception in 2003, would also be going to Honda came as a major shock.*

*Suppo will join Honda as marketing director, and he won't have a direct management role within the Repsol Honda team. Add in the decision to make satellite teams' bikes much closer in specification to the factory bikes in 2010 than was the case this year, plus the new chassis debuted at the post-Valencia test, and it's clear that Shuhei Nakamoto, HRC Vice-President and the man in charge on the ground, is getting serious. Nakamoto-san started his career at HRC as part of the team designing the RS125 and 250 production racers, and in 1990 he became Large Project Leader before moving to Honda's Formula 1 team in 2000.*

*Back with bikes from the start of this season, he has brought with him an uncompromising attitude to racing that many thought left HRC with the legendary Oguma-san, team manager in the era of Wayne Gardner and Mick Doohan. It cannot be long before Nakamoto brings this attitude to bear on the matter of rider recruitment. He was overtly critical of Andrea Dovizioso in mid-season, not something to be expected from Japanese management, and he's not convinced that Honda can win back the title with its current riders. Expect serious advances in the direction of Jorge Lorenzo and Casey Stoner very early next season.*

# VALENCIAN GP
## CIRCUITO RICARDO TORMO

### ROUND 17
November 8

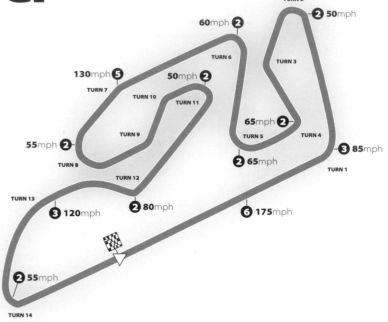

## RACE RESULTS

**CIRCUIT LENGTH** 2.488 miles
**NO. OF LAPS** 30
**RACE DISTANCE** 74.640 miles
**WEATHER** Dry, 19 C
**TRACK TEMPERATURE** 29°C
**WINNER** Dani Pedrosa
**FASTEST LAP** 1m 32.778s, 96.563mph, Dani Pedrosa
**LAP RECORD** 1m 32.582s, 96.767mph, Casey Stoner, 2008

## QUALIFYING

| | Rider | Nationality | Team | Qualifying | Pole + | Gap |
|---|---|---|---|---|---|---|
| 1 | Stoner | AUS | Ducati Marlboro Team | 1m 32.256s | | |
| 2 | Pedrosa | SPA | Repsol Honda Team | 1m 32.519s | 0.263s | 0.263s |
| 3 | Lorenzo | SPA | Fiat Yamaha Team | 1m 32.537s | 0.281s | 0.018s |
| 4 | Rossi | ITA | Fiat Yamaha Team | 1m 32.922s | 0.666s | 0.385s |
| 5 | Edwards | USA | Monster Yamaha Tech 3 | 1m 33.085s | 0.829s | 0.163s |
| 6 | Hayden | USA | Ducati Marlboro Team | 1m 33.154s | 0.898s | 0.069s |
| 7 | De Puniet | FRA | LCR Honda MotoGP | 1m 33.391s | 1.135s | 0.237s |
| 8 | Elias | SPA | San Carlo Honda Gresini | 1m 33.475s | 1.219s | 0.084s |
| 9 | Spies | USA | Sterilgarda Yamaha Team | 1m 33.539s | 1.283s | 0.064s |
| 10 | Dovizioso | ITA | Repsol Honda Team | 1m 33.678s | 1.422s | 0.139s |
| 11 | Kallio | FIN | Pramac Racing | 1m 33.809s | 1.553s | 0.131s |
| 12 | De Angelis | RSM | San Carlo Honda Gresini | 1m 33.844s | 1.588s | 0.035s |
| 13 | Capirossi | ITA | Rizla Suzuki MotoGP | 1m 34.097s | 1.841s | 0.253s |
| 14 | Toseland | GBR | Monster Yamaha Tech 3 | 1m 34.107s | 1.851s | 0.010s |
| 15 | Melandri | ITA | Hayate Racing Team | 1m 34.188s | 1.932s | 0.081s |
| 16 | Espargaro | SPA | Pramac Racing | 1m 34.308s | 2.052s | 0.120s |
| 17 | Talmacsi | HUN | Scot Racing Team MotoGP | 1m 34.357s | 2.101s | 0.049s |
| 18 | Vermeulen | AUS | Rizla Suzuki MotoGP | 1m 34.537s | 2.281s | 0.180s |

## FINISHERS

**1 DANI PEDROSA** Maintained his record of two race victories a year since coming to MotoGP, riding immaculately to lead every lap and round off a difficult season with a resounding win. He simply didn't put a foot wrong and even the Fiat Yamahas couldn't get within range.

**2 VALENTINO ROSSI** Went much better than expected after qualifying fourth. Unlike Estoril, the team found a magic bullet overnight so the bike had rear grip. An early dice with Elias and Lorenzo meant Dani was already 2s ahead when Vale got into second; he was happy to settle for that.

**3 JORGE LORENZO** Going well when a big mistake in a slow right-hander flicked Jorge violently out of the saddle, triggering the airbag in his leathers. It took a lap to go down, and it hurt. With composure recovered, he made it home for a rostrum finish – and second in the championship after Stoner's exit.

**4 COLIN EDWARDS** Shadowed Elias early on, then moved past into fourth to equal his best finish of the year. Also achieved his objective in the championship, with some help from fellow Texan Spies, who passed Dovizioso late in the race to ensure Colin was fifth overall – by a single point.

**5 NICKY HAYDEN** A second consecutive top-five finish to end the season: after a tough year he was getting to grips with the Ducati. Thought he should have been able to race with Edwards, but a slipping clutch and issues with grip meant he had to concentrate on keeping Elias behind him.

**6 TONI ELIAS** Another fighting race after a brilliant start from the third row. Into second place by Turn 2 after riding round the outside of Rossi in the first corner. Sixth was good enough to secure seventh in the championship – the main objective for Toni and the Gresini team.

**7 BEN SPIES** A brilliant wild-card debut for Yamaha. Played down his chances and got on with the job – a good start (which he didn't expect), followed by a difficult first half-dozen laps (which he

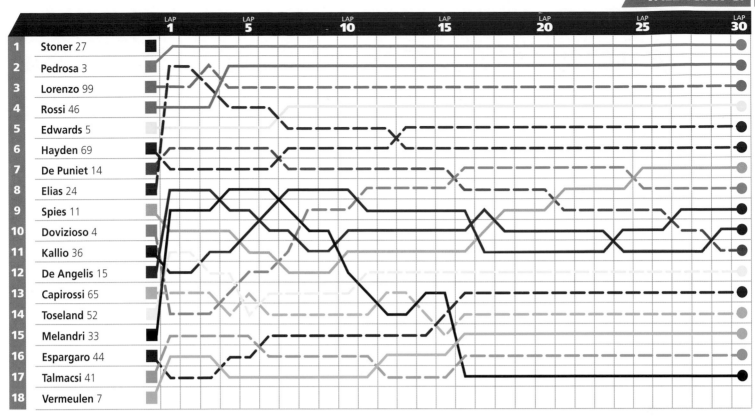

| | | | LAP 1 | | LAP 5 | | LAP 10 | | LAP 15 | | LAP 20 | | LAP 25 | | LAP 30 |
|---|---|---|---|---|---|---|---|---|---|---|---|---|---|---|---|
| 1 | Stoner 27 | | | | | | | | | | | | | | |
| 2 | Pedrosa 3 | | | | | | | | | | | | | | |
| 3 | Lorenzo 99 | | | | | | | | | | | | | | |
| 4 | Rossi 46 | | | | | | | | | | | | | | |
| 5 | Edwards 5 | | | | | | | | | | | | | | |
| 6 | Hayden 69 | | | | | | | | | | | | | | |
| 7 | De Puniet 14 | | | | | | | | | | | | | | |
| 8 | Elias 24 | | | | | | | | | | | | | | |
| 9 | Spies 11 | | | | | | | | | | | | | | |
| 10 | Dovizioso 4 | | | | | | | | | | | | | | |
| 11 | Kallio 36 | | | | | | | | | | | | | | |
| 12 | De Angelis 15 | | | | | | | | | | | | | | |
| 13 | Capirossi 65 | | | | | | | | | | | | | | |
| 14 | Toseland 52 | | | | | | | | | | | | | | |
| 15 | Melandri 33 | | | | | | | | | | | | | | |
| 16 | Espargaro 44 | | | | | | | | | | | | | | |
| 17 | Talmacsi 41 | | | | | | | | | | | | | | |
| 18 | Vermeulen 7 | | | | | | | | | | | | | | |

## RACE

| | Rider | Motorcycle | Race Time | Time + | Fastest Lap | Av Speed | B |
|---|---|---|---|---|---|---|---|
| 1 | Pedrosa | Honda | 46m 47.553s | | 1m 32.778s | 95.734mph | M/H |
| 2 | Rossi | Yamaha | 46m 50.183s | 2.630s | 1m 32.830s | 95.644mph | M/H |
| 3 | Lorenzo | Yamaha | 46m 50.466s | 2.913s | 1m 33.081s | 95.635mph | M/H |
| 4 | Edwards | Yamaha | 47m 20.068s | 32.515s | 1m 33.736s | 94.368mph | M/H |
| 5 | Hayden | Ducati | 47m 22.138s | 34.585s | 1m 33.865s | 94.569mph | S/H |
| 6 | Elias | Honda | 47m 22.441s | 34.888s | 1m 33.717s | 94.559mph | S/H |
| 7 | Spies | Yamaha | 47m 25.259s | 37.706s | 1m 34.015s | 94.465mph | M/H |
| 8 | Dovizioso | Honda | 47m 25.917s | 38.364s | 1m 34.050s | 94.444mph | M/H |
| 9 | Kallio | Ducati | 47m 30.044s | 42.491s | 1m 34.030s | 94.307mph | M/H |
| 10 | De Angelis | Honda | 47m 31.242s | 43.689s | 1m 33.982s | 94.267mph | S/H |
| 11 | De Puniet | Honda | 47m 33.571s | 46.018s | 1m 33.934s | 94.190mph | S/H |
| 12 | Toseland | Yamaha | 47m 37.779s | 50.226s | 1m 34.316s | 94.051mph | M/H |
| 13 | Espargaro | Ducati | 47m 44.721s | 57.168s | 1m 34.458s | 93.823mph | M/H |
| 14 | Capirossi | Suzuki | 47m 54.430s | 1m 06.877s | 1m 34.140s | 93.507mph | S/M |
| 15 | Vermeulen | Suzuki | 47m 59.254s | 1m 11.701s | 1m 34.871s | 93.350mph | S/H |
| 16 | Talmacsi | Honda | 48m 01.958s | 1m 14.405s | 1m 34.919s | 93.262mph | M/H |
| 17 | Melandri | Kawasaki | 48m 20.978s | 1m 33.425s | 1m 34.463s | 92.651mph | S/M |

## CHAMPIONSHIP

| | Rider | Team | Points |
|---|---|---|---|
| 1 | Rossi | Fiat Yamaha Team | 306 |
| 2 | Lorenzo | Fiat Yamaha Team | 261 |
| 3 | Pedrosa | Repsol Honda Team | 234 |
| 4 | Stoner | Ducati Marlboro Team | 220 |
| 5 | Edwards | Monster Yamaha Tech 3 | 161 |
| 6 | Dovizioso | Repsol Honda Team | 160 |
| 7 | Elias | San Carlo Honda Gresini | 115 |
| 8 | De Angelis | San Carlo Honda Gresini | 111 |
| 9 | Capirossi | Rizla Suzuki MotoGP | 110 |
| 10 | Melandri | Hayate Racing Team | 108 |
| 11 | De Puniet | LCR Honda MotoGP | 106 |
| 12 | Vermeulen | Rizla Suzuki MotoGP | 106 |
| 13 | Hayden | Ducati Marlboro Team | 104 |
| 14 | Toseland | Monster Yamaha Tech 3 | 92 |
| 15 | Kallio | Pramac Racing | 71 |
| 16 | Canepa | Pramac Racing | 38 |
| 17 | Talmacsi | Scot Racing Team MotoGP | 19 |
| 18 | Espargaro | Pramac Racing | 16 |
| 19 | Gibernau | Grupo Francisco Hernando | 12 |
| 20 | Spies | Sterilgarda Yamaha Team | 9 |
| 21 | Takahashi | Scot Racing Team MotoGP | 9 |

did). Once he had a feel for the tyres, he moved up smoothly and overtook Dovi to help Colin to fifth place overall.

**8 ANDREA DOVIZIOSO** Lost his fifth place in the standings thanks to starting from tenth on the grid and then getting a bad start – back in 14th place for the first three laps. Got up to seventh, half-way through the race, but was too far behind Hayden and Elias, and then succumbed to Spies.

**9 MIKA KALLIO** Not the best birthday present he'd ever had, but Mika made up for a bad start with a gritty race despite tyre problems and pain in his left arm.

**10 ALEX DE ANGELIS** Never happy

with set-up and suffered from the rear tyre sliding all race, but still did enough to secure eighth in the championship.

**11 RANDY DE PUNIET** Disappointed to finish outside the top ten after a good start. The left side of his rear tyre was the problem, as it was for several others.

**12 JAMES TOSELAND** Not the result he wanted in his last MotoGP race for Tech 3. It was looking much better at half-distance when James was in the battle for seventh. Then the rear tyre spun on the rim and he couldn't maintain his pace.

**13 ALEIX ESPARGARO** Again impressed as a stand-in for Canepa:

four rides on the Pramac Ducati, four points finishes. Not at all comfortable in practice or qualifying but showed his potential for 2010 by improving steadily in the race.

**14 LORIS CAPIROSSI** Suzuki had one of those weekends. The bike just won't work in wind and low temperatures, and the Ricardo Tormo circuit was windy and cool. Loris got all he could out of the bike.

**15 CHRIS VERMEULEN** Just like his team-mate, Chris had no chance of a decent ride in his final MotoGP race. There were also worries about his engine being able to go the distance. An unhappy way to leave the GP paddock.

**16 GABOR TALMACSI** Another difficult weekend to end Gabor's short sojourn in MotoGP. For 2010, he will be in the new Moto2 class.

**17 MARCO MELANDRI** His dream of securing seventh in the championship in Kawasaki's last MotoGP race was scuppered by a trip through a gravel trap at half-distance.

## NON-STARTERS

**CASEY STONER** A cold-tyre crash on the warm-up lap meant he couldn't go for a hat-trick of wins to round the season off. His pace in qualifying was awesome, though; Pedrosa would have had a much harder day if Casey had been there.

**NICCOLO CANEPA** Still not recovered from his operation after Phillip Island. Replaced by Aleix Espargaro.

# WORLD CHAMPIONSHIP CLASSIFICATION

## MotoGP

| | Rider | Nation | Motorcycle | QAT | JPN | SPA | FRA | ITA | CAT | NED | USA | GER | GBR | CZE | INP | RSM | POR | AUS | MAL | VAL | Points |
|---|---|---|---|---|---|---|---|---|---|---|---|---|---|---|---|---|---|---|---|---|---|
| 1 | Rossi | ITA | Yamaha | 20 | 20 | 25 | – | 16 | 25 | 25 | 20 | 25 | 11 | 25 | – | 25 | 13 | 20 | 16 | 20 | 306 |
| 2 | Lorenzo | SPA | Yamaha | 16 | 25 | – | 25 | 20 | 20 | 20 | 16 | 20 | – | – | 25 | 20 | 25 | – | 13 | 16 | 261 |
| 3 | Pedrosa | SPA | Honda | 5 | 16 | 20 | 16 | – | 10 | – | 25 | 16 | 7 | 20 | 6 | 16 | 16 | 16 | 20 | 25 | 234 |
| 4 | Stoner | AUS | Ducati | 25 | 13 | 16 | 11 | 25 | 16 | 16 | 13 | 13 | 2 | – | – | – | 20 | 25 | 25 | – | 220 |
| 5 | Edwards | USA | Yamaha | 13 | 4 | 9 | 9 | 10 | 9 | 13 | 9 | 7 | 20 | 9 | 11 | – | 11 | 11 | 3 | 13 | 161 |
| 6 | Dovizioso | ITA | Honda | 11 | 11 | 8 | 13 | 13 | 13 | – | – | – | 25 | 13 | 13 | 13 | 9 | 10 | – | 8 | 160 |
| 7 | Elias | SPA | Honda | 7 | 1 | 7 | 6 | 2 | – | 4 | 10 | 10 | – | 16 | 7 | 10 | 10 | 6 | 9 | 10 | 115 |
| 8 | De Angelis | RSM | Honda | 10 | 3 | 2 | 5 | 1 | 4 | 6 | 5 | 11 | 13 | 8 | 20 | – | – | 13 | 4 | 6 | 111 |
| 9 | Capirossi | ITA | Suzuki | – | 9 | 10 | 8 | 11 | 11 | 7 | – | 5 | 5 | 11 | 9 | 11 | – | 4 | 7 | 2 | 110 |
| 10 | Melandri | ITA | Kawasaki | 2 | 10 | 11 | 20 | 5 | 2 | 5 | 6 | 9 | 9 | – | – | 8 | 4 | 9 | 8 | – | 108 |
| 11 | De Puniet | FRA | Honda | 6 | 5 | 13 | 2 | 8 | 8 | 9 | 7 | – | 16 | 6 | 4 | 4 | 5 | 8 | – | 5 | 106 |
| 12 | Vermeulen | AUS | Suzuki | 9 | 6 | 6 | 10 | 6 | 5 | 11 | 8 | 3 | 3 | 5 | 5 | 7 | 6 | 5 | 10 | 1 | 106 |
| 13 | Hayden | USA | Ducati | 4 | – | 1 | 4 | 4 | 6 | 8 | 11 | 8 | 1 | 10 | 16 | – | 8 | 1 | 11 | 11 | 104 |
| 14 | Toseland | GBR | Yamaha | – | 7 | 3 | 7 | 9 | 3 | 10 | – | 6 | 10 | 7 | 10 | 6 | 7 | 2 | 1 | 4 | 92 |
| 15 | Kallio | FIN | Ducati | 8 | 8 | – | – | 3 | 7 | – | – | 2 | 6 | – | 8 | 9 | – | 7 | 6 | 7 | 71 |
| 16 | Canepa | ITA | Ducati | – | 2 | – | 1 | 7 | – | 2 | 4 | 4 | 8 | 4 | – | 3 | 3 | – | – | – | 38 |
| 17 | Talmacsi | HUN | Honda | – | – | – | – | – | – | – | – | 1 | 4 | 3 | 2 | 2 | 2 | 3 | 2 | – | 19 |
| 18 | Espargaro | SPA | Ducati | – | – | – | – | – | – | – | – | – | – | – | 3 | 5 | – | – | 5 | 3 | 16 |
| 19 | Gibernau | SPA | Ducati | 3 | – | 5 | – | – | 1 | 3 | – | – | – | – | – | – | – | – | – | – | 12 |
| 20 | Spies | USA | Yamaha | – | – | – | – | – | – | – | – | – | – | – | – | – | – | – | – | 9 | 9 |
| 21 | Takahashi | JPN | Honda | 1 | – | 4 | 3 | – | – | 1 | – | – | – | – | – | – | – | – | – | – | 9 |

## CONSTRUCTOR

| | Motorcycle | QAT | JPN | SPA | FRA | ITA | CAT | NED | USA | GER | GBR | CZE | INP | RSM | POR | AUS | MAL | VAL | Points |
|---|---|---|---|---|---|---|---|---|---|---|---|---|---|---|---|---|---|---|---|
| 1 | Yamaha | 20 | 25 | 25 | 25 | 20 | 25 | 25 | 20 | 25 | 20 | 25 | 25 | 25 | 25 | 20 | 16 | 20 | 386 |
| 2 | Honda | 11 | 16 | 20 | 16 | 13 | 13 | 9 | 25 | 16 | 25 | 20 | 20 | 16 | 16 | 16 | 20 | 25 | 297 |
| 3 | Ducati | 25 | 13 | 16 | 11 | 25 | 16 | 16 | 13 | 13 | 8 | 10 | 16 | 9 | 20 | 25 | 25 | 11 | 272 |
| 4 | Suzuki | 9 | 9 | 10 | 10 | 11 | 11 | 11 | 8 | 5 | 5 | 11 | 9 | 11 | 6 | -5 | 10 | 2 | 133 |
| 5 | Kawasaki | 2 | 10 | 11 | 20 | 5 | 2 | 5 | 6 | 9 | 9 | – | – | 8 | 4 | 9 | 8 | – | 108 |

## TEAM

| | Team | QAT | JPN | SPA | FRA | ITA | CAT | NED | USA | GER | GBR | CZE | INP | RSM | POR | AUS | MAL | VAL | Points |
|---|---|---|---|---|---|---|---|---|---|---|---|---|---|---|---|---|---|---|---|
| 1 | Fiat Yamaha Team | 36 | 45 | 25 | 25 | 36 | 45 | 45 | 36 | 45 | 11 | 25 | 25 | 45 | 38 | 20 | 29 | 36 | 567 |
| 2 | Repsol Honda Team | 16 | 27 | 28 | 29 | 13 | 23 | – | 25 | 16 | 32 | 33 | 19 | 29 | 25 | 26 | 20 | 33 | 394 |
| 3 | Ducati Marlboro Team | 29 | 13 | 17 | 15 | 29 | 22 | 24 | 24 | 21 | 3 | 10 | 24 | 9 | 28 | 26 | 36 | 11 | 341 |
| 4 | Monster Yamaha Tech 3 | 13 | 11 | 12 | 16 | 19 | 12 | 23 | 9 | 13 | 30 | 16 | 21 | 6 | 18 | 13 | 4 | 17 | 253 |
| 5 | San Carlo Honda Gresini | 17 | 4 | 9 | 11 | 3 | 4 | 10 | 15 | 21 | 13 | 24 | 27 | 10 | 10 | 19 | 13 | 16 | 226 |
| 6 | Rizla Suzuki MotoGP | 9 | 15 | 16 | 18 | 17 | 16 | 18 | 8 | 8 | 8 | 16 | 14 | 18 | 6 | 9 | 17 | 3 | 216 |
| 7 | Hayate Racing Team | 2 | 10 | 11 | 20 | 5 | 2 | 5 | 6 | 9 | 9 | – | – | 8 | 4 | 9 | 8 | – | 108 |
| 8 | Pramac Racing | 8 | 10 | – | 1 | 10 | 7 | 2 | 4 | 6 | 14 | 4 | 3 | 8 | 3 | 7 | 11 | 10 | 108 |
| 9 | LCR Honda MotoGP | 6 | 5 | 13 | 2 | 8 | 8 | 9 | 7 | – | 16 | 6 | 4 | 4 | 5 | 8 | – | 5 | 106 |
| 10 | Scot Racing Team MotoGP | 1 | – | 4 | 3 | – | – | 1 | – | 1 | 4 | 3 | 2 | 2 | 2 | 3 | 2 | – | 28 |
| 11 | Grupo Francisco Hernando | 3 | – | 5 | – | – | 1 | 3 | – | – | – | – | – | – | – | – | – | – | 12 |

**HONDA**
The Power of Dreams

# 2009 250cc World Champion

"I have been racing for 23 years, so I have been waiting for this moment for 23 years. It's incredible! I am very proud to win this title, and it makes it extra special that it's the last 250 title."

**Hiroshi Aoyama, Scot Honda**

www.hondaracing-eu.com

# 250 CHAMPIONSHIP
ANDY IBBOTT

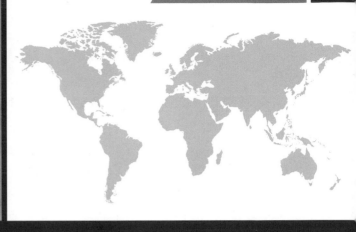

# LAST BUT NOT LEAST

**The last year of 250cc competition at World Championship level went down to the wire. Hiroshi Aoyama emerged from the pack to give Honda an unexpected title**

It promised to be an interesting year. Marco Simoncelli, World Champion in 2008, was hoping the successful combination of big hair and the Gilera/Aprilia would let him move up into MotoGP with another title under his belt, while Alvaro Bautista was looking to spoil the Italian's chances before he too found himself taking on the big boys in the top class in 2010. The Spaniard had come on strong over the early winter tests at Jerez, but then had a big off in the wet at Valencia, breaking his collarbone and putting himself on the back foot for the start of the season.

A whole bunch of old 250 hands and up and coming ex-125 riders also wanted the chance to prove that they too could have a pop at the title. Hector Barbera, Alex Debon and Thomas Luthi had all shown in the past that they could run with, and beat, the two favourites, although Barbera was still recovering from a bad crash in Japan plus an operation to remove a steel plate, the result of a past injury on his mountain bike. Hiroshi Aoyama, moving to Honda after a stint on the KTM in 2008, was getting used to his new bike at the start of testing. The 125 World Champion, Frenchman Mike di Meglio, was another likely contender who showed well in winter testing on the factory Aspar Aprilia, while other talented newcomers to come up from the 125 class included Hector Faubel and Raffaele de Rosa, both on Hondas.

There were changes to the rules for 2009. Gone now was the Friday qualifying session, and Friday mornings became a very quiet affair as nothing started on track until noon. At first the sessions themselves were shorter too, but grumblings from the big boys in MotoGP led to the time being restored, even though

**Above** Mattia Pasini had to contend with having his bike repossessed mid-season

**Top right** Alvaro Bautista celebrates his win in Barcelona with team principal Jorge 'Aspar' Martinez

**Right** Jules Cluzel was the revelation of the year. He got on the rostrum in the first race and ran with the leaders regularly – his enthusiasm could still get the better of him though

the Friday morning sessions were not. It was all in a bid to save money, but the hardcore fans probably thought it wasn't such a good idea.

It looked as if Aprilia would keep the title in their hands right from the off. The Hondas hadn't been updated from the previous year, and no-one wanted to spend a lot of R&D money on their bikes because in 2010 they would all be replaced by the new four-stroke Moto2 class. That said, Aprilia made sure they put out as many RSA bikes with seven-stage traction control as they could, for those who either had the talent or the money, or both, in a bid to spoil any chance Honda might have of winning the last ever two-stroke 250cc World Championship title, after 61 years of Grand Prix history.

But despite all the rumours about lack of development, once the season started all those Honda riders who had been written off started to be up at the front and winning. Fair enough with a talented rider like Aoyama, but when all the Hondas began to show a significant improvement over their 2008 positions, questions began to be asked.

### 1 – QATARI GP

With winter testing out of the way it was time to get serious. Hungarian Gabor Talmacsi headed the field on the first day of practice, which surprised a lot of people, but it wasn't to last. Come Saturday morning Hiroshi Aoyama was on top of the pile and looking for a good opening round with the 'unchanged' Honda. However, Alvaro Bautista put his bike on pole in the 'afternoon' session. Meanwhile World Champion Simoncelli was down in 14th place in the 'morning', suffering with his wrist injury. He didn't take part in final qualifying, or race on the Sunday, leaving the Aspar pair of Bautista and Mike di Meglio to battle it out with Aoyama.

On Sunday the race was delayed due to rain (yes, in Qatar!) and it was then shortened to 13 laps in order not to affect the start time of the MotoGP race. A mad dash to the finish ensued, with a surprise victory for Hector Barbera on his return from a bad injury; privateer Jules Cluzel came second and di Meglio third. The top six also featured Aoyama, Raffaele de Rosa and Thomas Luthi, who all finished within half a second of di Meglio.

### 2 – JAPANESE GP

Having missed Qatar, World Champion Simoncelli was keen to get back in the fray, and he started in fine style by leading the lone Friday practice session. He was lucky to be able to hold on to this position when bad weather again played havoc with the 250 class; qualifying positions were decided on the basis of combined times from the two free practice sessions.

In the race it was Bautista who took the win after battling hard with home boy Aoyama for a good ten laps. Racing was difficult, as part of the track still had water running across it, even though 99 per cent was dry. One of these wet patches caught out di Meglio, and then Simoncelli managed to clip one of the kerbs so heavily that he took his front tyre off the rim and had to come in for a wheel change. He finished 17th and out of the points. For the second year running, Simoncelli failed to score points in the opening two rounds.

### 3 – SPANISH GP

Back for the traditional first European round at Jerez, it was Bautista who continued his assault on the championship, setting the fastest time on Friday. The weather looked unlikely to play a part, although unpredictable winds were causing some riders problems.

On Saturday Alex Debon made it three Spanish riders on pole in the three World Championship categories. He was followed by the ever-threatening Barbera and then Simoncelli, who crashed twice during the Saturday sessions. Bautista completed the front row and Aoyama was in sixth.

The race was a real thriller, with four riders dicing for most of the time. The lead changed constantly, between Aoyama, Bautista and Simoncelli, and they finished in that order, but the Italian faded away slightly in the final laps. He was just 0.063s ahead of fourth-placed Barbera, who had harassed the World Champion towards the finish. Aoyama won thanks to his astonishing ability on the brakes after a great last-lap fight with Bautista.

Pole-man Debon lobbed his bike away with 16 laps to go and left Luthi and Mattia Pasini in their own private battle, with the Swiss crossing the line 0.004s in front of the Italian to take fifth.

### 4 – FRENCH GP

Everything seemed to be going Bautista's way as he set another pole position despite a strong challenge from Luthi at his favourite circuit. The Swiss rider rather upset the applecart by putting himself on the front row, pushing Barbera down to the third row. Simoncelli and Aoyama joined them on the front row, thus keeping the battle for the title alive and well after the first three rounds.

It was another wet race, which helped Simoncelli take his second podium in two outings, and his first win of the year, going some way towards making up for his abortive visits to Qatar and Japan.

Marco brought his Gilera home a massive 18s ahead of ex-125 rider Hector Faubel, who recorded his first 250cc podium. Also avoiding any errors in the wet conditions was Simoncelli's team-mate Roberto Locatelli, who came home third, having not been on the rostrum since 2006. It could be argued, though, that this was only because of an unfortunate incident when Debon brought down Luthi with ten laps to go. Bautista was now leading the championship by a single point from Aoyama, with Barbera lying third and World Champion Simoncelli fourth.

### 5 – ITALIAN GP

Talmacsi had now been officially replaced in the Aspar team by another Hungarian rider, Balazs Nemeth. It was his first appearance in the World Championship in any class, but he didn't last very long.

The session on Friday saw the two leading championship contenders in first and second places, with Simoncelli down in a lowly eighth position. Come the end of Saturday, though, all four leading riders were sitting across the front row ready for a titanic fight in Sunday's race. Also mixed into the melting pot on the second row were fierce rivals Debon and Luthi, as well as the ever-improving Honda rider Wilairot and Pasini.

The rain poured down for the race and this led to Pasini eventually coming out on top, by a 0.117s margin, from second-placed Simoncelli, whom he brilliantly held off on the final lap. With ten laps to go, however, a big incident saw rivals Bautista and Simoncelli clashing at high speed. Both riders ran off track, and this allowed Pasini to push through to the front. Bautista eventually finished third, with Luthi a distant fourth, 24s behind Pasini, to go some way towards making up for his Le Mans disappointment. Barbera was fifth, and Aoyama lost ground in the championship by finishing in sixth place.

**Above** Alvaro Bautista tailgates Hiro Aoyama at the Assen chicane

'What have you done to your 250s, Mr Honda?' 'Nothing' was the reply all season, and yet Honda riders were not only doing well, but outsider Aoyama was actually challenging for the title! No development? Not convinced on that one! The only concession to be disclosed was that Aoyama got 'some new parts' mid-season. What these were no-one really knew – and no-one was saying anything either.

There were various dramas during the season, starting with 2008 champion Simoncelli missing testing in Qatar – and then sitting out the opening race – after fracturing his scaphoid in a motocross crash. Then Talmacsi split from his team before the French GP in a 'dispute over image rights', and went on to ride for Scot Honda in the MotoGP class, pushing out Japanese rider Takahasi in an alleged 'I've got more money than you' deal.

Perhaps the biggest drama occurred at Estoril, when it seemed that a long-running dispute between Team Toth

## 6 – CATALAN GP

The weather couldn't have been more different for the second Spanish race of the year, with the paddock enjoying soaring temperatures and brilliant sunshine. And the weather wasn't the only news: Simoncelli announced that he would be moving up to MotoGP in 2010, and di Meglio had surgery to get rid of his forearm pump problems.

There were no problems for Debon on Friday, as he put his Aprilia on the front row and sent a warning shot across the bows of the other riders, but it was Bautista who led the morning session on Saturday and Barbera who finally took pole position from Bautista, Simoncelli and Luthi. Marco was lucky to be uninjured after a big off in the final session. Aoyama also crashed but qualified on the second row in sixth place.

Bautista won the race, crossing the finishing line seven seconds ahead of his nearest rival, Aoyama, and extending his lead to 12 points at the top of the table. Simoncelli retired with a mechanical problem after crashing on the second lap, meaning that the Italian trailed the Spaniard by 47 points after six races. Team-mate Locatelli had come from 16th on the grid up into fourth position, but he ruined it all when he crashed out after 14 laps, making it a miserable day for the Metis Gilera team.

## 7 – DUTCH TT

Another round, another change… replacement rider Nemeth crashed during testing and needed surgery to treat a broken bone in his left hand, which gave Aleix Espargaro the chance to return to the 250 class for the Balatonring team. Catalunya winner Bautista kept up his momentum on Friday, posting fastest time, but his success was overshadowed by the news that Pasini's participation was in doubt after a financial wrangle between his Team Toth outfit and bike supplier Aprilia; a last-minute deal allowed the Italian to compete.

However, it was a second consecutive pole for Barbera, with Aoyama and Bautista in second and third, and Simoncelli completing the front row. The second row was also packed with talent, as stand-in Espargaro impressed to head Debon, de Rosa and Pasini.

The race saw Aoyama take the victory and the lead in the points standings, proving that consistency is the way to win world titles – and that a bit of luck helps too. Bautista had smashed into the back of Aoyama's Honda at the last chicane, ending his own race but leaving the Japanese to stay upright and take the win. The Spaniard's late exit meant the battle behind became one for the runner-up spot, with pole-man Barbera eventually getting the better of reigning champion Simoncelli.

## 8 – GERMAN GP

Barbera came back from the three-week break for the 250cc class by putting his name at the top of the first timesheet. The Spaniard was nearly half a second quicker than rival Simoncelli, but that didn't last long because the champion put his Gilera on pole ready for the race on Sunday. Joining him on the front row in a wet qualifying session were Barbera, Bautista and Aoyama. It would make for a very interesting race, provided the rain held off.

In the event, the rain came but also went again, leaving all the riders with a very difficult choice regarding tyres for the race. It looked as if those who made the bravest choice would win the day, but in fact only Karel Abraham, fifth on the grid, stayed with his initial choice of wets while the rest of the pack swapped to dry tyres. The race was restarted after an initial lap when rain fell.

Simoncelli brought it home, with Debon in hot pursuit. Bautista got close on the final lap but couldn't make a move on Debon, despite putting in a circuit record lap, but he did get past his title rival and the series leader, Hiroshi Aoyama, to cut the gap in the standings to ten points.

## 9 – BRITISH GP

And once more the weather played a part in the race for the title. On Friday at Donington Debon moved his Aprilia to the front of the grid, temporarily upsetting the title chasers – Bautista, Aoyama and Simoncelli. There was also another name change: Ralf Waldmann, at the age of 43, replaced Russian rider Vladimir Leonov, who had picked up a hand injury in Germany. Ralf was 18th in his first day of World Championship riding since 2002. In the end it was to be Barbera who took pole position, but only just, as he was a mere 0.094s quicker than Simoncelli; Aoyama was third and Debon fourth. Bautista ended his 100 per cent record of front-row starts after suffering the after-effects of two crashes in previous sessions.

As Sunday came, so did the rain, but for the 250 class it was to turn into a fine drizzle that made tyre choice possibly the hardest it could ever be. The race was declared wet before the start, so full wet tyres were the only real choice, but by half-distance a dry line had appeared. It was Aoyama on the 'softer'-engined Honda who did the best job in the awful conditions and he finished first, taking his lead in the championship to 15 points over Bautista.

## 10 – CZECH REPUBLIC GP

After the traditional summer break it was Barbera who seemed to have benefited the most, for he put himself in provisional pole position on Friday. But, as ever, the title leaders had other ideas and by the close of play on Saturday it was Simoncelli on pole with Aoyama, Barbera and Debon completing the front row. Bautista was eighth after crashing his bike with four minutes of the final session remaining.

Czech rider Abraham caused concerns when he crashed into the luckless Luthi on the very first corner, but the debris was cleared before the end of the first lap, allowing Simoncelli to roar away to another victory and bring himself closer to a title bid for the second year running. The track temperature rose to a staggering 51 degrees during the race, and Bautista's and Aoyama's tyres did not cope as well as those of their Italian rival. They came in third and fourth, behind Pasini who'd stolen vital points from them. The result meant that Simoncelli now trailed Aoyama by just 32 points and Bautista by 20 points, with six races remaining.

Once more Aoyama was lucky in the race. Di Meglio clipped the back of his bike in a similar incident to the Assen coming-together with Bautista, but this time both riders stayed on the track.

**Above** Reigning champion Simoncelli lost his title at the last race of the year

**Right** At his home track Hector Barbera won the last ever 250 GP race and in the process took second in the championship off Simoncelli

and an unpaid-for Aprilia came to a head. The big boys came in and took the bikes away, leaving paddock and punters' favourite Mattia Pasini with nothing to ride. Imre Toth was given a stock bike to use and Pasini caught up with some sunshine until he was allowed to use it. Oddly, Thomas Luthi's sponsors came to the rescue and secured the bike back for him for the remaining four rounds, although he had to pay for his own mechanics.

Bautista didn't endear himself to his team when he did a 'Biaggi' across the start/finish line at Brno – but without the Italian's luck, because Alvaro flipped his bike, smashing it to pieces and writing it off completely, just when the team needed to pack it into a crate and send it off to the USA for the Indy round. A bag would have been better than a box, given the number of pieces the bike was in.

Reigning 125cc World Champion and 250cc rookie Mike di Meglio underwent surgery to treat 'arm pump' in his right forearm, following a start to the 2009 season in which he had been plagued by the condition. 'Arm pump' is something that's seen in a lot of riders coming from the junior class, and a mid-season operation isn't always the ideal solution.

Finally there were musical chairs within the teams, due to injuries in most cases. Russian rider Vladimir Leonov picked up a hand injury in Germany and the Viessmann Kiefer Racing team turned to old hand Ralf Waldmann for the British Grand Prix. Spaniard Aleix Espargaro replaced an injured Balazs Nemeth, who had himself replaced Gabor Talmasci.

The title came down to a last-round confrontation between Aoyama and Simoncelli, Honda versus Aprilia. After one of the most dramatic races imaginable, Hiro Aoyama beame the last 250cc World Champion. You would have got very long odds against a Honda rider winning a race, let alone the title, back at the start of the season, but the combination of a fine rider and a team that has worked with Hondas for years gave the Japanese company their first world title since 2006.

## 11 – INDIANAPOLIS GP

After the appalling weather at Indy last year, which resulted in the 250 race being cancelled, Friday didn't get off to a good start because conditions were again wet and windy. However, this did allow riders with less power to shine, with Cluzel, in particular (of whom very little had been heard since his excellent race in Qatar), pushing to the front. Czech rider Abraham also managed to get himself up to fourth, even though he crashed while pushing too hard towards the end of the session.

But even though the weather cleared and the track was dry on the second day, it was di Meglio who placed his bike at the front ready for the race the following day. He was one of the few on the grid who'd actually raced at Indy as he'd been in the 125 class the previous year. Aoyama clinched the second slot and Simoncelli was third, lucky to get into the session at all after crashing both his bikes.

Simoncelli took the win but was pushed by Aoyama, at least until the Japanese rider lost the front end of his bike. He stayed on but any chance of catching the Italian rider was gone. Bautista completed the podium, but his lack of first and second places was starting to cost him championship-wise. By the end of the US round Simoncelli had clawed back to within 27 points of title leader Aoyama and 11 points of Bautista.

## 12 – SAN MARINO GP

After the US trip it was back to Italy and another home advantage for Simoncelli, who was gaining ground on the two riders in front of him in the championship, but once again on Friday Barbera put his bike at the front of the field, leaving over a second for championship contenders Aoyama and Bautista to find overnight.

Aoyama took pole – his first of the season, despite leading the championship – but it was a close-run thing as Barbera pushed him hard all the way and the gap in the end was a paper-thin 0.008s – less than half the width of a front wheel! Two-tenths of a second behind were local riders Simoncelli and Pasini, with Bautista left struggling in eighth place.

The race turned out to be as hot as the weather, which was scorching, but didn't involve the expected riders as Simoncelli crashed out on lap 12 while fighting for the lead. This left a tremendous battle to rage between Barbera and home boy Pasini which went right down to the wire, with a fraught last lap ending with the Spaniard crossing the line just four-hundredths of a second in front of the Italian.

The fight for the last podium position, between Bautista and Aoyama, also went to the last corner – and it was the Spanish rider who succeeded to go 13 points behind Aoyama, the championship leader.

## 13 – PORTUGUESE GP

During the penultimate European round it wasn't Bautista or Simoncelli or Aoyama who would be showing the way around the Portuguese circuit; that honour went to Barbera, who set the fastest time on Friday and followed that up by being fastest in second free practice and quickest again in the qualifying session to put himself on pole for the race. The three championship contenders filled the remaining front-row positions. Pasini had to wait until he was bailed out by Luthi's sponsors before he could ride, but did manage to get himself on to the second row.

Simoncelli won the race, however, with di Meglio and Barbera completing the podium. They'd crossed the line side by side, and although they were given exactly the same race time di Meglio was awarded second place because he had the quicker fastest lap in the race. A good fourth-place finish for Aoyama saw him extend his title lead to 26 points over Bautista, but only because the Spaniard crashed out early on, when his engine seized on the fourth lap.

It was Simoncelli's fifth win of the year – and his fourth in the last six rounds – and it put him just two points behind his Spanish rival and closer to Aoyama.

## 14 – AUSTRALIAN GP

Barbera began practice in a strong first place, but his weekend was marred by a highside. Luckily he only suffered from bruising to his back. The other contenders didn't fare so well either, with Simoncelli down in 10th, Aoyama 11th and Bautista 12th. Thankfully both Simoncelli and Aoyama managed to get their acts together and set up their bikes well enough to achieve front-row places for the race, but surprisingly it was de Rosa who took pole position after rain caused havoc during the session. Debon and Pasini were caught out early on when they crashed, but made it on to the second row. However, qualifying was disastrous for Bautista – third row on the grid – presenting him with a difficult challenge to keep close to Aoyama and in front of Simoncelli for the title race.

A red flag with only six laps to go finally settled the positions on race day. It was unlucky for some, with Locatelli highsiding and lying on the track (the cause of the red flag), Aoyama ending up in seventh and Bautista crashing out while holding second place (he did remount to finish the race), but good luck for Simoncelli, who took the race win, overtook Bautista in the title chase and closed the gap on the Japanese rider to just 12 points.

## 15 – MALAYSIAN GP

With the championship closer than ever the pressure was on for all three contenders to keep their bikes upright and gain valuable points at the Sepang circuit. In the first practice session Aoyama had a lead of just 0.013s over Debon, with Wilairot in fine form, setting third-quickest time a further 0.039s behind, and Bautista fifth. A dispute involving Barbera and his team management was quickly resolved, and the Spaniard got on track after missing the first ten minutes.

It was Aoyama who did the business again in the vital qualifying session, setting a new 250cc lap record. Cluzel, di Meglio and Barbera completed the front row, which helped the Japanese rider's championship ambitions; Simoncelli qualified in eighth, Bautista was fifth. Aoyama was also victorious in the race after a superlative head-to-head battle with Simoncelli, who placed third after a photo finish with Barbera. The Japanese also set a new track record of 2m 07.597s on the 16th lap. With a six-second advantage by the end of the race, Aoyama extended his lead in the championship to 21 points over Simoncelli.

The result left Aoyama needing an 11th-place finish or better in Valencia to secure the 2009 title ahead of Simoncelli, while Barbera rose to third in the standings after Bautista crashed out again.

**Above** The first corner of the last race: Aoyama is third, Simoncelli sixth

**Right** The moment when it could have all gone so wrong – Aoyama speeds through the gravel trap at Valencia's first corner

**Far right** Hiroshi Aoyama – the last 250cc World Champion

## 16 – VALENCIAN GP

Everyone was watching Simoncelli and Aoyama, but it was Debon who sneaked under the radar and put himself on pole. He had been strong in both free practice sessions, running second to Barbera and then di Meglio, but during qualifying his engine seized at the end of the front straight, going into the first turn, so he had to put the bike down in the gravel as he headed towards the tyre wall; he damaged several ribs and put himself out of the race. Simoncelli qualified second and Aoyama headed the second row, but Debon's absence, of course, moved everyone up the grid for the race, putting Simoncelli on pole and Aoyama on the front row.

The last ever 250cc two-stroke race was a belter. Aoyama only had to finish, but it was clear he wanted the win to secure his title. Simoncelli had to finish first and hope Aoyama would make a mistake.

As it was, the Japanese did just that on the ninth lap, going into the first turn too hard and off the track in a cloud of dust. Luckily he stayed on board and rejoined the race in that all-important 11th position. Simoncelli was leading, so Aoyama couldn't afford to make any more mistakes. Then Simoncelli lost the back of the bike coming out of Turn 5. He recovered, only to lose the front in the very next turn, and crashed out, handing the title to Aoyama and the race win to Barbera.

| | Rider | Nation | Team | Motorcycle | Points |
|---|---|---|---|---|---|
| 1 | Hiroshi Aoyama | JPN | Scot Racing Team 250cc | Honda | 261 |
| 2 | Hector Barbera | SPA | Pepe World Team | Aprilia | 239 |
| 3 | Marco Simoncelli | ITA | Metis Gilera | Gilera | 231 |
| 4 | Alvaro Bautista | SPA | Mapfre Aspar Team | Aprilia | 218 |
| 5 | Mattia Pasini | ITA | Team Globalgest | Aprilia | 128 |
| 6 | Raffaele de Rosa | ITA | Scot Racing Team 250cc | Honda | 122 |
| 7 | Thomas Luthi | SWI | Emmi – Caffe Latte | Aprilia | 120 |
| 8 | Mike di Meglio | FRA | Mapfre Aspar Team | Aprilia | 107 |
| 9 | Hector Faubel | SPA | Honda SAG | Honda | 105 |
| 10 | Alex Debon | SPA | Aeropuerto-Castello-Blusens | Aprilia | 101 |
| 11 | Roberto Locatelli | ITA | Metis Gilera | Gilera | 85 |
| 12 | Jules Cluzel | FRA | Matteoni Racing | Aprilia | 82 |
| 13 | Ratthapark Wilairot | THA | Thai Honda PTT SAG | Honda | 81 |
| 14 | Karel Abraham | CZE | Cardion AB Motoracing | Aprilia | 74 |
| 15 | Lukas Pesek | CZE | Auto Kelly – CP | Aprilia | 74 |
| 16 | Alex Baldolini | ITA | WTR San Marino Team | Aprilia | 41 |
| 17 | Shoya Tomizawa | JPN | CIP Moto – GP250 | Honda | 32 |
| 18 | Gabor Talmacsi | HUN | Balatonring Team | Aprilia | 28 |
| 19 | Shuhei Aoyama | JPN | Racing Team Germany | Honda | 27 |
| 20 | Aleix Espargaro | SPA | Balatonring Team | Aprilia | 22 |
| 21 | Valentin Debise | FRA | CIP Moto – GP250 | Honda | 18 |
| 22 | Imre Toth | HUN | Team Toth Aprilia | Aprilia | 12 |
| 23 | Balazs Nemeth | HUN | Balatonring Team | Aprilia | 11 |
| 24 | Vladimir Leonov | RUS | Viessmann Kiefer Racing | Aprilia | 9 |
| 25 | Bastien Chesaux | SWI | Matteoni Racing | Aprilia | 3 |
| 26 | Axel Pons | SPA | Pepe World Team | Aprilia | 3 |
| 27 | Toby Markham | GBR | C&L Racing | Aprilia | 2 |
| 28 | Kazuki Watanabe | JPN | Bardral Racing with SJ-R | Yamaha | 2 |
| 29 | Stevie Bonsey | USA | Milar – Juegos Lucky | Aprilia | 1 |

# 125 CHAMPIONSHIP

ANDY IBBOTT

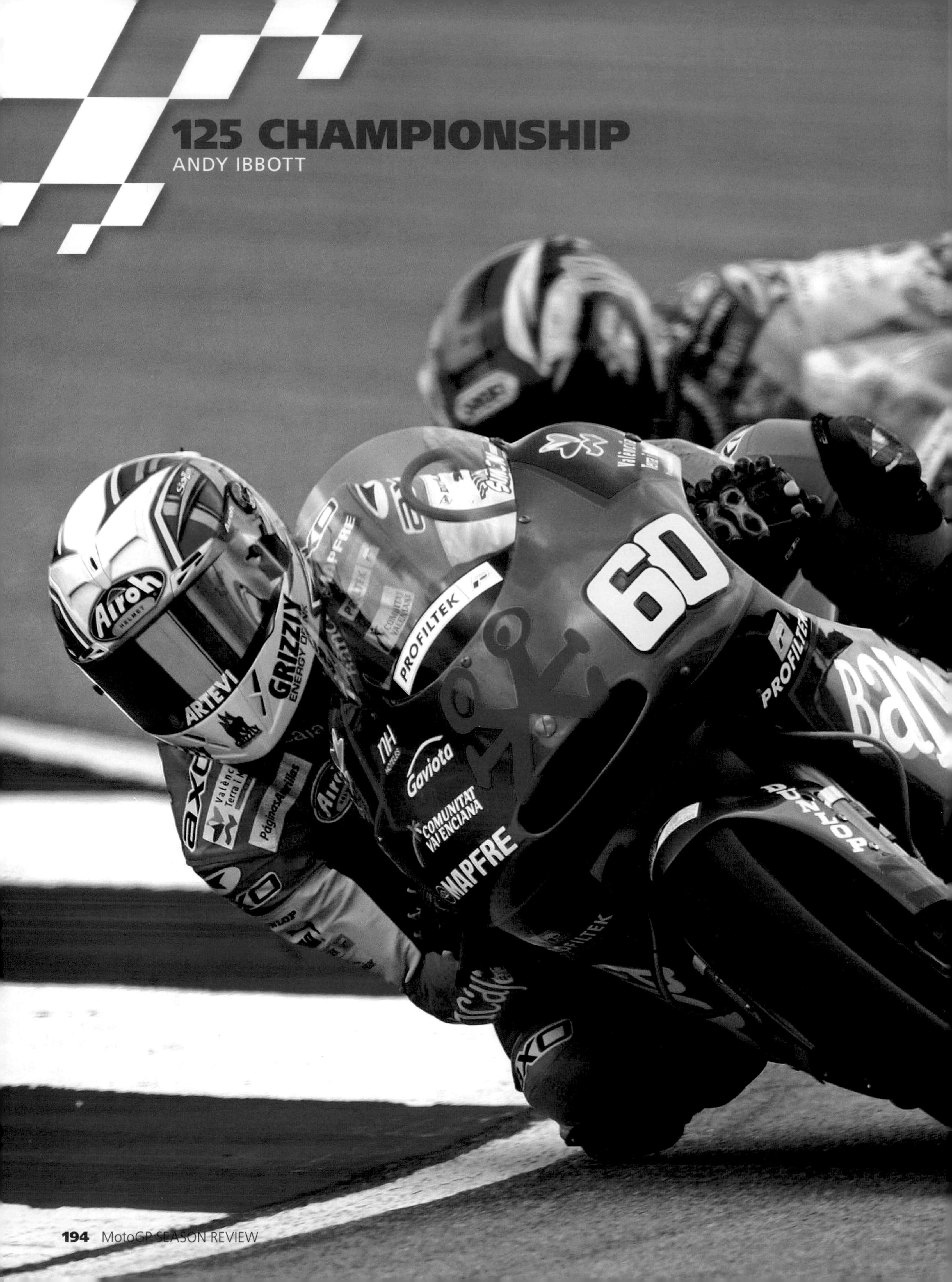

# ASPAR'S ARMADA

**Team-mates Julian Simon and Bradley Smith were the stand-out riders of the year, with Simon the worthy champion**

The 2009 season looked likely to be a good one as, unlike in previous years, there were several riders who were clear contenders for the title. They could best be grouped into two levels – those with a really good shot at the title and those with slightly more of an outside chance.

The favourites had to include Julian Simon, who'd spent a year in 250s with KTM but was coming back to the smaller machines on an Aprilia for the Aspar team, one of the strongest outfits in the paddock in both this and the 250 class. His team-mate, Britain's Bradley Smith, was also in with a shout for the same reasons, and had been looking increasingly strong with each passing year in 125s. Also in there were 2008 runner-up Simone Corsi, who had stated publicly that he wanted to move up to the next class as a champion, as well as Andrea Iannone and Nicolas Terol; all three had shown increasing maturity in the previous season.

On the 'B' list – but still strong contenders – were the German riders Stefan Bradl and Sandro Cortese (both now with new teams), old hand Sergio Gadea (who was also in the strong Aspar team for another year), and the Spanish riders Joan Olive and Pol Espargaro, the latter an up-and-coming youngster.

Others who might not have been title contenders but could certainly upset the apple cart were British rider Scott Redding, who had proved his worth with a win at the Donington GP in 2008, tiny Marc Marquez on the KTM and another Brit, Danny Webb, who could always be counted on for a strong finish.

The big pre-season test was held at Estoril, and featured nearly all the top contenders, all eyeing each other up to see who was likely to be in contention for the

**Above** Marc Marquez rode as hard as ever and gave KTM two pole positions in their final year of GP competition

top position. Unfortunately injury is always a risk when testing in cold conditions in Europe during the winter. Derbi rider Efrén Vazquez crashed whilst testing his new machine, becoming entwined with the bike's front wheel, causing an ankle fracture and damage to his Achilles tendon. He also underwent surgery to help him overcome 'arm pump', caused by compartmental syndrome, which

he had been experiencing in his left arm. Other riders suffered injuries too.

As expected Simon and Smith racked up good times in Estoril, both marking themselves out as firm favourites for the title. They didn't test on the third day, though, which allowed Iannone to top the charts, with Cortese and Espargaro following close behind.

## 1 – QATARI GP

Maintaining their dominance from pre-season testing, new team-mates Simon and Smith opened the first free practice session of the season by securing provisional first and second places. This continued into the night, on Saturday, as Simon set a time of 2m 06.974s, putting him on pole, just 0.133s ahead of Smith, who was unable to repeat his 2008 Qatar pole. Joining the Aspar pair on the front row were Italian rider Iannone and Spaniard Terol, with Cortese, Gadea, Bradl and Pol Espargaro on the second row.

However, just four laps were run because heavy rain saw the race red-flagged, with Andrea Iannone declared the winner as he held the lead at the time of the disruption. He'd battled with Simon, who was second when the flag came out but then crashed, although he was still awarded the runner-up place. The final podium slot went to Cortese, who'd started in fifth but had made it up to third before rain stopped play. Smith was fifth.

A big highside for Marquez just before the red flag meant a no-score for the lead KTM rider, although he'd been in the top five when he suffered the accident. The riders were awarded half points.

## 2 – JAPANESE GP

The weather in Japan wasn't much better for the 125 riders, even though they found themselves on the other side of the world for the second round of the season. The Friday session was dry, with Iannone fastest, and he took pole position on Saturday, ahead of Simon, Bradl and Rabat, with Terol, Aegerter, Smith and Espargaro on the second row.

Iannone also took the victory, and the championship lead, in a race decided by tyre choice due to the changeable weather and track conditions, but he'd had to battle his way to the front after getting a terrible start. Eight laps before the end Simon caught up with early race leader Danny Webb, and the race between the riders on slick tyres was on, with the Spaniard taking second and his compatriot Espargaro third.

## 3 – SPANISH GP

It was back to Europe for round three, and one of the championship's main test tracks – indeed, many riders actually refer to Jerez as their home track rather than one in their own countries. The qualifying session on Saturday saw Simon taking top spot in his home race with a best lap of 1m 48.237s, ahead of team-mate Smith, Iannone and Marquez, with the Aspar team's third rider, Gadea, in fifth, missing the front row by just 0.024s. Aegerter, Redding and Webb made up the second row.

The race was rain-free but in true Jerez style the wind got up and caused some unpredictable conditions for the riders – not that it bothered most of them as they are full of youthful exuberance and seem to have no fears about crashing!

It was a good weekend for Bradley Smith, who took his first ever GP win at one of his Spanish team's home circuits, and he did it in style with over 13s on his rivals. Team-mate Simon managed to highside himself out of the race on the fifth lap, leaving the way open for Gadea and Marquez to take the other podium slots. Iannone crashed but remounted to finish way down the field. Germany's Jonas Folger was an unexpected star: he came from 35th and last on the grid to battle for the podium in the final stages but crashed out on the penultimate lap.

## 4 – FRENCH GP

Rain seemed to be almost a permanent racing feature in 2009, although it was dry at Le Mans for the first Friday session, allowing Iannone to make up for his crash in Jerez by setting fastest time. Come Saturday, though, and it was KTM rider Marquez who secured pole position, followed by Scott Redding and then Terol and Aegerter. All the championship hopefuls, including Simon and Smith, had to put up with the second row, while series leader Iannone qualified in 23rd position after a crash.

On race day the conditions weren't ideal, with the rain making the track slippery for all the riders, but it was Simon who got his set-up spot on and took the win by a staggering 27 seconds, putting him at the top of the championship table. In a surprising second place was 15-year-old German Jonas Folger, who battled from 16th on the grid to take his first podium in just his tenth race. Gadea completed the podium places, with team-mate Smith in fourth place collecting more valuable championship points.

## 5 – ITALIAN GP

Another circuit renowned for its changeable weather conditions is the fantastic track at Mugello, where it can be glorious Italian sunshine one minute and pouring with rain the next as the clouds come hurtling in over the surrounding mountains. Nothing deterred Simon, though, as he put his Aprilia at the head of the front row on Friday, with team-mates Gadea and Smith close behind, but it was the Brit who pulled it out of the hat on Saturday. Bradley set a new pole record with a 1m 58.134s lap, beating Lukas Pesek's time from 2006 by 0.068s. He was joined on the front row by the up-and-coming Redding, Simon and Gadea.

With the pole record under his belt, the young Brit set about dominating the Mugello track and his fellow competitors to win the Italian round and also take control of the series leaderboard, but he was pushed hard by Terol, who fought him all the way to the line and only lost out on the top step by a mere 0.2s. Simon, meanwhile, was a further seven seconds back in third, with Espargaro fourth. Iannone, meanwhile, was gradually ruling himself out of championship contention as he failed to finish yet another race.

**Above** Nico Terol and Andrea Iannone, both winners in 2009, sandwich Julian Simon at Brno

**Left** Bradley Smith, second in the championship and double GP winner

**Right** Scott Redding celebrates third place at Donington Park

## 6 – CATALAN GP

The Catalan circuit near Barcelona was blessed with extremely pleasant but very hot weather for the whole of the race weekend, and it was clear that Simon badly wanted to win, not only for the series but also for the Spanish crowd – and the crowd was pleased on Friday that the top four slots featured Simon, plus Gadea, Terol and Espargaro, who all lapped within a second of the leader.

On Saturday, as the temperatures soared into the high thirties, it was again Simon who kept his cool to set pole, with Derbi rider Espargaro missing out by just 0.02s at his home venue; Pol could ride to and from the circuit on a scooter, as his home is only a short distance away. Folger was a surprising third, with Krummenacher an equally unexpected fourth.

The Catalan circuit normally provides a dramatic race in all GP classes and this was no exception. Simon led for most of the race but as he crossed the finishing line on the penultimate lap he slowed and celebrated his 'win' – only to realise there was one more lap to go! Dropping to eighth place, he had a desperate fight to get back in touch with the leaders on the final lap. To add insult to injury, he thought he'd crossed the line in third and went to the podium, only to discover that in a video replay of the results he was actually fourth behind Iannone, Terol and Gadea.

## 7 – DUTCH TT

Assen is another track that seems to lend itself to exciting, close racing, particularly in the slipstreaming 125 class. As the race takes place on a Thursday, the first free practice was on Thursday and three Spanish riders again took the top slots – Simon, Gadea and Terol – with Smith in fourth.

But this all changed on Friday when German rider Cortese took his first ever pole position from Simon by a very tight 0.11s margin, with Terol and Bradl making up the rest of the front row, leaving Smith at the front of the second row with Iannone, Corsi and Espargaro.

In the race Smith got the holeshot but soon lost ground and found himself scrapping with Iannone for what he thought would be fourth place. As Gadea crossed the line for his first win of the season, Simon and Terol were fighting for second, with Terol finally beaten into third – but not before a questionable overtake. Although Terol ended up on the podium, Race Direction decided his attempted move on Simon had been a bit risky and demoted him to fifth, making the final result Gadea, Simon, Smith, Iannone and Terol. The fact that Gadea had started from the third row of the grid made his victory even more impressive.

## 8 – GERMAN GP

The weather was again to play its part in the proceedings on Friday at the Sachsenring. With just over half the session gone the heavens opened and most of the riders decided to call it a day and sit in their pit boxes as the rain pelted down. In the short dry start to the session it had been Simon who ended up with provisional pole.

The rain continued to fall on Saturday, so by the time it came to qualifying Simon set probably the slowest pole time ever for the German track. He was followed by title rival Smith, and they were the only two riders to put in a time below 1m 40s. Marquez qualified third and German rider Marcel Schrotter, a wild-card entry, was fourth on a Honda, just proving that the rain was indeed an equaliser for all the riders.

As it was, the race turned out to be dry and it was Simon who took full advantage of the grippy conditions to bring his Aprilia home in first place. This helped him to extend his championship lead as Smith crashed not once but twice. Gadea took the second spot on the podium with fellow Spaniard Olive third. Gadea's second place helped him to move further up the championship table to get within reach of Simon and overtake Smith.

## 9 – BRITISH GP

If the riders didn't get enough wet-weather practice in Germany, then the British round helped them to hone their rain skills even further. The Friday session started dry – for the first five minutes – and then the heavens opened. Saturday wasn't much better, so the riders had to splash round the Donington circuit to get the best times they could muster on its notoriously slippery surface. Smith put in the best time to take pole at his home track, much to the delight of the local crowd, with Marquez, Simon and Gadea behind him to prove that riders from hot countries can also cut it in bad British weather.

The weather hadn't really improved by Sunday, even though the start of the race was dry. After 11 laps the race was stopped because of heavy rain, then restarted as a five-lap dash for the cash. Simon once again proved victorious and further extended his lead in the championship. Joining him on the rostrum were Corsi and Scott Redding, who'd won the race in 2008. It wasn't such good news for Smith, who went off track early on and remounted for a pointless 20th place – all watched by Royalty, in the shape of Prince Harry.

## 10 – CZECH REPUBLIC GP

The Czech GP is the busiest meeting of the year and, while not as hot as the race in Barcelona, it did prove difficult at Brno for the 125 riders to find the right tyre, with the track getting steadily hotter as the weekend progressed. On the first day Smith took the initiative from Marquez, with Simon and Terol behind the front runners. Come Saturday and Iannone took his second pole of the year; having started the season well, the Italian had dropped out of the running after a series of DNFs and inconsistent results. Joining him on the front row were Terol, Cortese and Simon. Smith couldn't repeat his Friday performance, ending up at the head of the second row with Gadea even lower, in seventh.

On race day it was Terol who took the chequered flag, having fought with Simon for most of the race and produced an excellent last-lap manoeuvre on the Aspar rider. It was his first win of the 2009 season. Iannone came third, after a lonely race where he was unable to keep up with the leaders. It was the same story for Smith, in fourth, who had a big gap in front and behind him. The result extended Simon's championship advantage to 54.5 points, with Terol moving into second place in the standings.

At the IRTA tests in Jerez, Simon and Smith again took top spot, before the whole GP circus moved to a much hotter Qatar for more tests, shortly before the first race of the season. Smith also found time to help up-and-coming British riders with his project team called the KRP-Bradley Smith Racing team in the British Championship.

For some other riders it wasn't setting up new teams that held their attention but leaving their current team. Simone Corsi, 125cc World Championship runner-up in 2008, parted company with the Jack & Jones WRB team; poor results and the failure of either party to find a solution to problems were the reasons cited for the split.

As well as tried and tested riders, there was also a new team looking to make their mark, the Chinese-backed Haojue outfit, being run by GP team legend Garry Taylor, and helped with chassis development by British company Harris, who have a long pedigree building race and road chassis. However, the team was to be plagued with difficulties over the season, starting in Japan where they pulled out of the race due to 'technical' problems that they couldn't fix – an engine that was both unreliable and slow was the problem. Things didn't improve, and by July the team had folded following the decision of the Haojue management to sit out three championship rounds, with the subsequent cancellation of contracts for riders Micky Ranseder and Matthew Hoyle.

KTM took the decision during the season to withdraw from the 125 championship at the end of 2009, meaning that in three years the Austrian company had gone from involvement in all three GP classes to a complete pull-out.

One statistic of particular note in 2009 was the incredible total of 32 crashes at the Le Mans round, a record for the highest number of crashes in a single race or session. The previous record was 28 crashes in the 125cc race in Portugal in 2002.

## 11 – INDIANAPOLIS GP

With all the bikes packed up and delivered to Indy, everyone was wondering what the weather held in store for them at the US track. In 2008 the meeting had been hit by a hurricane, which meant officials were forced to cancel the 250 race. Thankfully this year wasn't too bad, allowing Brno winner Terol to keep his confidence high and put himself on top of the pile on Friday. He was joined by Corsi, Smith and Cortese, but then rain fell in the final part of the session, causing most riders to stay in their pit boxes.

The sun shone on Saturday, much to everyone's relief. Simon put his bike on pole, but another 12 riders were within one second of his time by the end of the session, with Germany's Cortese a mere 0.05s behind the Spaniard. Terol and Espargaro completed the front row; Smith and Gadea were fifth and seventh.

It was Pol Espargaro, however, who took his bike across the line first at the Brickyard, his first ever win in the 125 class. Smith was second, with Corsi coming in third and Simon down in fifth, although he still walked away from the US circuit with a healthy lead of 52.5 points in the championship. Smith's second place brought the gap to Terol down to a single point.

## 12 – SAN MARINO GP

There was no rain in Misano, but conditions were extremely hot and humid throughout the meeting. Smith once again started the weekend at the front, with Simon only 0.3s behind and snapping at his heels, followed by Iannone and Bradl. By Saturday the humidity was even higher as riders tried for their fastest times, and Smith was superb – he managed not only to secure pole position but also set the fastest ever 125 lap time round the Misano circuit. Simon was right behind him again, just 0.016s shy of first place.

Sunday saw the heat becoming a little more bearable for the race, a good job as the battles going on around the track could only be described as titanic. Iannone and Espargaro locked horns from the off and by the last lap of the race it was clear this was definitely going to be a 'win it or bin it' result, with pass after pass, and everyone out of their seats with excitement. But the two riders came into the last turn only to take each other off the track and hand Simon his fourth victory of the season. Podium places were also handed out to Terol and Smith.

It was now a mathematical possibility that Simon could secure the title in Estoril.

## 13 – PORTUGUESE GP

With the title so close, the pressure was on for Simon to 'do the business', but with three rounds left after this one he could quite easily bide his time – to a degree. Being a true racer, though, Simon wasn't about to sit back. He finished Friday leading the pack, showing he was prepared to try and secure the crown at the earliest opportunity. He was further helped towards his goal as Smith crashed and was sitting in 18th place with a bruised ankle.

Then, come qualifying on Saturday, Simon showed the world and the paddock that he really did want to secure that title as soon as possible by setting pole position. Smith had recovered from his fall to take third spot, with Espargaro between them. Marquez completed the front row.

But the pressure that Simon seemed to have under control over the first two days fell to pieces in the race when he made a mistake and ended up on the floor. After being over five seconds ahead of the rest of the field, the result was just four points for his weekend's work – but he was still 50.5 points ahead in the standings. His mistake handed another victory to Espargaro, who'd had a tight battle with Cortese and Smith.

## 14 – AUSTRALIAN GP

Phillip Island has been a traditional 'make or break' racetrack when it comes to a racer securing a world title. Many have won here, but many have lost too. After his lowly showing at Estoril, Simon needed to make sure he remained calm and in control for the whole weekend.

Victorious in two out of the previous three rounds, Espargaro was trying to keep up his winning streak and set the best time on Friday. Smith and Terol, meanwhile, kept the pressure on with second and third positions, while Simon had to settle for fourth on the first day. On Saturday Espargaro retained his composure and took pole position with Terol in second and Simon and Corsi behind him. Smith wasn't helping his chances in the title race as he crashed out late in the session.

On race day Simon took a calculated view and waited until the very last lap to overtake his team-mate and championship rival Smith, claiming victory and the World Championship, and thus vindicating his decision to move 'down' and 'back' to the 125 class.

Smith finished second, with Cortese taking a well-deserved and hard-fought third position.

## 15 – MALAYSIAN GP

With the title secured, Simon could get on with the job of just racing, almost for fun, rather than having to ride around thinking of what points were needed and where he should finish to gain those points. It was Smith who now needed to count, as Terol was only 21 points behind him in the championship and Bradley was determined to clinch second after Simon had taken the title at Phillip Island. With this in mind, Smith threw down the gauntlet by taking fastest time on Friday, with Terol a close fourth behind Marquez and newly crowned champion Simon.

It was Marquez, however, who secured the front row on Saturday as Smith and Espargaro crashed out, Smith's highside causing a break in his foot. Despite that, Smith managed to qualify in third while Espargaro, who lost time while his brake lever was fixed after his crash, ended up 11th. Simon got the second spot, Cortese was fourth and Terol fifth.

Come race day the battle was to be between the two Aspar riders, as Simon showed his team-mate exactly why he was the World Champion in a last-lap fight to the finish. With Smith finishing second and Terol down in fifth, second place in the title race was also secured for Bradley and the Aspar team. Espargaro managed a fine third place with Gadea taking fourth.

**Above** Andrea Iannone (right) and Julian Simon dominated the start and finish of the season respectively

**Right** Aleix Espargaro looks after younger brother Pol on the grid

**Far right** German teenager Marcel Schrotter had three wild-card rides and scored points each time

**Opposite** Julian Simon celebrates his title with a fancy-dress crash helmet at Phillip Island

## 16 – VALENCIAN GP

The first and second places in the championship were now secure, but the weather still had a part to play in the final round at Valencia. The challenge for the riders wasn't the wet or the cold but something that arguably was even worse – strong, blustery winds.

Simon fired the first shot with fastest time on Friday. Terol was up there too, but the big shock came from German wild-card rider Schrotter, who put himself in third on his Honda. With the wind still gusting on Saturday, it was again Simon who popped in the fastest time, with Corsi, Smith and Marquez completing the front row. Olive and Terol headed the second row, but Schrotter was still strong in seventh with Espargaro completing row two.

By Sunday's race the wind was at its worst and a real challenge for the riders of the lightweight 125s. Smith very nearly failed to make the start, as his bike stopped on the warm-up lap. He got it going with the help of some marshals and managed a blinding start. A group quickly set about chasing him, but they tripped over each other and Smith was gone. In the end only Simon could break away from the group and catch him. But for a mistake by Bradley when he ran wide, it looked like he had this final race in the bag, but Simon seized the opportunity and took the win. Espargaro, in third, was a long way behind them.

| | Rider | Nation | Team | Motorcycle | Points |
|---|---|---|---|---|---|
| 1 | Julian Simon | SPA | Bancaja Aspar Team 125cc | Aprilia | 289 |
| 2 | Bradley Smith | GBR | Bancaja Aspar Team 125cc | Aprilia | 233.5 |
| 3 | Nicolas Terol | SPA | Jack & Jones Team | Aprilia | 179.5 |
| 4 | Pol Espargaro | SPA | Derbi Racing Team | Derbi | 174.5 |
| 5 | Sergio Gadea | SPA | Bancaja Aspar Team 125cc | Aprilia | 141 |
| 6 | Sandro Cortese | GER | Ajo Interwetten | Derbi | 130 |
| 7 | Andrea Iannone | ITA | Ongetta Team I.S.P.A. | Aprilia | 125.5 |
| 8 | Marc Marquez | SPA | Red Bull KTM Moto Sport | KTM | 94 |
| 9 | Joan Olive | SPA | Derbi Racing Team | Derbi | 91 |
| 10 | Stefan Bradl | GER | Viessmann Kiefer Racing | Aprilia | 85 |
| 11 | Simone Corsi | ITA | Fontana Racing | Aprilia | 81 |
| 12 | Jonas Folger | GER | Ongetta Team I.S.P.A. | Aprilia | 73 |
| 13 | Dominique Aegerter | SWI | Ajo Interwetten | Derbi | 70.5 |
| 14 | Efran Vazquez | SPA | Derbi Racing Team | Derbi | 54 |
| 15 | Scott Redding | GBR | Blusens Aprilia | Aprilia | 50.5 |
| 16 | Takaaki Nakagami | JPN | Ongetta Team I.S.P.A. | Aprilia | 43 |
| 17 | Danny Webb | GBR | Degraaf Grand Prix | Aprilia | 38.5 |
| 18 | Esteve Rabat | SPA | Blusens Aprilia | Aprilia | 37 |
| 19 | Lorenzo Zanetti | ITA | Ongetta Team I.S.P.A. | Aprilia | 37 |
| 20 | Johann Zarco | FRA | WTR San Marino Team | Aprilia | 32.5 |
| 21 | Randy Krummenacher | SWI | Degraaf Grand Prix | Aprilia | 32 |
| 22 | Luis Salom | SPA | Jack & Jones Team | Aprilia | 21 |
| 23 | Marcel Schrotter | GER | Toni – Mang Team | Honda | 18 |
| 24 | Tomoyoshi Koyama | JPN | Loncin Racing | Loncin | 17 |
| 25 | Michael Ranseder | AUT | CBC Corse | Aprilia | 9 |
| 26 | Lorenzo Salvadori | ITA | Junior GP Racing Dream | Aprilia | 7 |
| 27 | Riccardo Moretti | ITA | Ellegi Racing | Aprilia | 3 |
| 28 | Jasper Iwema | NED | Racing Team Germany | Honda | 3 |
| 29 | Cameron Beaubier | USA | Red Bull KTM Moto Sport | KTM | 3 |
| 30 | Martin Glossop | GBR | KRP/Bradley Smith Racing | Honda | 2 |
| 31 | Marvin Fritz | GER | LHF-Project Racing | Honda | 2 |
| 32 | Gregory di Carlo | FRA | Equipe de France | Honda | 2 |
| 33 | Dani Kartheininger | GER | Freudenberg Racing Team | Honda | 1 |

## RED BULL ROOKIES
PETER CLIFFORD

**Above** Daijiro Hiura, Sturla Fagerhaug and Jake Gagne are congratulated by Valentino Rossi after the Rookies' Assen race

The fastest group of teenagers ever assembled contested the third Red Bull Rookies Cup over eight races at six GP venues across Europe. Ten new rookies joined the established racers from the previous two seasons. Pre-season favourite Sturla Fagerhaug returned alongside previous race winners Mathew Scholtz and Daijiro Hiura but they were eclipsed at the final race by 16-year-old Czech Jakub Kornfeil, who won in front of his home crowd at Brno to take the title in his second year as a Red Bull Rookie.

Everything came down to the last lap of the last race. Kornfeil took the win in Brno from Fagerhaug and stole the points lead when it counted, ending a classic year of great action as the pair had arrived at the final double race weekend tied on points.

The first race of the Brno dénouement saw a ten-man battle for the lead go all the way to the line, as 17-year-old Norwegian Fagerhaug picked up a three-point advantage with fifth place to Kornfeil's eighth. In the second race, though, Kornfeil got the best of a five-man scrap to cross the line in first place and take the Red Bull Rookies Cup.

No-one would have predicted at the start of the year

that Kornfeil, then only 15, would be able to fight back from 46 points down halfway through the eight-race season. Fagerhaug had started his third Rookies season full of confidence, having won two races in 2008 and finished a close third in the Cup. Sturla looked great in pre-season testing and, thanks to a little bit of good fortune, scored a win and a second from the opening weekend in Jerez. He claimed back-to-back victories at Mugello and Assen and began to look unstoppable, yet Kornfeil had already taken a very important step forward as he'd chased the Cup leader all the way to the flag in Italy.

For the Czech youngster that race in Mugello was the turning point of his season. 'I proved to myself that I could race with him. I saw that he was not unbeatable even though I didn't win that day,' recalled Kornfeil. The race had been a battle between the two of them, but there was a seven-man scrap for the win in Holland, and while Fagerhaug broke free to take the victory, Kornfeil remained tangled in the group and crossed the line in fifth.

That Assen group contained many of the top 2009 Rookies, including Danny Kent, up to that point of the

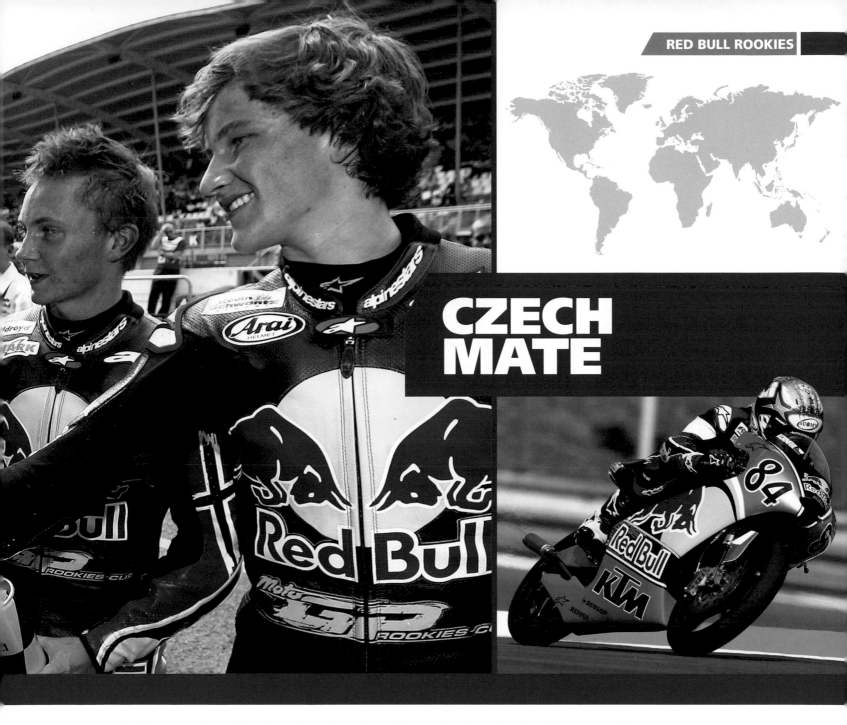

# CZECH MATE

**Above** The 2009 Red Bull Rookies Cup winner Jakub Kornfeil on his home circuit at Brno

season the only rider to have beaten Fagerhaug: he took victory in race two at Jerez. The 15-year-old Briton crashed out while trying to match Fagerhaug's breakaway in Holland, leaving the 14-year-old Japanese rider Daijiro Hiura to claim second, his best result of the year. He backed that up with three third places.

Third in Assen was 15-year-old Californian Jake Gagne. When he made his debut in the 2008 US Rookies Cup the motocrosser was just beginning his tarmac career, but he learnt quickly, winning at both Road Atlanta and Indianapolis. Moving to the MotoGP Cup for 2009 brought fresh challenges, with new circuits and international competition, but Gagne stepped up with three third places to finish sixth overall in the Cup.

Next across the line in Assen was Florian Marino. The French rider had just turned 16 and was very frustrated to miss out on the podium for the third consecutive race. Fifth in Germany and sixth in Britain saw him continue that disappointing trend, but he came through with a brilliant win in the first of the two races at Brno.

Kornfeil had also been frustrated in Holland, but he just let that motivate him more for the next round, in Germany, a race run in the most tricky of conditions.

The track was cold and wet, but Kornfeil was masterful from the start; he was the only one who looked in control. Fagerhaug crashed trying to chase him and the others either fell or accepted the fact that the Czech was in a class of his own. South African 16-year-old Mathew Scholtz finished second after a great battle on a drying track with Danny Kent, who crashed at the final corner.

At Donington Kornfeil romped away again, with Spain's Daniel Ruiz making a great charge through from 20th on the grid to take second ahead of Hiura. For Fagerhaug it was another disaster, another crash. Just four points from the two races meant Kornfeil was now level with him on points.

Perhaps the Norwegian had become too confident, or maybe his wild-card GP rides with the Red Bull KTM team had diluted his focus. Coming to the final weekend in Brno the pressure switched to Kornfeil and the Czech rider admitted it affected his performance in the first race. 'I did feel the pressure for the first race, but for the second I just ignored everything and concentrated on riding. It worked – and it was an unbelievable feeling to win the Cup.'

## Best Location and Exclusive Privileges

Situated at the heart of the action, either directly above the Pit Lane or in a smart village area, MotoGP VIP VILLAGE puts you as close as you can get to the world's top motorcycle racers.

Privileged Parking, excellent views, race coverage on closed-circuit TV, Pit Lane Walk, Paddock Tour, Service Road Tour and complimentary Official Programme on Sunday.

The MotoGP VIP VILLAGE Game will offer all guests the chance to win the possibility to view races from the pit wall, a service road tour and one of the many licensed MotoGP products.

## Best Service and Excellent Cuisine

Hospitality is of the highest quality, from the buffet breakfast in the morning to gourmet lunch and afternoon petit fours, with a complimentary bar all day.

# RIDERS FOR HEALTH
### BARRY COLEMAN

# ANNUAL REPORT

**H**ere's a surprise. As the 2009 season ended, Randy Mamola turned 50. Of course that's only a surprise for the relatively elderly and mentally unreliable who think they remember that the whole point of Randy Mamola, when first we heard his name, was that he was 15. He went to New Zealand for some sort of international race meeting and beat quite a handful of established Grand Prix stars. As a reward he went home with one of those lengthy adjectives so beloved of the motorcycle press of the day: 'Sensational tousled-haired freckle-faced tiny California schoolkid Randy Mamola'. Among the living compound adjectives he beat down there, I remember, was 'Yamaha-mounted globe-trotting ex-public-schoolboy Chas Mortimer'. In other words, Randy was good.

Back then, pronouncing his perfectly simple name was a serious problem. Inexplicably, when he showed up for the Match Races, most commentators chose to add another syllable: 'Randy Mamanola'. Even getting the stress on the correct one of the original three was evidently challenging. I remember Randy's manager, Jim Doyle, giving Murray Walker lessons, mouth open wide for correct emphasis: 'Mamohla, Murray, Mamohla.'

What a long way that kid has come. What a long way the sport has come. And, along with them both, what a very long way Riders for Health has come.

It started with Randy's wish to help (other) children. Then came Somalia with Save the Children in '88 and the positively biblical revelation to Randy that the world didn't consist exclusively of American suburbs and racetracks. But when he got that, boy did he get it. We started working on the question of how motorcycle racing could save the world during the course of the next year. You know all about that now.

So how are we doing? In a word or two, pretty well. The Bill and Melinda Gates Foundation and the Skoll Foundation for Social Entrepreneurship (founded by the delightful genius Jeff Skoll, who was also responsible for an interesting enterprise called eBay) have adopted our strategy as their strategy in finding and securing ways actually to deliver health care in Africa (as opposed to just talking about it). And another partner, none other than the Indianapolis Motor Speedway, has adopted Riders for Health as one of their three charities. In 2010 the Day of

Health-care worker Bubacarr Jallow visits a mother and child in the Gambia on his Riders-managed motorcycle

riders

Riders is an international humanitarian organisation – born out of the world of motorcycle racing – which works to improve the delivery of health care in Africa. Our vision is of a world in which no-one will die of an easily preventable or curable disease because barriers of distance, terrain or poverty prevent them from being reached. Our mission is to strengthen health systems by addressing one of the most neglected, yet vital, aspects of development for the health of Africa – transport and logistics.

Riders began work in 1989 when its founders – Grand Prix racer Randy Mamola, and Barry and Andrea Coleman – became determined to find a solution to the problem that they recognised as undermining the development of Africa: the lack of appropriate transportation infrastructure.

They realised that vehicles themselves were not the answer – the key was to have sound management systems and regular maintenance to keep the vehicles running day in, day out.

Today, Riders employs over 300 local staff in Africa and helps to maintain over 1,400 vehicles used by professional health workers and local community organisations. In total, our programmes are helping over 10 million people across Africa to receive regular, reliable health care.

Thanks to the support of MotoGP in 2009, we have been able to expand our work in Kenya, start an innovative motorcycle courier service that is helping to get thousands more people into treatment for HIV and tuberculosis, and initiate a brand-new programme in Zambia.

Champions will be at Silverstone. Thank you, Donington, for 18 fabulous years. We're moving along, but without forgetting for a second where we came from.

So, back to Randy's involvement with Riders. Just after his scary 2009 birthday, we surprised him. We took him to Lesotho, a country he first visited with Kevin Schwantz, among others, in 1993. Lesotho, starting in 1991, was the first national-scale Riders for Health programme and it ran for seven years. Recently we were invited back, supported by the Elton John AIDS Foundation (EJAF), to set up a new and much bigger programme. Randy's treat was to be part of a ride through the country with a selected group of supporters to launch our 'Experience Africa' adventures. What he saw, from very close up, was one of the world's most beautiful countries.

But Lesotho can claim some other, not so nice, superlatives – the world's highest rate of HIV/AIDS infection, for example. Which is exactly why your very own charity, Riders for Health, is there again, working with the Ministry of Health, EJAF, the Clinton Foundation, Partners in Health and many others.

Among the Riders programmes Randy saw was our brand-new service, a professional motorcycle courier network dedicated to collecting blood and sputum samples from health centres, delivering them to labs and returning the results. Almost unbelievably, this has never been done in Africa before. Its introduction in Lesotho has transformed HIV care. People are put on treatment in a couple of weeks of being tested, as opposed to months, if at all. For next year (2010), working with the Clinton Foundation, we are rolling out the service in new countries, starting in Zambia. In January you will be able to see a

**Opposite** Riders technician carries out a monthly out-reach service on Bubacarr Jallow's motorcycle

**Opposite below** Randy Mamola auctioning a set of his factory Cagiva leathers at Day of Champions

**Right** Blood samples await testing at Mokhotlong Hospital, Lesotho

**Below** New motorcycles for Riders' Asset Management Programme in the Gambia

## FOCUS ON...SAMPLE TRANSPORT

One of the main challenges to managing the disease burden across Africa, and particularly the HIV crisis, is in detection of the disease and therefore in the testing of the population. However, testing remains low as the average wait for results is four months. Knowing your status and beginning anti-retroviral treatment (ARVs) is vital, but this wait is reducing the number of people who are willing to be tested. Put very simply, the delays are due to the inadequate and/or inappropriate transport available. The health organisations with which Riders works have described this as being one of the greatest current obstacles to improving public health.

In Lesotho, together with the Elton John AIDS Foundation and the Clinton Foundation HIV/AIDS Initiative, Riders has this year developed a specialist motorcycle courier service which significantly speeds up the processes of testing and diagnosis. Riders is currently replicating this service in Zambia's Eastern Province, where nearly 16 per cent of the population is already known to be HIV positive.

'I think this programme will be very useful,' said Davis Ndovi, nurse and officer in charge at Miti Rural Health Centre in Zambia. 'We panic sometimes because we have no way to get to the laboratory, or we are so busy and cannot take the samples to the lab. But if we take samples from the patient and waste them because we can't get them to the lab in time, how do we tell the patients? I cannot leave all the patients at the health centre waiting for treatment while I cycle to the lab.' (In August 2009 Miti RHC had 880 patients visiting the centre – an average of 42 a day – with only two health staff working there.)

30-minute BBC World film about Riders and the new programme. Better yet, perhaps, you might want to consider a Riders 'Experience Africa' ride – perhaps in Kenya, a country with which MotoGP and Riders are establishing a special 'racing to health' relationship.

It's 38 years since Randy started racing a motorcycle. Without him, there would have been no Riders for Health and thus no hope for those people in the Lesotho highlands who are now on anti-retroviral treatment and will therefore live.

Not bad. So to celebrate the first 50 years, let's give him some new adjectives: 'Crowd-pleasing utterly determined humanity-loving sensitive polite no-hair-at-all world-changing life-saving freckle-faced Randy Mamola.'

Let's hear it for the kid. And for the only sport in which it could all have been possible.

# MotoGP on DVD!

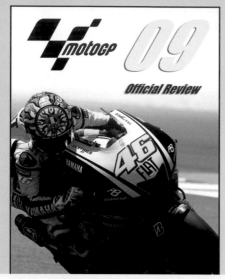

**MotoGP official Season Review 2009** The Official Review of the 2009 MotoGP season brings you the comprehensive and action-packed story of the knife-edge championship battle between the legendary Valentino Rossi and his sensational Fiat Yamaha teammate Jorge Lorenzo. There's breathtaking footage featuring the epic battles, vital moments, action-packed racing and shocking crashes from every round, plus interviews and bonus features including an exclusive interview with 2009 MotoGP World Champion Valentino Rossi and complete on-board laps of all 17 circuits featured in the 2009 championship.

**MotoGP Evolution of a Species** Discover the incredible story of how today's state-of-the-art MotoGP motorcycles have evolved since the first days of the 4-stroke machines. This fascinating DVD charts the development of the iconic machines of the premier class from 2002 right through to 2009, revealing the changes, the challenges and the influence of electronics. Features the Ducati Desmosedici, Honda RCV, Kawasaki Ninja ZX-RR, Suzuki GSV-R and Yamaha YZR-M1, and we hear from crew chiefs, top engineers and racing greats including Valentino Rossi, Casey Stoner, Mick Doohan, Freddie Spencer, Dani Pedrosa, Colin Edwards and Nicky Hayden.

DVD 180+mins No.1844 *RRP: £24.46*
**Duke Club Price: £19.99**
Redeem with 1000 Duke Club points

DVD 105mins No.1845 *RRP: £19.56*
**Duke Club Price: £16.99**
Redeem with 800 Duke Club points

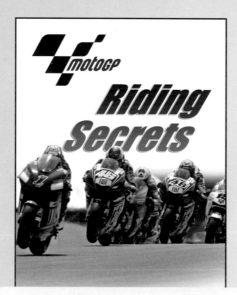

DVD 180+mins No.1850 *RRP: £24.46*
**Duke Club Price: £19.99**
Redeem with 1000 Duke Club points

DVD 114mins No.1761 *RRP: £19.56*
**Duke Club Price: £16.99**
Redeem with 800 Duke Club points

DVD 71mins No.1744 *RRP: £19.56*
**Duke Club Price: £16.99**
Redeem with 800 Duke Club points

To join the Duke Club please place your order and we will send you your Duke Club Card. Membership is FREE and, as a member, you earn points every time you shop. Duke Reward points can be redeemed against hundreds of action-packed titles - so start collecting today*!

For any Duke Club enquiries, please email: club@dukevideo.com

**Call 01624 640 000**

**FREE 2010 catalogue out now with over 12,000 products to fuel your passion!**

**Shop online at www.DukeVideo.com**